AN OUTLINE OF
OCCULT SCIENCE

AN OUTLINE OF OCCULT SCIENCE

by
Rudolf Steiner

1972
ANTHROPOSOPHIC PRESS, INC.
Spring Valley, N.Y.

This volume is a translation of *Die Ge-
heimwissenschaft in Umriss* (Vol. 13 in the
Bibliographic Survey, 1961). Translated
by Maud and Henry B. Monges and re-
vised for this edition by Lisa D. Monges.

This edition of
AN OUTLINE OF OCCULT SCIENCE
commemorates the fiftieth anniversary
of the founding of
THE ANTHROPOSOPHIC PRESS
by Henry B. Monges.
1922 – 1972

CONTENTS

Preface

SIXTEENTH TO TWENTIETH EDITION

NOW, fifteen years after the first edition of this book, I may well be allowed to say something publicly about the state of soul out of which it arose.

Originally, it was my plan to add its essential content as final chapters to my book *Theosophy*, which had been published previously. This proved to be impossible. At the time of the publication of *Theosophy* the subject matter of *Occult Science* did not yet live in me in its final form as was the case with *Theosophy*. In my imaginative perceptions the spiritual nature of individual man stood before my soul and I was able to describe it; the cosmic relationships, however, which had to be presented in *Occult Science* did not yet live in my consciousness in the same way. I perceived details, but not the complete picture.

I, therefore, decided to publish *Theosophy* with the content I had seen as the nature of the life of individual man, and then to carry through *Occult Science* in the near future, without undue haste.

The contents of this book had, in accordance with my soul mood at that time, to be given in thoughts that are further elaborations of the thoughts employed in natural science, suited for the presentation of the spiritual. In the preface to the first edition, reprinted in this book, it will be noted how strongly responsible I felt toward natural science in all that I wrote at that time about the science of the spirit.

What reveals itself to spiritual perception as the world of spirit cannot, however, be presented in such thoughts alone. For this revelation does not fit into a mere thought content. He who has experienced the nature of such revelation knows that the thoughts of ordinary consciousness are only suited to express what is perceived by the senses, not what is seen by the spirit.

The content of what is spiritually perceived can only be reproduced in pictures (imaginations) through which inspirations speak, which have their origin in spiritual entity intuitively perceived.[1]

But he who describes imaginations from the world of spirit cannot at present merely present these imaginations. For in doing so he would be presenting something that would stand as quite a different content of consciousness alongside the content of knowledge of our age, without any relationship whatsoever to it. He has to fill modern

---

[1] All that it is necessary to know concerning the nature of imagination, inspiration, and intuition is to be found in this book, *Occult Science*, in my book, *Knowledge of the Higher Worlds and Its Attainment*, also in *The Stages of Higher Knowledge*.

consciousness with what can be recognized by another consciousness that perceives the world of spirit. His presentation will then have this world of spirit as content, but this content will appear in the form of thoughts into which it flows. Through this it will be completely comprehensible to ordinary consciousness, which thinks in terms of the present day but does not yet behold the world of spirit.

This comprehensibility will only then be lacking if we ourselves raise barriers against it, that is, if we labor under the prejudices that the age has produced regarding "the limits of knowledge" through an incorrectly conceived view of nature.

In spiritual cognition everything is immersed in intimate soul experience, not only spiritual perception itself, but also the understanding with which the unseeing, ordinary consciousness meets the results of clairvoyant perception.

Those who maintain that anyone who believes he understands is merely suggesting the understanding to himself have not the slightest inkling of this intimacy.

But it is a fact that what expresses itself merely in concepts of truth and error within the scope of comprehension of the physical world becomes *experience* in regard to the spiritual world.

Whoever permits his judgment to be influenced—be it ever so slightly—by the assertion that the spiritually perceived is incomprehensible to the everyday, still unperceiving consciousness—because of its limitations—will find his comprehension obscured by this judgment as though by a dark cloud, and he really cannot understand.

What is spiritually perceived is fully comprehensible to the unprejudiced, unperceiving consciousness if the seer gives his perceptions thought form. It is just as comprehensible as the finished picture of the painter is to the man who does not paint. Moreover, the comprehension of the spirit world is not of the nature of artistic feeling employed in the comprehension of a work of art, but it bears the stamp of thought employed in natural science.

In order, however, to make such a comprehension really possible, the one who presents what he perceives spiritually must bring his perceptions up to a point where he can pour them into thought form without loss of their imaginative character within this form.

All this stood before my soul as I developed my *Occult Science.*

In 1909 I felt that, under these premises, I might be able to produce a book which, in the first place, offered the content of my spiritual vision brought, to a sufficient degree, into thought form, and which, in the second place, could be understood by every thinking human being who allows no obstructions to interfere with his understanding.

I say this today, stating at the same time that in 1909 the publication of this book appeared to be a risk. For I knew indeed that professional scientists are unable to call up in themselves the necessary impartiality, nor are the numerous personalities able to do so who are dependent on them for their judgment.

But, before my soul there stood the very fact that at the time when the consciousness of mankind was furthest removed from the world of spirit, the communications from that world would answer a most urgent necessity.

I counted upon the fact that there are human beings who feel, more or less desperately, the remoteness from all spirituality as a grave obstacle to life that causes them to seize upon the communications of the spiritual world with inner longing.

During the subsequent years this has been completely confirmed. *Theosophy* and *Occult Science,* books that presume the goodwill of the reader in coping with a difficult style of writing, have been widely read.

I have quite consciously endeavored not to offer a "popular" exposition, but an exposition that makes it necessary for the reader to study the content with strict effort of thought. The character I impressed upon my books is such that their very study is the beginning of spiritual training. For the calm, conscious effort of thought that this reading makes necessary strengthens the forces of the soul and through this makes them capable of approaching the spirit world.

The fact that I have entitled this book *Occult Science* has immediately called forth misunderstandings. From many sides was heard, "What claims to be *science* must not be secret, *occult*." How little thought was exercised in making such an objection! As though someone who reveals a subject matter would want to be secretive about it. This entire book shows that it was not the intention to designate anything "occult," but to bring everything into a form that renders it as understandable as any science. Or do we not wish to say when we employ the term "natural science" that we are dealing with the knowledge of "nature"? Occult science is the science of what occurs occultly insofar as it is not perceived in external nature, but in that region toward which the soul turns when it directs its inner being toward the spirit.

Occult Science is the antithesis of *Natural Science.*

Objections have repeatedly been made to my perceptions of the spiritual world by maintaining that they are transformed reproductions of what, in the course of the ages, has appeared in human thought about the spirit world. It is said that I had read this or that, absorbed what I read into the unconscious, and then presented it in the belief that it originated in my own perception. I am said to have gained my expositions from the teachings of the Gnostics, from the poetic records of ancient oriental wisdom, and so on.

These objections are superficial.

My knowledge of things of the spirit is a direct result of my own perception, and I am fully conscious of this fact. In all details and in the larger surveys I had always examined myself carefully as to whether every step I took in the progress of my perception was accompanied by a fully awake consciousness. Just as the mathematician advances from thought to thought without the unconscious or auto-suggestion playing a role, so—I told myself—spiritual perception must advance from objective imagination to objective imagination without anything living in the soul but the spiritual content of clear, discerning consciousness.

The knowledge that an imagination is not a mere subjective picture, but a representation in picture form of an objective spiritual content is attained by means of healthy inner experience. This is achieved in a psycho-spiritual way, just as in the realm of sense-perception one is able with a healthy organism to distinguish properly between mere imaginings and objective perceptions.

Thus the results of my perception stood before me. They

xiv

were, at the outset, "perceptions" without names. Were I to communicate them, I needed verbal designations. I then sought later for such designations in older descriptions of the spiritual in order to be able to express in words what was still wordless. I employed these verbal designations freely, so that in my use of them scarcely *one* coincides with its ancient meaning.

I sought, however, for such a possibility of expression in every case *only after* the content had arisen in my own perception.

I knew how to exclude what had been *previously read* from my own perceptive research by means of the state of consciousness that I have just described.

Now it was claimed that in my *expressions* reminiscences of ancient ideas were to be found. Without considering the content, attention was fixed on the expressions. If I spoke of "lotus flowers" in the astral body of man, that was a proof, to the critic, that I was repeating the teachings of ancient India in which the expression is to be found. Indeed, if I spoke of "astral body," this was the result of my reading the literature of the Middle Ages. If I employed the expressions "Angeloi," "Archangeloi," and so forth, I was simply renewing the ideas of Christian Gnosis.

I found such entirely superficial thinking constantly opposing me.

I wanted to point to this fact, too, now that a new edition of *Occult Science* is to be published, for the book contains the outline of Anthroposophy as a whole. It will, therefore, be chiefly beset by the misunderstandings to which Anthroposophy is exposed.

Since the time when the imaginations that this book presents merged into a complete picture in my soul, I have advanced uninterruptedly in my ability to investigate, by means of soul and spirit perception, the historical evolution of mankind, the cosmos, and so forth. In the details I have continuously arrived at new results. But what I offered as an outline in *Occult Science* fifteen years ago remains for me basically undisturbed. Everything I have been able to say since then, if inserted in this book in the proper place, appears as an amplification of the outline given at that time.

RUDOLF STEINER

January 10, 1925
Goetheanum
Dornach, Switzerland

PREFACE

SEVENTH TO FIFTEENTH EDITION

I N THIS new edition of *An Outline of Occult Science*, I
have almost entirely reshaped the first chapter, "The
Character of Occult Science." I believe that, as a result,
there will now be less cause for the misunderstandings I
saw arising from the earlier wording of this chapter. From
many sides I could hear, "Other sciences offer proofs;
what here is offered as science says simply, 'Occult Science
states this or that.' " It is quite natural for such prejudice to
arise, since the proofs of supersensible cognition cannot
obtrude themselves upon us with the exposition as is the
case with the exposition of relationships of sense-perceptible reality. I have, however, sought, by means of a revision
of the first chapter of this book, to make clearer than I
seem to have succeeded in doing in the earlier editions,
that we have to contend here merely with prejudice.—In
the other chapters I have attempted, through amplifica-
tions, to elaborate some items of my presentation more

clearly. Throughout the entire book I have taken pains to make numerous changes in the wording of the content, which seemed to me necessary after renewed experience of the subject matter..

RUDOLF STEINER

Berlin, May 1920.

FOURTH EDITION

ANYONE attempting an exposition of the results of spiritual science as recorded in this book must, above all, take into account the fact that at present these results are universally looked upon as something quite impossible. For things are said in the following exposition that the supposedly exact thinking of our age affirms to be "probably entirely indeterminable by human intelligence." He who knows and appreciates the reasons why so many earnest persons are lead to maintain this impossibility will wish to make ever new attempts to show the misconceptions upon which is based the belief that entrance into supersensible worlds is denied to human knowledge.

For two things offer themselves for consideration. First, any human soul, by reflecting deeply, will in the long run be unable to disregard the fact that its most important questions concerning the meaning and significance of life must remain unanswered if there be no access to supersensible worlds. We may theoretically deceive ourselves about this fact, but the depths of the soul-life will not tolerate this self-delusion.—If we do not wish to listen to these depths of the soul, we shall naturally reject any statement about supersensible worlds. Yet there are human beings—really not few in number—who find it impossible to remain deaf to the demands coming from these soul depths. Such people must always knock at the door that conceals, according to the opinion of others, the "inconceivable."

Second, the statements resulting from "exact thinking" are not at all to be underrated. He who occupies himself with them will certainly appreciate their seriousness where they are to be taken seriously. The writer of this book would not like to be looked upon as one who light-heartedly passes over the tremendous thought activity that has been employed in determining the limits of the human intellect. This thought activity cannot be disposed of by a few phrases about "academic wisdom" and the like. In many cases its source rests in true striving for knowledge and in genuine acumen.—Indeed, even more may be admitted: reasons have been brought forward to show that the knowledge considered scientific today cannot penetrate into the spirit world, and these reasons *are in a certain sense irrefutable.*

Since this is admitted without hesitation by the writer of this book himself, it may appear to many quite strange that he, nevertheless, undertakes to make statements about supersensible worlds. It appears, indeed, to be almost impossible that someone in a certain sense admits the reasons for the inapprehensibility of the supersensible worlds and yet at the same time continues to speak about them.

It is possible, nevertheless, to have this attitude, and it is possible, at the same time, to understand that it will appear contradictory. For not everyone concerns himself with the experiences one has if one approaches the supersensible realm with the human intellect. There it becomes evident that the proofs of this intellect may well be irrefutable, and that, in spite of their irrefutability, they need not be decisive for reality. Instead of all theoretical arguments, the attempt shall be made here to bring about an understanding by means of a comparison. The fact that comparisons themselves are not proof is readily conceded; yet this does not prevent their making comprehensible what is to be expressed.

Human cognition, as it acts in everyday life and in ordinary science, is really so constituted that it cannot penetrate into supersensible worlds. This can be irrefutably proved, but this proof can have no more value for a certain kind of soul-life than the proof that is undertaken to show that the natural human eye with its power of perception cannot penetrate into the smallest cells of a living body, or into the constitution of distant celestial bodies. Just as the declaration is true and demonstrable that the ordinary power of sight does not penetrate as far as the cells, so also is the other statement correct and provable that ordinary cognition is unable to penetrate into supersensible worlds. Yet the proof that the ordinary power of sight must stop short of the cells does not decide anything against research into the cells. Why should the proof that the ordinary power of cognition must halt before supersensible worlds decide anything against the possibility of research into these worlds?

We can appreciate the feeling aroused in many a person by this comparison. We are even able to sympathize with those who doubt whether somebody who confronts the thought activity mentioned with such a comparison has even the slightest idea of the seriousness of this activity. Nevertheless, the author of this book is not only imbued with this seriousness, but he is of the opinion that this thought activity is to be counted among the noblest achievements of mankind. To prove that the human power of sight cannot penetrate to the cell structure without the aid of instruments would be, to be sure, an unnecessary undertaking; to become conscious, through exact thinking, of the nature of this thinking is a necessary spiritual activity. It is only too understandable that those who give themselves up to such thought activity do not notice that reality can refute them. The present preface of this book cannot be the place to go into the various "refutations" of the first editions on the part of persons who lack all understanding of what this book strives for, or who direct their false attacks at the person of the author. It must, however, be strongly emphasized that only those can suspect in this book any underrating of serious scientific thought activity who wish to close their eyes to the real character of the expositions.

The human power of cognition can be strengthened and enhanced, just as the faculty of eyesight can be strengthened. The means, however, for strengthening cognition are of an entirely spiritual nature; they are purely inner soul functions. They consist in what is described in this book as meditation and concentration (contemplation). Ordinary soul-life is bound to the instruments of the body, the strengthened soul-life frees itself from them. To certain modern schools of thought such a declaration must appear quite senseless and based only upon self-delusion. From their point of view, it will be found easy to prove that "all soul-life" is bound up with the nervous system. A person holding the point of view out of which this book is written will completely understand such proofs. He understands the people who say that only the superficial can maintain that there may be some sort of soul-life independent of the body, and who are entirely convinced that for such soul experiences a connection with the life of the nerves exists that "spiritual scientific amateurishness" fails to perceive.

Here certain entirely comprehensible habits of thought confront what is described in this book so sharply that they preclude at present any prospect of coming to an understanding. We are here at a point where the wish must make itself felt that in the present age it should no longer be in keeping with spiritual life to decry a direction of research as fantastic and visionary because it diverges abruptly from our own.—On the other hand, however, we have the fact that there are a number of human beings who have an understanding for the supersensible mode of research presented in this book. They are individuals who realize that the meaning of life does not reveal itself in general terms about soul, self, and so forth, but only through the real entering upon the results of supersensible research. It is not from lack of modesty, but with joyful satisfaction that the author of this book feels deeply the necessity of this fourth edition after a relatively brief time since the last edition appeared.

The author does not accentuate this from lack of modesty, because he feels only too clearly how little even the new edition corresponds to what it really ought to be as an "outline of a supersensible world conception." In preparing this new edition, the whole subject matter has been re-studied and re-worked with considerable amplification at important points. Clarification was also striven for. Nevertheless, in numerous places the author became conscious of how inadequate the means of presentation available to him prove to be in comparison with what supersensible research shows. Hence, scarcely more than a *way* could be indicated for acquiring the concepts that in this book are given for the *Saturn, Sun,* and *Moon* evolutions. An important point of view, also in this domain, has been briefly treated anew in this edition. But the experiences in regard to such things diverge so greatly from all the experiences in the domain of the senses that the exposition must of necessity struggle continually for expressions that appear sufficiently adequate for the purpose. Anyone who is willing to go into the exposition attempted here will perhaps notice that much that is impossible to say in dry words is striven for by the *manner* of the description. This manner is, for example, one thing for the *Saturn* evolution, but quite another for the *Sun* evolution, and so forth.

The second part of this book, which deals with knowledge of the higher worlds, was greatly supplemented and amplified by its author. He endeavored to present clearly the character of the inner soul processes through which knowledge frees itself from its limits present in the sense world and fits itself for experiencing the supersensible world. The author attempted to show that this experiencing of the supersensible, although acquired entirely through inner ways and means, does not have a merely subjective significance for the individual who acquires it. The presentation was to show that, *within* the soul, its singularity and personal peculiarity are stripped off and an experience is reached which is similar in every human being who effects his development in the right manner out of his subjective experiences. Only when the knowledge of supersensible worlds is conceived of as possessing this character is it possible to distinguish it from all experiences of mere subjective mysticism and the like. Of such mysticism it may well be said that it is, more or less, a subjective concern of the mystic. The spiritual scientific training of the soul that is meant here, however, strives for objective experiences, the truth of which is indeed recognized entirely inwardly, the universal validity of which, however, is discernible for that reason.—Here again is a point where it is quite difficult to come to an understanding with many a thought habit of our age.

In conclusion, the author of this book should like to observe that also the well-intended reader should accept these expositions as they offer themselves by virtue of their own content. Today numerous attempts have been made to give to this or that spiritual movement this or that ancient historical name. To many, only then does it appear of value. The question, however, may be asked: What have the expositions of this book to gain by designating them "Rosicrucian" or the like? The important point is that here, with the means that are possible and adequate for the soul in this present period of evolution, an insight is attempted into supersensible worlds, and that from this point of view the riddles of human destiny and of human existence beyond the limits of birth and death are observed. It is not the question of a striving bearing this or that ancient name, but of a striving for truth.

On the other hand, opponents have also employed terms for the world conception presented in this book. Apart from the fact that the terms used in order to deal the author the heaviest possible blow and to discredit him are absurd and objectively false, such terms characterize themselves in their unworthiness by the fact that they attempt to discredit a completely *independent* striving for truth by failing to judge it on its own merits, and by endeavoring to impose their dependence upon ideas derived from this or that trend of thought as judgment upon others. Although these words are necessary in the face of many attacks against the author, nevertheless, he is loath here to go further into this matter.

RUDOLF STEINER

June 1913.

FIRST EDITION

IN OFFERING to the public a book like the present one, its author should be able to anticipate, with utter calmness, any kind of criticism that is possible in our time. Someone, for example, might begin to read the presentation given here of this or that matter, about which he has thought in accordance with the results of research in science, and he might come to the following conclusion: It is astonishing how such assertions are at all possible in our age. The author treats the simplest scientific concepts in a manner that shows the most inconceivable ignorance concerning even the most elementary facts of scientific knowledge. For example, he treats concepts, such as "heat," in a way only possible for someone who has permitted the whole modern mode of thinking in physics to pass over his head without having the least effect. Anyone who knows even the elementary facts of this science could show him that what he says here does not even deserve the designa-

tion "amateurishness," but can only be called "absolute ignorance." Many sentences could be quoted that express
this kind of possible criticism. One could imagine that
someone might arrive at the following conclusion:
"Whoever has read a few pages of this book will, according
to his temperament, lay it aside either with a smile or with
indignation, and say to himself, 'It is certainly queer what
eccentricities can be brought forth by a wrong trend of
thought in the present day. It is best that such expositions
be laid aside with many other freaks of the human
mind.' "—What, however, does the author of this book say
if he really experienced such criticism? Must he not, from
his standpoint, simply regard the critic as a reader lacking
the faculty of judgment or as someone who has not the
goodwill to form an appreciative opinion?—The answer to
that is emphatically, No! the author does not do that in
every case. He is able to imagine that his critic may be a
very clever person and also a trained scientist, someone
who forms his judgments in quite a conscientious way. For
the author of this book is able to enter with his thinking
into the soul of such a person and into the reasons that can
lead the latter to such a judgment. A certain necessity
arises to clarify what the author really says. Although in
general he considers it highly improper to discuss anything
of a personal nature, it seems essential to do so in regard to
this book. To be sure, nothing will be brought forward that
is not concerned with the decision to write this book. What
is said in such a book would certainly have no reason for
existence were it to bear only a personal character. It must
contain views that *every* human being may acquire, and
these must be expressed without any personal coloring as

far as this is humanly possible. The introduction of the personal element is only to make clear how the author is able to comprehend the above-mentioned criticism of his expositions, yet nevertheless was still able to write this book. There would be one way, to be sure, of avoiding mention of the personal element: that of presenting, explicitly, every detail that proves that the statements in this book really agree with every forward step of modern science. This would necessitate, however, the writing of many volumes of introductory matter. Since this at present is out of the question, it seems necessary for the author to describe the personal circumstances through which he feels justified in believing himself in agreement with modern science.—Never, for example, would he have undertaken to publish all that is said in this book about heat phenomena were he not able to affirm that, thirty years ago, he was in the position to make a thorough study of physics, which had ramifications into the various fields of that science. The expositions belonging to the so-called "Mechanical Theory of Heat" ("Theory of Thermodynamics") occupied at that time the central point of his studies in the field of heat phenomena. This theory was of special interest to him. The historical development of the interpretations associated with such names as Julius Robert Mayer, Helmholtz, Joule, Clausius, and others, formed a part of his continuous studies. He thus laid the proper foundation and created the possibility of being able to follow—right up to the present—all the advances of science in the domain of the physical theory of heat. Hence there are no difficulties to overcome when he investigates what modern science has achieved in this field. His confession of inability to do this would have been sufficient reason for leaving the matters advanced in this book unsaid and unwritten. He has truly made it a principle to speak or write only about those subjects in the field of spiritual science about which he would be sufficiently able to say what modern science knows about them. This statement, however, is not meant as a general prerequisite for everyone. Others may, with justice, feel impelled to communicate and publish what their judgment, healthy sense of truth, and feelings indicate, although they may not know the point of view of contemporary science in such matters. The author of this book, however, intends to hold to the above expressed principle for himself. He would not, for example, write about the human glandular or nervous system as he does, were he not at the same time in the position also to discuss these matters from the point of view of natural science.—Thus in spite of the fact that it is possible to conclude that anyone who discusses "heat" in the manner of this book knows nothing about the fundamental laws of modern physics, the author believes himself fully justified in what he has done, because he is striving really to know modern research, and he would have refrained from speaking in this way were the results of this research unknown to him. He knows that the motive for stating such a principle might easily be confused with lack of modesty. In regard to this book it is necessary, however, to state such things, in order that the author's true motives be not mistaken still further. This further mistaking might be far worse than to be accused of immodesty.

Criticism could also be possible from a philosophical standpoint. It might occur in the following way. A philosopher who reads this book might ask himself, "Has the author entirely neglected to study the present day achievements in the field of epistemology? Has he never heard of the existence of a man named Kant, according to whom it is simply philosophically inadmissible to advance such views?" Again, we could continue in this direction. The following critical conclusion, however, might also be drawn: "For the philosopher, such uncritical, naive, amateurish stuff is unbearable and to deal with it further would be nothing but a waste of time."—From the same motive indicated above, in spite of all the misunderstandings that might arise from it, the author would again like to advance something personal here. His study of Kant began in his sixteenth year, and today he believes himself truly capable of judging quite objectively—from the Kantian standpoint—what has been advanced in the present book. From this aspect also, he would have had a reason for leaving this book unwritten did he not know what moves a philosopher to find naive what is written here if he applies the measuring rod of modern criticism. It is, however, possible really to know how, in the sense of Kant, we pass here beyond the limits of possible knowledge. It can also be known how Herbart might discover in this book a "naive realism" that has not yet attained to the "elaboration of concepts," and so forth. It is even possible to know how the modern pragmatism of James, Schiller, and others would find that this book has gone beyond the bounds of "true representations" which "we are able to make our own, to assert, to put into action, and to verify." [1] All of

---

[1] This includes an earnest consideration and study of the philosophy of the "As If," the Bergsonian philosophy, and the *Critique of Speech*.

this may be realized and in spite of that realization, indeed because of it, one may feel justified in writing the expositions presented here. The author has dealt with philosophical trends of thought in his writings: *The Theory of Knowledge Based on Goethe's World Conception* (*Erkenntnistheorie der Goetheschen Weltanschauung*); *Truth and Science* (*Wahrheit und Wissenschaft*); *Philosophy of Freedom* (*Philosophie der Freiheit*); *Goethe's Conception of the World* (*Goethe's Weltanschauung*); *Views of the World and Life in the Nineteenth Century* (*Welt- und Lebensanschauungen im neunzehnten Jahrhundert*); *Riddles of Philosophy* (*Die Raetsel der Philosophie*).

Many kinds of possible criticism could still be cited. There might be critics who have read the earlier writings of the author, for example, *Views of the World and Life in the Nineteenth Century*, or perhaps the brochure on *Haeckel and His Opponents*. Some such critic might say, "It is incomprehensible how one and the same man can write *these* books and then, besides the already published book, *Theosophy*, also write this present book. How is it possible that someone can defend Haeckel and then turn around and discredit what results from Haeckel's research as healthy 'monism'? It might be comprehensible had the author of this *Occult Science* combatted Haeckel 'with fire and sword,' but, that he has defended him, indeed, has even dedicated *Views of the World and Life in the Nineteenth Century* to him, is the most monstrous thing imaginable. Haeckel would have unmistakably declined this dedication had he been conscious of the fact that the dedicator might some day write such stuff as this *Occult Science* with its exposition of a more than crude dualism."—The author of this book, however, is of the opinion that while it is possible to understand Haeckel very well, it is, nevertheless, not necessary to believe that he is only to be understood by one who considers nonsensical everything that is not derived from Haeckel's own concepts and hypotheses. Furthermore, he is of the opinion that it is possible to come to an understanding of Haeckel only by entering upon what he has achieved for science and not be combatting him "with fire and sword." Least of all does the author believe that Haeckel's opponents are right, against whom, for example in his brochure, *Haeckel and His Opponents*, he has defended the great natural philosopher. Indeed, if the writer of this brochure goes far beyond Haeckel's hypotheses and places the spiritual point of view of the world alongside Haeckel's merely naturalistic one, his opinion need not therefore coincide with the opinion of the latter's opponents. If the facts are looked at correctly, it will be discovered that the author's present day writings are in complete accord with his earlier ones.

The author also understands quite well the critic who generally regards the descriptions in this book as an outpouring of wild fancy or a dreamlike play of thoughts. All that is to be said in this regard, however, is contained in the book itself. It is shown there how, in full measure, thought based on reason can and must become the touchstone of what is presented. Only the one who applies to this book the test of reason in the same way he would apply it, for example, to the facts of natural science, will be able to determine what reason proves in such a test.

After saying so much about personalities who from the outset refute this book, a word may also be spared for those who have reason to agree with it. For them the most essential is to be found in the first chapter, *The Character of Occult Science.* Something more, however, is to be said here. Although the book deals with the results of research that lie beyond the power of the intellect bound to the sense world, yet nothing is offered that cannot be comprehended by anyone possessing an unprejudiced reason, a healthy sense of truth, and the wish to employ these human faculties. The author says without hesitation that he would like, above all, to have readers who are not willing to accept on blind faith what is offered here, but who endeavor to examine what is offered by means of the knowledge of their own soul and through the experiences of their own lives.[1] He would like to have above all *cautious* readers who only accept what can be logically justified. The author knows his book would have *no* value, were it dependent only on blind faith; it is only useful to the degree it can be vindicated before unbiased reason. Blind faith can so easily mistake the foolish and superstitious for the true. Many who are gladly satisfied with a mere belief in a "supersensible world" will perhaps find that this book makes too great a demand on the powers of thought. Yet concerning the communications given here, it is not merely a question of communicating something, but that the communication be in conformity with a conscientious view of the sphere of life in question. For it is indeed the sphere in which the highest things and the most unscrupulous charlatanry, in which knowledge and crass su-

---

[1] Here is not only meant the spiritual scientific test by supersensible methods of research, but primarily the test that is possible by healthy, unprejudiced thought and common sense.

perstition so easily meet in actual life, and where, above all, they can be so easily confused with one another.

Anyone acquainted with supersensible research will, in reading this book, notice that it has been the endeavor of its author sharply to mark the limits between what can and ought to be communicated from the sphere of supersensible knowledge at present and that which is to be presented at a later period, or at least in another form.

RUDOLF STEINER

December 1909.

AN OUTLINE OF
OCCULT SCIENCE

I

THE CHARACTER
OF OCCULT SCIENCE

OCCULT science, an ancient term, is used for the contents of this book. This term can arouse in various individuals of the present day feelings of the most contrary character. For many, it possesses something repellent; it arouses derision, pitying smiles, perhaps contempt. These people imagine that the kind of thinking thus designated can only be based upon idle, fantastic dreaming, that behind such "alleged" science there can lurk only the impulse to renew all sorts of superstitions that are properly avoided by those who understand "true scientific methods" and "pure intellectual endeavor." The effect of this term upon others is to cause them to think that what is meant by it must bring them something that cannot be acquired in any other way and to which, according to their nature, they are attracted by a deep, inner longing for knowledge, or by the soul's sublimated curiosity. In between these sharply con-

3

trasting opinions there exists every possible kind of intermediate stage of conditional rejection or acceptance of what this or that person imagines when he hears the term, "occult science."—It is not to be denied that for many the term, occult science, has a magical sound because it seems to satisfy their fatal passion for knowledge of an "unknown," of a mysterious, even of an obscure something that is not to be acquired in a natural way. For many people do not wish to satisfy the deepest longings of their souls by means of something that can be clearly understood. Their convictions lead them to conclude that besides what can be known in the world there must be something that defies cognition. With extraordinary absurdity, which they do not observe, they reject, in regard to the deepest longing for knowledge, all that "is known" and only wish to give their approval to something that cannot be said to be known by means of ordinary research. He who speaks of "occult science" will do well to keep in mind the fact that he is confronted by misunderstandings caused by just such defenders of a science of this kind—defenders who are striving, in fact, not for knowledge, but for its antithesis.

This work is intended for readers who will not permit their impartiality to be taken away from them just because a word may arouse prejudice through various circumstances. It is not here a question of knowledge which, in any respect, can be considered to be "secret" and therefore only accessible to certain people through some special favor of fate. We shall do justice to the use of the term, occult science, employed here, if we consider what Goethe has in mind when he speaks of the "revealed secrets" in the phenomena of the universe. What remains "secret"—unrevealed—in these phenomena when grasped only by means of the senses and the intellect bound up with them will be considered as the content of a supersensible mode of knowledge.[1]—What is meant here by "Occult Science" does not constitute science for anyone who only considers "scientific" what is revealed through the senses and the intellect serving them. If, however, such a person wishes to understand himself, he must acknowledge that he rejects occult science, not from well-substantiated insight, but from a mandate arising from his own personal feelings. In order to understand this, it is only necessary to consider how science comes into existence and what significance it has in human life. The origin of science, in its essential nature, is not recognized by means of the subject matter it is dealing with, but by means of the human soul-activity arising in scientific endeavor. We must consider the attitude of the soul when it elaborates science. If we acquire the habit of exercising this kind of activity only when we are concerned with the manifestation of the senses, we might easily be led to the opinion that this sense-manifestation is the essential thing, and we do not become aware that a certain attitude of the human soul has been employed only in re-

---

[1] It has happened that the term "occult science," as used by the author in earlier editions of this book, has been rejected for the reason that a science cannot be "something hidden." That would be correct if the matter were meant in this way. But such is not the case. The science of nature cannot be called a "natural" science in the sense that it belongs by "nature" to everyone, nor does the author consider occult science as a "hidden" science, but one that has to do with the unrevealed, the concealed, in the phenomena of the world for ordinary methods of cognition. It is a science of the "mysteries," of the "revealed secrets." This science, however, should not be a secret for anyone who seeks knowledge of it by the proper methods.

gard to the manifestation of the senses. It is possible, however, to rise above this arbitrary self-limitation and, apart
from special application, consider the characteristics of
scientific activity. This is the basis for our designating as
"scientific" the knowledge of a non-sensory world-content.
The human power of thought wishes to occupy itself with
this *latter* world-content just as it occupies itself, in the
other case, with the world-content of natural science. Occult science desires to free the natural-scientific method
and its principle of research from their special application
that limits them, in their own sphere, to the relationship
and process of sensory facts, but, at the same time, it wants
to retain their way of thinking and other characteristics. It
desires to speak about the non-sensory in the same way
natural science speaks about the sensory. While natural
science remains within the sense world with this method of
research and way of thinking, occult science wishes to consider the employment of mental activity upon nature as a
kind of self-education of the soul and to apply what it has
thus acquired to the realms of the non-sensory. Its method
does not speak about the sense phenomena as such, but
speaks about the non-sensory world-content in the way the
scientist talks about the content of the sensory world. It retains the mental attitude of the natural-scientific method;
that is to say, it holds fast to just the thing that makes natural research a science. For that reason it may call itself a
science.

When we consider the significance of natural science in
human life, we shall find that this significance cannot be
exhausted by acquiring a knowledge of nature, since this
knowledge can never lead to anything but an experiencing

of what the human soul itself is *not*. The soul-element does not live in what man knows about nature, but in the process of acquiring knowledge. The soul experiences itself in its occupation with nature. What it vitally achieves in this activity is something besides the knowledge of nature itself; it is self-development experienced in acquiring knowledge of nature. Occult science desires to employ the results of this self-development in realms that lie beyond mere nature. The occult scientist has no desire to undervalue natural science; on the contrary, he desires to acknowledge it even more than the natural scientist himself. He knows that, without the exactness of the mode of thinking of natural science, he cannot establish a science. Yet he knows also that after this exactness has been acquired through genuine penetration into the spirit of natural-scientific thinking, it can be retained through the force of the soul for other fields.

Something, however, arises here that may cause misgivings. In studying nature, the soul is guided by the object under consideration to a much greater degree than is the case when non-sensory world contents are studied. In the latter study, the soul must possess to a much greater degree, from purely inner impulses, the ability to hold fast to the scientific mode of thinking. Since many people believe, unconsciously, that this can be done only through the guidance of natural phenomena, they are inclined, through a dogmatic declaration, to make their decisions accordingly; as soon as this guidance is abandoned, the soul gropes in a void with its scientific method. Such people have not become conscious of the special character of this method. They base their judgment for the most part upon errors that must arise if the scientific attitude is not sufficiently strengthened by observation of natural phenomena and, in spite of this, the soul attempts a consideration of the non-sensory regions of the world. It is self-evident that in such cases there arises much unscientific talk about non-sensory world contents. Not, however, because such talk, in its essence, is incapable of being scientific, but because, in such an instance, scientific self-education in the observation of nature has been neglected.

Whoever wishes to speak about occult science must certainly, in connection with what has just been said, be fully awake in regard to all the vagaries that arise when, without the scientific attitude, something is determined concerning the revealed mysteries of the world. It would, however, be of no avail if, at the very beginning of an occult-scientific presentation, we were to speak of all kinds of aberrations, which in the souls of prejudiced persons discredit all research in this direction, because they conclude, from the presence of really quite numerous aberrations, that the entire endeavor is unjustified. Since, however, in the case of scientists, or scientifically minded critics, the rejection of occult science rests in most instances solely upon the above mentioned dogmatic declaration, and the reference to the aberrations is only an often unconscious pretext, a discussion with such opponents will be fruitless. Nothing, indeed, hinders them from making the certainly quite justifiable objection that, at the very outset, there is nothing that can definitely determine whether the person who believes others to be in error, himself possesses the above characterized firm foundation. Therefore, the person striving to present occult science can simply offer what in his estimation he has a right to say. The judgment concerning his justification can only be formed by other persons; indeed, only by those who, avoiding all dogmatic declarations, are able to enter into the nature of his communications concerning the revealed mysteries of cosmic events. To be sure, he will be obliged to show the relationship between his presentations and other achievements in the field of knowledge and life; he will have to show what oppositions are possible and to what degree the direct, external, sensory reality of life verifies his observations. He should, however, never attempt to present his subject in a way that produces its effect by means of his art of persuasion instead of through its content.

The following objection is often heard in regard to the statements of occult science: "These latter do not offer proof; they merely assert this or that and say that occult science ascertains this." The following exposition will be misjudged if it is thought that any part of it has been presented in this sense. Our endeavor here is to allow the capacity of soul unfolded through a knowledge of nature to evolve further, as far as its own nature will allow, and then call attention to the fact that in such development the soul encounters supersensible facts. It is assumed that every reader who is able to enter into what has been presented will necessarily run up against these facts. A difference, however, is encountered with respect to purely natural-scientific observation the moment we enter the realm of spiritual science. In natural science, the facts present themselves in the field of the sense world; the exponent of natural science considers the activity of the soul as something that recedes into the background in the face of the relationships and the course of sensory facts. The exponent of spiritual science must place his soul activity into the foreground; for the reader only arrives at the facts if he makes this activity of the soul his own in the right way. These facts are not present for human perception *without* the activity of the soul as they are—although uncomprehended —in natural science; they enter into human perception only *by means of* soul activity. The exponent of spiritual science therefore presumes that the reader is *seeking* facts mutually with him. His exposition will be given in the form of a narration describing how these facts were discovered, and in the manner of his narration not personal caprice but scientific thinking trained by natural science will prevail. It will also be necessary, therefore, to speak of the means by which a consideration of the non-sensory, of the supersensible, is attained.—Anyone who occupies himself with an exposition of occult science will soon see that through it concepts and ideas are acquired that previously he did not possess. Thus he also acquires new thoughts concerning his previous conception of the nature of "proof." He learns that for an exposition of natural science, "proof" is something that is brought to it, as it were, from without. In spiritual-scientific thinking, however, the activity, which in natural-scientific thinking the soul employs for proof, lies already in the search for facts. These facts cannot be discovered if the path to them is itself not already a proof. Whoever really travels this path has already experienced the proving in the process; nothing can be accomplished by means of a proof applied from without. The fact that this is not recognized in the character of occult science calls forth many misunderstandings.

10

The whole of occult science must spring from two thoughts that can take root in every human soul. For the occult scientist, as he is meant here, these two thoughts express facts that can be experienced if we use the right means. For many people these thoughts signify extremely controversial statements about which there may be wide differences of opinion; they may even be "proved" to be impossible.

These two thoughts are the following. First, behind the visible there exists an invisible world, *concealed* at the outset from the senses and the thinking bound up with the senses; and second, it is possible for man, through the development of capacities slumbering within him, to penetrate into this hidden world.

One person maintains that there is no such hidden world, that the world perceived by means of the human senses is the only one, that its riddles can be solved out of itself, and that, although the human being at present is still far from being able to answer all the questions of existence, a time will surely come when sense experience and the science based upon it will be able to give the answers.

Others state that we must not maintain there is no hidden world behind the visible, yet the human powers of cognition are unable to penetrate into it. They have limits that cannot be overstepped. Let those who need "faith" take refuge in a world of that kind: a true science, which is based upon assured facts, cannot concern itself with such a world.

There is a third group that considers it presumptuous if a man, through his cognitive activity, desires to penetrate into a realm about which he is to renounce all "knowledge" and be content with "faith." The adherents of this opinion consider it wrong for the weak human being to want to penetrate into a world that is supposed to belong to the religious life alone.

It is also maintained that a common knowledge of the facts of the sense world is possible for everyone, but that in respect of supersensible facts it is only a matter of the personal opinion of the individual, and that no one should speak of a generally valid certainty in these matters.

Others maintain still other things.

It can become clear that the observation of the visible world presents riddles that can never be solved out of the facts of that world themselves. They will never be solved in this way, although the science concerned with these facts may have advanced as far as is possible. For the visible facts, through their very inner nature, point clearly to a hidden world. Whoever does not discern this closes his mind to the riddles that spring up everywhere out of the facts of the sense world. He *refuses* to perceive certain questions and riddles; he, therefore, thinks that all questions may be answered by means of the sensory facts. The questions he *wishes* to propound can indeed *all* be answered by means of the facts that he expects will be discovered in the future. This may be readily admitted. But why should a person wait for answers to certain things who does not ask any questions? Whoever strives for an occult science merely says that for him these questions are self-evident and that they must be recognized as a fully justified expression of the human soul. Science cannot be pressed into limits by forbidding the human being to ask unbiased questions.

12

The opinion that there are limits to human cognition that cannot be overstepped, compelling man to stop short before an invisible world, must be replied to by saying that there can be no doubt about the impossibility of finding access to the invisible world with the kind of cognition referred to here. Whoever considers that form of cognition to be the only possible one cannot come to any other opinion than that the human being is denied access to a possibly existent higher world. Yet the following may also be stated. If it is possible to develop *another* kind of cognition, *this* then may well lead into the supersensible world. If this kind of cognition is considered to be impossible, then we reach a point of view from which all talk about a supersensible world appears as pure nonsense. From an impartial viewpoint, however, the only reason for such an opinion can be the fact that the person holding it has no knowledge of this other kind of cognition. Yet how can a person pass judgment upon something about which he himself admits his ignorance? Unprejudiced thinking must hold to the premise that a person should speak only of what he *knows* and should not make statements about something he does *not* know. Such thinking can only speak of the right that a person has to communicate what he himself has experienced, but it cannot speak of the right that somebody declare impossible what he does not know or does not wish to know. We cannot deny anyone the right to ignore the supersensible, but there can never be any good reason for him to declare himself an authority, not only on what *he himself* can know, but also on all that a man can *not* know.

In the case of those who declare that it is presumptuous

13

to penetrate into the domain of the supersensible an occult-scientific exposition has to call attention to the fact that this can be done, and that it is a transgression against the faculties bestowed upon man if we allow them to stagnate, instead of developing and making use of them.

Whoever thinks, however, that the views concerning the supersensible world must belong entirely to personal opinion and feeling denies what is common to all human beings. It is certainly true that the insight into these things must be acquired by each person for himself, but it is also a fact that *all* human beings who go far enough arrive, not at different opinions about these things, but at the same opinion. Differences of opinion exist only as long as human beings wish to approach the highest truths, not by a scientifically assured path, but by way of personal caprice. It must again be admitted, however, that only that person is able to acknowledge the correctness of the path of occult science who is willing to familiarize himself with its characteristics.

At the proper moment, every human being can find the way to occult science who recognizes, or even merely assumes or divines, out of the manifest world, the existence of a hidden world and who, out of the consciousness that the powers of cognition are capable of development, is driven to the feeling that the concealed is able to reveal itself to him. To a person who has been led to occult science by means of these soul experiences there opens up not only the prospect of finding the answer to certain questions springing from his craving for knowledge, but also the quite different prospect of becoming the victor over all that hampers and weakens life. It signifies, in a certain higher sense, a weakening of life, indeed a death of the soul, when a human being sees himself forced to turn away from the supersensible, or to deny it. Indeed, under certain conditions it leads to despair when a man loses hope of having the hidden revealed to him. This death and despair in their manifold forms are, at the same time, inner soul opponents of occult-scientific striving. They appear when the inner force of the human being dwindles. Then all force of life must be introduced from without if such a person is to get possession of any life force at all. He then perceives the things, beings, and events that appear before his senses; he analyses these with his intellect. They give him pleasure and pain, they drive him to the actions of which he is capable. He may carry on in this way for a while yet at some time he must reach a point when he inwardly dies. For what can be drawn from the world in this way becomes exhausted. This is not a statement derived from the personal experience of one individual, but the result of an unbiased consideration of all human life. What guards against this exhaustion is the concealed something that rests within the depths of things. If the power to descend into these depths, in order to draw up ever new life-force, dies away within the human being, then finally also the outer aspect of things no longer proves conducive to life.

This question by no means concerns only the individual human being, only his personal welfare and misfortune. Precisely through true occult-scientific observations man arrives at the certainty that, from a higher standpoint, the welfare and misfortune of the individual is intimately bound up with the welfare or misfortune of the whole world. The human being comes to understand that he injures the whole universe and all its beings by not developing *his* forces in the proper way. If he lays waste his life by losing the relationship with the supersensible, he not only destroys something in his own inner being—the decaying of which can lead him finally to despair—but because of his weakness he creates a hindrance to the evolution of the whole world in which he lives.

The human being can deceive himself. He can yield to the belief that there is no hidden world, that what appears to his senses and his intellect contains everything that can possibly exist. But this deception is only possible, not for the deeper, but for the surface consciousness. Feeling and desire do not submit to this deceptive belief. In one way or another, they will always crave for a concealed something, and if this is withdrawn from them, they force the human being into doubt, into a feeling of insecurity of life, indeed, into despair. A cognition that reveals the hidden is capable of overcoming all hopelessness, all insecurity, all despair, in fact all that weakens life and makes it incapable of the service required of him in the cosmos.

This is the beautiful fruit of the knowledge of spiritual science that it gives strength and firmness to life, and not alone gratification to the passion for knowledge. The source from which this knowledge draws its power to work and its trust in life is inexhaustible. No one who has *once* really approached this source will, by repeatedly taking refuge in it, go away unstrengthened.

There are people who wish to hear nothing about this knowledge because they see something unhealthy in what has just been said. Such people are quite right in regard to the superficial and external side of life. They do not wish to see stunted what life offers in its so-called reality. They consider it weakness when a person turns away from reality and seeks his salvation in a hidden world that to them appears as a fantastic, imaginary one. If, in our spiritual-scientific striving, we are not to fall into an unhealthy dreaminess and weakness, we must acknowledge the partial justification of such objections. For they rest upon a healthy judgment that leads, not to a whole, but only to a half-truth through the very fact that it does not penetrate into the depth of things, but remains on the surface.— Were the striving for supersensible knowledge likely to weaken life and to estrange men from true reality, then such objections would certainly be strong enough to remove the foundation from under this spiritual trend.

Also concerning such points of view, spiritual-scientific endeavors would not take the right path if they wished to "defend" themselves in the usual sense of the word. Here also they can only speak out of their own merit, recognizable to every unprejudiced person, when they make evident how they increase the vital force and strength in those who familiarize themselves with them in the right way. These endeavors cannot turn man into a person estranged from the world, into a dreamer; they give him strength from the sources of life out of which his spirit and soul have sprung.

Many a man encounters still other intellectual obstacles when he approaches the endeavors of occult science. For it is fundamentally true that the reader finds in the presentation of occult science a description of soul experiences through the pursuit of which he can approach the supersensible world-content. But in practice this must present itself as a kind of ideal. The reader must at first absorb a comparatively large number of supersensible experiences in the form of communications, experiences that he, however, has not yet passed through himself. This cannot be otherwise and will also be the case with this book. The author will describe what he believes he knows about the nature of man, about his conduct between birth and death, and in his disembodied state in the spiritual world; in addition, the evolution of the earth and of mankind will be described. Thus it might appear as though a certain amount of alleged knowledge were presented in the form of dogmas for which belief based on authority were demanded. This is not the case. What can be known of the supersensible world-content is present in him who presents the material as a living content of the soul, and if someone becomes acquainted with this soul-content, this then enkindles in his own soul the impulses that lead to the corresponding supersensible facts. While reading the communications concerning spiritual-scientific knowledge, we live in a quite different manner than we do while reading those concerning external facts. If we read communications from the outer sense world, we are reading *about* them. But if we read communications about supersensible facts in the right way, we are living into the stream of spiritual existence. In absorbing the results we, at the same time, enter upon our own inner path to them. It is true that what is meant here is often not at all observed by the reader. Entrance into the spiritual world is imagined in a way too similar to an experience of the senses; therefore, what is experienced when reading about this world is considered to be much too much of the nature of thought. But if we have *truly* absorbed these thoughts we are already within this world and have only to become quite clear about the fact that we have already experienced, unnoticed, what we thought we had received merely as an intellectual communication.— Complete clarity concerning the real nature of what has been experienced will be gained in carrying out in practice what is described, in the second and last part of this book, as the "path" to supersensible knowledge. It might easily be thought that the opposite would be the right way; that this path should be described first. That is not the case. For anyone who only carries out "exercises" in order to enter the supersensible world, without directing the attention of his soul to definite facts concerning it, that world remains an indefinite, confused chaos. We learn to become familiar with that world naïvely, as it were, by gaining information about certain of its facts, and then we account for the way in which we ourselves, abandoning naïveté, fully consciously acquire the experiences about which we have gained information. If we penetrate deeply into the descriptions of occult science we become convinced that this is the only sure path to supersensible knowledge. We shall also realize that the opinion that supersensible knowledge might at first have the effect of a dogma through the power of suggestion, as it were, is unfounded. For the content of this knowledge is acquired by a soul activity that takes from it all merely suggestive power and only gives it the possibility of appealing to another person in the same way in which all truths speak to him that offer themselves to his thoughtful judgment. The reason the other person does not at first notice that he is living in the spiritual world does not lie in a thoughtless, suggestive absorption of what he has read, but in the subtlety and unfamiliarity of what he has experienced in his reading.—Therefore, by first absorbing the communications as given in the first part of this book, we become participators in the knowledge of the spiritual world; by means of the practical application of the soul exercises given in the second part, we become independent knowers of this world.

In the spirit and true sense of the word, no real scientist will be able to find a contradiction between his science built upon the facts of the sense world and the method by which the supersensible world is investigated. The scientist makes use of certain instruments and methods. He produces his instruments by transforming what "nature" offers him. The supersensible method of knowledge also makes use of an instrument. This instrument is man himself. This instrument, too, must first be made ready for higher research. The capacities and forces given to man by nature, without his assistance, must be transformed into higher capacities and powers. Man is thereby able to make himself the instrument for research in the supersensible world.

II

THE ESSENTIAL NATURE OF MANKIND

IN THE OBSERVATION of man from the point of view of a supersensible mode of cognition, the general principles of this method become immediately applicable. This observation rests upon the recognition of the "revealed mystery" within the individual human being. Only a part of what supersensible cognition apprehends as the human being is accessible to the senses and to the intellect dependent upon them, namely, *the physical body*. In order to elucidate the concept of this physical body, our attention must first be turned to that phenomenon which, as the great riddle, lies spread out over all observation of life, that is, to death and, in connection with it, to so-called lifeless nature—the mineral kingdom—which always bears death within it. We have, thereby, referred to facts that are only fully explainable through supersensible knowledge, and to which a large part of this volume must be devoted. Here,

21

however, a few thoughts must first be offered for the sake of orientation.

Within the manifest world, the physical body is the part of man having the same nature as the mineral world. On the other hand, what differentiates man from the mineral cannot be considered as physical body. Especially important in an unbiased consideration is the fact that death lays bare the part of man that, after death, is of the same nature as the mineral world. We can point to the corpse as that part of man subject to the processes of the mineral realm. It can be emphasized that in this member of man's being, the corpse, the same substances and forces are active as in the mineral realm, but it is necessary to emphasize, equally strongly, the fact that at death the decay of the physical body occurs. Yet we are also justified in saying that while it is true that the same substances and forces are active in both the human physical body and the mineral, their activity during life is dedicated to a higher purpose. Only when death has occurred is their activity similar to that of the mineral world. They then appear as they must appear, according to their own nature, namely, as the dissolver of the physical bodily form.

Thus, in man we have to differentiate sharply between the visible and the concealed. For during life the concealed must wage constant battle against the substances and forces of the mineral element in the physical body. When this battle ceases, the mineral activity comes to the fore.— We have thereby drawn attention to the point where the science of the supersensible must enter. It must seek that which wages the above-mentioned battle. It is just this that is hidden from sense-observation and is only accessible to

22

supersensible observation. In a later chapter of this work we shall consider how the human being is able to reach the point where this hidden something becomes manifest to him just as the phenomena of the senses are manifest to the ordinary eye. Here, however, we shall describe the result of supersensible observation.

It has already been indicated that the descriptions of the path on which man attains to a higher perception can be of value to him only after he has become acquainted in simple narrative form with the disclosures of supersensible research. For in regard to the supersensible realm it is possible to *comprehend* what has not yet been *observed*. Indeed, the right path toward perception is that which proceeds from comprehension.

Even though that hidden something, which in the physical body carries on the battle against disintegration, is only observable by higher perception, yet its *effects* are clearly evident to the reasoning power that limits itself to the manifest. These effects express themselves in the *form* or shape into which the mineral substances and forces of the physical body are fashioned during life. This form disappears by degrees and the physical body becomes a part of the rest of the mineral world when death has occurred. Supersensible perception, however, is able to observe, as an independent member of the human entity, what prevents the physical substances and forces during life from taking their own path, which leads to dissolution of the physical body. Let us call the independent member the *ether* or *lifebody*.—In order to prevent misunderstandings from the very beginning, two things should be borne in mind concerning this designation of a second member of the human entity. The word "ether" is used here in a sense quite different from the one in use in present day physics, which, for example, designates the vehicle of light as ether. Here, however, the word will be limited to the meaning given above. It will be used for what is accessible to higher perception and for what is recognizable to sense-observation only in its effects, that is, through its ability to give a definite form and shape to the mineral substances and forces existing in the physical body. The word "body" also must not be misunderstood. In designating the higher things of existence, it is necessary to use the words of ordinary language, and for sense-observation these words express only the sensory. From the standpoint of the senses, the ether body is, naturally, nothing of a bodily nature, however tenuous we may picture it.[1]

Having reached, in the presentation of the supersensible, the mention of this ether body or life body, the point has also been reached where such a concept will have to encounter the opposition of many present-day opinions. The evolution of the human spirit has led to the point where in our age the discussion of such a member of the human organism must be considered as something unscientific. The materialistic mode of thought has reached the point of seeing in the living body nothing but a combination of physical substances and forces, like those to be found in the so-called lifeless body, in the mineral. The combination in the living is supposed to be more complicated than in the lifeless, however. Not so long ago, ordinary science,

---

[1] In his book, *Theosophy,* the author has discussed the fact that with the designation "ether body" or "life body" he has no intention of renewing the old concept of "life force" discarded by natural science.

too, held still other points of view. Whoever has followed the writings of many serious scientists of the first half of the nineteenth century realizes that at that time "real natural scientists" were conscious of the fact that something exists in the living body besides what is present in the lifeless mineral. They spoke of a "life force." This "life force," to be sure, is not visualized as having the nature of the life-body designated here, but an inkling that something of the kind exists, underlies such a concept. This "life force" was thought of as though supplementing in the living body the physical substances and forces as the magnetic force supplements the mere iron in the magnet. Then came the time when this "life force" was discarded from the store of scientific concepts. Purely physical and chemical causes were to suffice for everything. In this respect, a reaction has set in today among many modern scientific thinkers. It is admitted on many sides that the assumption of something similar to "life force" is not, after all, pure nonsense. The scientist who admits this, however, will not be inclined to make common cause with the point of view presented here concerning the life body. It is useless, as a rule, to enter into a discussion, from the standpoint of supersensible knowledge, with people holding such views. It ought rather be the concern of this knowledge to recognize that the materialistic mode of thought is a necessary concomitant phenomenon of the great progress in natural science in our age. This progress rests upon an enormous improvement in the means of sense-observation, and it lies in the nature of man, during his evolution, at times to bring to a certain degree of perfection particular faculties at the cost of others. Exact sense-observation, which has developed so significantly through natural science, caused the cultivation of those human capacities that lead into "hidden worlds" to retreat into the background, but the time has come again when this cultivation is necessary. Acknowledgment of the concealed, however, will not be won by contending against opinions that result with logical accuracy from the denial of the concealed, but by placing the concealed itself in the proper light. Then those for whom "the time has come" will acknowledge it.

It was necessary to speak of this here in order to keep people from assuming that the author is ignorant of the viewpoint of natural science when he speaks of an "ether body" that in many circles is considered as something purely fantastic.

This ether body, then, is a second member of the human entity. For supersensible cognition, it possesses a higher degree of reality than the physical body. A description of its appearance to supersensible perception can only be given in a subsequent chapter of this book after the sense in which such descriptions are to be taken has become clear. For the present it may suffice to say that the ether body penetrates the physical completely and that it is to be looked upon as a kind of architect of the latter. All organs are preserved in their form and shape by means of the currents and movements of the ether body. The physical heart is based upon an "etheric heart," the physical brain upon an "etheric brain," and so forth. The ether body is organized like the physical body, only with greater complexity. Wherever in the physical body separated parts exist, in the ether body everything is in living, interweaving motion.

The human being possesses this ether body in common

with the plants, just as he possesses the physical body in common with the mineral element. Everything living has its ether body.

Supersensible observation advances from the ether body to a further member of the human entity. In order to aid the student in forming a visualization of this member, it points to the phenomenon of sleep, just as it pointed to the phenomenon of death when it spoke of the ether body.— All human endeavor rests upon activity in the waking state, in so far as the manifest is concerned. This activity, however, is only possible if man again and again gathers new strength for his exhausted forces from sleep. Action and thought disappear in sleep; all suffering, all pleasure are submerged for conscious life. As though out of hidden, mysterious depths, conscious forces arise out of the unconsciousness of sleep as man awakens. It is the same consciousness that sinks into shadowy depths when we go to sleep and arises again when we awaken. The power that awakens life again and again out of a state of unconsciousness is, according to supersensible cognition, the third member of the human entity. We may call it the *astral body*. Just as the physical body is unable to retain its form by means of the mineral substances and forces contained in it, but only by being interpenetrated by the ether body, so likewise the forces of the ether body are unable, by themselves, to illuminate this body with the light of consciousness. An ether body, left entirely to itself, would have to remain in a continuous state of sleep. We might also say: it could only maintain a plant-existence within the physical body. An awakened ether body is illuminated by an astral body. For sense-observation, the activity of

27

the astral body disappears when man sinks into sleep. For supersensible observation, the astral body still exists, but it appears to be separated or withdrawn from the ether body. Sense-observation is not concerned with the astral body itself, but only with its effects within the manifest, and during sleep these effects are not directly present. In the same sense that man has his physical body in common with the minerals, his ether body with the plants, he is, in regard to his astral body, of the same nature as the animals. Plants are in a continuous state of sleep. A person who does not judge accurately in these things can easily fall into the error of ascribing a kind of consciousness also to plants that is similar to that of animals and men in their waking state. That, however, can happen only if he has an unclear idea of the nature of consciousness. It is then stated that if an external stimulus is applied to the plant it makes certain movements like the animal. One speaks of the "sensitivity" of some plants that, for example, contract their leaves if certain outer stimuli act upon them. Yet it is not the characteristic of consciousness that a being reacts to certain stimuli, but that the being experiences something in its inner nature that adds something new to the mere reaction. Otherwise, one could also speak of consciousness when a piece of iron expands under the influence of heat. Consciousness is present only when, through the effect of heat, the being, for example, inwardly experiences pain.

The fourth member of his being that supersensible cognition must ascribe to man has nothing in common with the world of the manifest surrounding him. It is what distinguishes him from his fellow-creatures and through which he is the crown of creation belonging to him. Supersensible cognition forms a conception of this additional member of the human entity by calling attention to the essential difference in the experiences of waking life. This difference appears at once when man realizes that in the waking state he stands, on the one hand, always in the midst of experiences that *of necessity* come and go, and that, on the other hand, he has experiences in which this is not the case. This becomes especially clear when human and animal experiences are compared. The animal experiences with great regularity the influences of the outer world, and under the influence of heat and cold, pain and pleasure, under certain regularly recurring processes of its body, it becomes conscious of hunger and thirst. The life of man is not exhausted with such experiences. He can develop passions and desires that transcend all this. In the case of the animal it would always be possible, were we able to go far enough, to show where the cause for an action or sensation lies, outside of or within the body. With man this is by no means the case. He can produce desires and passions for whose origin neither the cause within nor without his body is sufficient. We must ascribe a special source to everything that falls within this domain. In the light of supersensible science this source can be seen in the human *ego*. The *ego* can, therefore, be called the fourth member of the human entity.—If the astral body were left to itself, pleasure and pain, feelings of hunger and thirst would take place in it; but what would not occur is the feeling that there is something *permanent* in all this. Not the permanent as such is here called the "ego," but what experiences this permanency. We must formulate the concepts precisely in this realm, if misunderstandings are not to arise. With the becoming aware of something enduring, something permanent in the change of the inner experiences the dawning of the "ego feeling" begins. The fact that a being feels hunger, for example, cannot give it an ego feeling. Hunger arises when the renewed causes of it make themselves felt within the being in question. It pounces upon its food just because these renewed causes are present. The ego feeling appears when not only these renewed impulses drive the human being to seek food, but when pleasure has arisen at a previous appeasement of hunger and the consciousness of this pleasure has remained, thus making not only the *present* experience of hunger, but the *past* experience of pleasure the driving force in the human being's search for food.—Without the presence of the ether body, the physical body would decay. Without the illumination by the astral body, the ether body would sink into unconsciousness. In like manner the astral body would have to let the past sink, again and again, into *oblivion,* were it not for the "ego" to carry this past over into the present. What death is for the physical body, and sleep for the ether body, *oblivion* is for the astral body. One might also say that *life* belongs to the ether body, *consciousness* to the astral body, and *memory* to the ego.

It is even easier to fall into the error of ascribing memory to animals than it is to ascribe consciousness to plants. It is very natural to think of memory when a dog recognizes its master whom he has not seen perhaps for a long time. Yet, in reality, this recognition does not rest upon memory, but upon something quite different. The dog feels a certain attraction to its master. This attraction proceeds

30

from the master's personality. This personality causes pleasure in the dog when the master is in its presence, and every time the master's presence reoccurs, it causes a renewal of this pleasure. Memory, however, is only present when a being not only feels with its experiences in the present, but when it retains also those of the past. One might acknowledge this and still fall into the error of thinking that the dog has memory. For it might be said that the dog mourns when its master leaves it, therefore it has retained a memory of him. That also is an incorrect conclusion. Through sharing the master's life, his presence becomes a need to the dog and it, therefore, experiences his absence in the same way that it experiences hunger. Whoever does not make these distinctions, will not arrive at clarity concerning the true relationships of life.

Out of certain prejudices, one might object to this exposition by maintaining that it cannot be known whether or not there exists in the animal anything similar to human memory. Such an objection, however, is the result of untrained observation. Anyone who can observe quite factually how the animal behaves in the complex of its experiences notices the difference between its behavior and that of the human being, and he realizes that the animal's behavior corresponds to the non-existence of memory. For supersensible observation this is quite clear. Yet, what arises as direct experience in supersensible observation may also be known *by its effects* in this domain through sense-perception permeated by thought activity. If one says that man is aware of *his* memory through inner soul-observation, something he cannot carry out in the case of the animal, one states something based upon a fatal error.

31

What man has to say to himself about his capacity for memory he cannot derive from inner soul-observation, but only from what he experiences with himself in relation to the things and occurrences of the outer world. Man has these experiences *with himself* and with another human being and also with animals in exactly the same way. He is blinded by pure illusion when he believes that he *judges* the existence of memory merely by means of inner observation. The power underlying memory may be called an inner power; the *judgment* concerning this power is acquired, also in regard to one's own person, through the outer world by directing one's attention to the relationships of life. Just as one is able to judge these relationships in regard to oneself, so one can judge them in regard to the animal. In regard to such things our current psychology suffers from its wholly untrained, inexact ideas, deceptive to a great degree because of errors in observation.

Memory and oblivion signify for the ego what waking and sleeping signify for the astral body. Just as sleep permits the cares and troubles of the day to disappear into nothingness, oblivion spreads a veil over the bad experiences of life, blotting out a part of the past. Just as sleep is necessary for the restoration of the exhausted life forces, so man has to eradicate certain parts of the past from his memory if he is to approach new experiences freely and without bias. But precisely through forgetting, strength develops for perception of the new. Consider certain facts, like that of learning to write. All the details the child has to experience in learning to write are forgotten. What remains is the ability to write. How would man be able to write if at every stroke of the pen all the past experiences in learning to write were to arise again in the soul as memory?

Memory appears in various stages. Its simplest form occurs when a person observes an object and, after turning away, is able to call up its *mental image,* is able to visualize it. He has formed this image while perceiving the object. A process has taken place between his astral body and his ego. The astral body has aroused the consciousness of the outer impression of the object. Yet knowledge of the object would last only as long as the latter is present, if the ego were not to absorb this knowledge and make it its own.—It is at this point that supersensible perception separates the bodily element from the soul nature. One speaks of the *astral body* as long as one considers the arising of knowledge of an object that is present. What, however, gives permanence to this knowledge one designates as *soul.* From what has been said we can see at the same time how closely the human astral body is connected with that part of the soul that gives permanence to knowledge. Both are united into one member of the human entity. This union, therefore, may also be called astral body. If we desire an exact designation, we may call the human astral body the *soul body;* the soul, in so far as it is united with this soul body, we may call the *sentient soul.*

The ego rises to a higher stage of its being when it directs its activity toward what it has made its own out of the knowledge of the objects. This is the activity by which the ego severs itself more and more from the objects of perception in order to work within what it has made its own. The part of the soul in which this occurs may be designated the *intellectual* or *mind soul.*—It is characteristic of both the sentient and intellectual souls that they work with what they receive through the impressions of the objects perceived by the senses, and what is retained from this in memory. The soul is here completely surrendered to what is external to it. What it makes its own through memory it has also received from outside. But it can pass beyond all this. It is not alone sentient soul and intellectual soul. For supersensible perception it is easiest to give an idea of this passing beyond by pointing to a simple fact, the comprehensive significance of which, however, must be appreciated. This fact is the following: In the whole range of language there is one name that, through its very nature, distinguishes itself from every other name. That name is "I." Every other name may be given by *every* man to the object or being to whom it applies. The "I" as designation for a being has meaning only when this being applies it to itself. The name "I" can never resound to the ear of a human being from without as his designation; only the being himself can apply it to himself. "I am an 'I' to myself only. For every other person I am a 'you' and everyone else is for me a 'you.'" This fact is the outer expression of a deeply significant truth. The true nature of the "I" is independent of all that is external; *therefore* its name "I" cannot be called to it by anything external. Those religious denominations that have consciously maintained their relationship with supersensible perception designate the "I" as the "Ineffable Name of God." By using this expression, reference is made to what has been indicated. Nothing of an external nature has access to that part of the soul with which we are concerned here. Here is the "hidden sanctuary" of the

34

soul. Only a being with whom the soul is of like nature can gain entrance there. The God who dwells within man speaks when the soul becomes aware of itself as an I. Just as the sentient and intellectual souls live in the outer world, so a third soul member immerses itself in the Divine when the soul gains a perception of its own being.

The above conceptions may easily be misunderstood as an attempt to *identify* the I with God. But it has not been stated that the I *is* God, but only that it is of the same nature and essence as the Divine. Would anyone contend that a drop of water is the sea when he says that the drop is of the same essence or substance as the sea? If we wish to use a comparison, we may say that the drop of water has the same relationship to the sea that the I has to the Divine. Man can find the Divine within himself because his innermost being is drawn from the Divine. Thus he acquires, through this, the third member of his soul, an inner knowledge of himself, just as he gains through his astral body a knowledge of the outer world. Therefore, occult science can call this third member of the soul the *consciousness soul;* and, in this sense, the soul consists of three members: the sentient soul, the intellectual soul, and the consciousness soul, just as the corporeal part of man consists of three members—the physical body, the ether body, and the astral body.

Psychological errors of observation, similar to those already mentioned concerning the judging of the capacity of memory, make it difficult to gain the proper insight into the nature of the I. Much that people believe they understand can be regarded as a refutation of the above, yet it is in reality a confirmation. This is the case, for example, with the remarks about the I which Eduard von Hartmann makes in his *Outline of Psychology*:[1] "In the first place, consciousness of self is more ancient than the word I. Personal pronouns are a rather late product of the evolution of languages and have only the value of abbreviations. The word I is a short substitute for the speaker's own name, but a substitute that each speaker, as such, uses for himself, no matter by what proper name others may call him. Consciousness of self can be developed in animals and in uneducated deaf and dumb persons to a high degree, even without reference to a proper name. Consciousness of the proper name can fully replace the lack of use of the word I. With this insight the magical nimbus is eliminated which for many people envelops the little word I; it cannot add the slightest thing to the concept of self-consciousness, but receives its whole content solely from the latter." It is possible to be quite in agreement with such points of view; also with the contention that no magical nimbus be bestowed upon the little word, I, which would only dim a thoughtful consideration of the matter. But the nature of a *thing* is not decided by the way the *verbal designation* for this thing has gradually been brought about. The important point is the fact that the essential nature of the ego in self-consciousness is "more ancient than the word I" and that man is compelled to use *this* little word—endowed with the qualities belonging to it alone—for what he experiences, in his reciprocal relationship with the outer world, differently from the way the animal can experience

---

[1] Eduard von Hartmann, *Grundriss der Psychologie,* Vol. III, p.55. Bad Sachsa, 1908.

it. Nothing can be known concerning the nature of the triangle by showing how the "word" triangle has been evolved; likewise, nothing can be decided concerning the nature of the I by knowing how this word has taken form in the *evolution of language* out of a different verbal usage.

The true nature of the I reveals itself only in the consciousness soul. For while the soul sinks itself into other things in feeling and intellect, as consciousness soul it takes hold of its own being. Therefore this I can be perceived by the consciousness soul only through a certain inner activity. The visualizations of external objects are formed just as these objects come and go, and these visualizations continue to work in the intellect by means of their own force. But if the I is to observe itself, it cannot simply *surrender* itself; it must, through inner activity, first lift its being out of its own depths in order to have a consciousness of it. With the perception of the I, with *self-contemplation,* an inner activity of the I begins. Through this activity, the perception of the I within the consciousness soul has a significance for man quite different from the observation of all that reaches him through the three corporeal members and the two other members of the soul. The force that discloses the I within the consciousness soul is indeed the same force that manifests in all the rest of the world. This force does not, however, appear directly in the body and in the lower members of the soul, but reveals itself by degrees in its effects. The lowest manifestation is the manifestation through the physical body; this then mounts up by stages to what fills the intellectual soul. One might say that, with each step upward, one of the veils that envelop the hidden falls away. In what fills the consciousness soul, the hidden

37

enters unveiled into the innermost temple of the soul. Yet it appears there only like a drop out of the ocean of all-pervading spirituality. Here, however, man must first take hold of this spirituality. He must recognize it in himself; then he will be able to find it also in its manifestations.

What here like a drop penetrates into the consciousness soul, occult science calls the *spirit*. Thus the consciousness soul is united with the spirit, which is the *hidden* in all that is manifest. If man wishes to take hold of the spirit in all manifestation, he must do it in the same way he takes hold of the ego in the consciousness soul. He must direct the activity that has led him to the perception of this I toward the manifest world. He, thereby, develops to higher stages of his being. He adds something new to the corporeal and soul members. The next thing is that he, himself, also conquer what lies hidden within the lower members of his soul, and this happens through his work on his soul, proceeding from the ego. How man is engaged in this work becomes evident if one compares a person who still surrenders himself to his lower passions and so-called sensual lust, with a noble idealist. The latter develops out of the former if he rids himself of certain low inclinations and turns toward nobler ones. In doing so he has worked on his soul, ennobling and spiritualizing it *out of his ego*. The ego has become master within the soul-life. This can be carried so far that no desire, no enjoyment can gain entrance into the soul without the I being the power that makes the entrance possible. In this way, the whole soul now becomes a manifestation of the I, as this was previously the case with the consciousness soul alone. In fact, all cultural life and all spiritual human endeavor consists in a work that has as its aim this rulership of the ego. *Every* human being living in the present age is engaged in this work whether he wants it or not, whether he is conscious of it or not.

Through this work, however, higher stages of the being of man are reached. Through it, man develops new members of his being. These lie as the concealed behind what is manifest to him. Not only can he become master of the soul by working on the latter through the power of the ego so that the soul drives the concealed into manifestation, but he can also extend this work. He can extend it to the astral body. The I thus takes possession of this astral body by uniting itself with the latter's hidden nature. This astral body, overcome and transformed by the ego, may be called the *spirit self.* (This is what, in connection with oriental wisdom, is called "manas.") In the spirit self we have a higher member of man's being, one which, so to speak, exists within it as a germ and which emerges more and more as it actively works upon itself.

Just as the human being conquers his astral body by penetrating to the hidden forces standing behind it, so, too, in the course of evolution, does this happen with the ether body. The work upon the ether body is, however, more intensive than the work upon the astral body, for what is concealed in the former is enveloped by two veils, while the concealed in the astral body is veiled by only one. It is possible to form a concept of the difference in the work on these two bodies by pointing to certain changes that can take place in man in the course of his development. Let us call to mind how certain human soul qualities develop when the ego is working upon the soul; how passion and desire, joy and sorrow may change. It is only necessary to

39

think back to the time of childhood. At that time, what was man's source of pleasure? What caused him pain? What has he learned in addition to what he was able to do in childhood? All this is only an expression of the way the ego has gained mastery over the astral body. For this body is the bearer of pleasure and pain, of joy and sorrow. Compare this with how little certain other qualities of man change in the course of time, for example, his temperament, the deeper peculiarities of his character, and so forth. A person, hot-tempered as a child, will often retain certain aspects of this violent temper in later life. This is such a striking fact that there are thinkers who wholly deny the possibility of any change in the fundamental character of a human being. They assume that this is something that remains unchanged throughout life, manifesting in one way or another. Such a judgment is merely based upon lack of observation. Anyone who has the capacity of observing such things can perceive clearly that also man's temperament and character change under the influence of his ego. To be sure, this change is slow when compared with the change in the qualities described above. The relationship between the two kinds of changes may be compared with the advancing of the hour hand of a clock in relation to the minute hand. The forces that bring about this change of character or temperament belong to the hidden realm of the ether body. They are of like nature with the forces that rule in the kingdom of life, that is to say, with the forces of growth and nutrition and those that bring about reproduction. Subsequent explanations in this book will shed the right light upon these matters.—The I is not working upon the astral body if the human being simply gives himself up to pleasure and pain, joy and sorrow, but if the peculiarities of these soul qualities change. Likewise, the work extends to the ether body if the ego applies its activity to the changing of its traits of character, of its temperament, and so forth. Also on this latter change every human being is working, whether he is conscious of it or not. The strongest impulses producing this change in ordinary life are the religious ones. When the I allows the impulses that flow from religion to act upon it again and again, they form within it a power that works right into the ether body and transforms it in much the same way that lesser life-impulses cause a transformation of the astral body. These lesser impulses of life, which come to man through study, contemplation, ennobling of the feelings, and so forth, are subject to the manifold changes of existence; religious experiences, however, imprint upon all thinking, feeling, and willing a uniform character. They shed, as it were, a common, uniform light over the entire soul-life. A man thinks and feels this way today, tomorrow differently. The most varied causes bring this about. But if a person through his religious feelings, whatever they may be, divines something that persists throughout all changes, he will relate his current soul experiences of thinking and feeling to that fundamental feeling just as he does with his soul experiences of tomorrow. Religious creed, therefore, has a far-reaching effect upon the whole soul-life; its influence becomes ever stronger in the course of time, because it works by means of constant repetition. It therefore acquires the power of working upon the ether body.—The influence of true art has a similar effect upon the human being. If, through outer form, through color and tone of a

41

work of art, he penetrates to its spiritual basis with thought and feeling, then the impulses that the I thus receives work down even into the ether body. If we think this thought through to the end we can estimate what a tremendous significance art has for all human evolution. We have referred here only to a few instances that give to the I the impulse to act upon the ether body. There are many similar influences in human life that are not so apparent to the observing eye as those that have been mentioned. But from these it is evident that hidden within man there is another member of his being that the I gradually develops. This member may be called the second spiritual member, the *life spirit.* (It is called "buddhi" in oriental wisdom.) The expression "life spirit" is the appropriate term for the reason that the same forces are active in what it designates as in the "life body"; only, in these forces, when they manifest themselves as life body, the human ego is not active. If they manifest as life spirit, however, they are permeated by the activity of the I.

The intellectual development of man, his purification and ennobling of the utterances of feeling and will are the measure of his transformation of the astral body in spirit self; his religious and many other experiences imprint themselves upon the ether body and transform it into life spirit. In the usual course of life this occurs more or less unconsciously. On the other hand, what is called *initiation* of man consists in his being directed by supersensible knowledge to the means that enable him to undertake this work on the spirit self and life spirit in full consciousness. These means will be discussed in later parts of this book. For the present, it was a question of showing that, beside the soul and the body, the spirit is also active within the human being. We shall see later how this spirit, in contrast to the transient body, belongs to the Eternal in man.

The activity of the I is not exhausted with its work upon the astral and ether bodies; it extends also to the physical body. A trace of the influence of the I upon the physical body can be seen when, for example, under certain circumstances a person blushes or turns pale. In this case the I is actually the cause of a process in the physical body. If, through the activity of the I, changes take place in man in respect of its influence upon the physical body, the I is actually united with the hidden forces of this physical body, with the same forces that cause the physical processes to take place. It can be said, then, that the I, through this activity, works upon the physical body. This expression must not be misunderstood. It must not be imagined that this activity is something grossly material. What appears in the physical body as gross matter is only the manifested part of it. Behind this manifested part lie the hidden forces of its being, and these forces are of a spiritual nature. We are not speaking here of work upon a material substance, of which the physical body seems to consist, but of the spiritual work upon the invisible forces that bring this body into existence and allow it to decay. In ordinary life this work of the I on the physical body enters human consciousness indistinctly. Complete clarity of consciousness in this respect is acquired only if man, under the influence of supersensible knowledge, takes this activity consciously in hand. Then the fact emerges that there is still a third spiritual member in man. It is what may be called *spirit man,* in contrast to the physical man. (In oriental wisdom this spirit-man is called "atma.")

It is easy to be misled in respect of the spirit man, owing to the fact that in the physical body we see the lowest member of man's being, and it is, therefore, hard to be reconciled to the idea that work on the physical body brings into being the highest member of the human entity. But just because the physical body conceals the active spirit within it behind three veils, the highest form of human endeavor is needed to unite the I with this hidden spirit.

Thus in occult science man presents himself as a being composed of various members. Those of a corporeal nature are the physical body, the ether body, and the astral body. Those belonging to the soul are sentient soul, intellectual soul, and consciousness soul. The I, the ego, spreads out its light within the soul. The members possessing a spiritual nature are spirit self, life spirit, and spirit man. We see from the above descriptions that the sentient soul and the astral body are closely united and in a certain respect form a whole. In a similar manner, consciousness soul and spirit self are a whole, for the spirit flashes up within the consciousness soul and from there rays through the other members of human nature. With this in mind, we can also speak of the following membering of the human being. We may combine astral body and sentient soul into a single member, likewise consciousness soul and spirit self, and the intellectual soul we may call the I, since it partakes of the I nature and, in a certain respect, is already the I that has not yet become conscious of its spiritual nature. We have, therefore, seven members of man: 1. physical body, 2. ether or life body, 3. astral body, 4. I, 5. spirit self, 6. life spirit, and 7. spirit man.

Even for those who are accustomed to materialistic ideas this membering of man according to the number seven would not possess anything "vaguely magical," which they often ascribe to it, if they but held to the meaning of the above description and did not, from the very outset, themselves introduce this magical element into the matter. It is from the standpoint of a higher form of observing the world and in no other way that we ought to speak of these seven members of man, just as we speak of the seven colors of light or of the seven tones of the scale, (considering the octave as a repetition of the tonic.) Just as light appears in seven colors, and tone in a sevenfold scale, so does the *homogeneous* human nature appear in the above-mentioned seven members. Just as the number seven in tone and color bears nothing of "superstition" in it, so is this also the case in regard to the sevenfold membering of the human being. (On one occasion, when this question was discussed verbally, it was said that in the case of colors the number seven does not hold good, since beyond red and violet there are other colors that are not visible to the eye. Even in this respect, however, the comparison with the colors agrees, for the being of man extends beyond the physical body on the one side and spirit man on the other, only these extensions are "spiritually invisible" to the spiritual means of observation in the same way that the colors beyond red and violet are invisible to the physical eye. This comment had to be made because the opinion so easily arises that supersensible perception is

45

not particular with respect to natural scientific thinking, that it is amateurish in this regard. But whoever pays strict attention to what is meant by the statements made here will find that, in fact, they are nowhere in contradiction to true natural science—neither when facts of natural science are used for illustration nor when, in the remarks made here, a direct relationship to natural-scientific research is indicated.)

III

SLEEP AND DEATH

IT IS NOT possible to penetrate into the nature of waking consciousness without observing the state through which the human being passes during sleep, and it is impossible to solve the riddle of life without considering death. For a human being in whom there is no feeling for the significance of supersensible knowledge, doubts may arise in regard to such knowledge because of the way in which it carries on its considerations regarding sleep and death. Supersensible knowledge is able to understand the motives that give rise to such a distrust. For it is quite comprehensible when someone says that man is here for an active, purposeful life and his accomplishments are based upon his devotion to it; furthermore, that the occupation with states such as sleep and death can only result from an inclination to idle dreaming and can only lead to empty imaginings. The rejection of what is thus held to be "fantastic" may readily be looked upon as the expression of a

47

healthy soul, and an inclination toward "idle dreaming" of this kind as something unhealthy, characteristic of persons lacking in vital energy and the joy of life, and who are incapable of "real accomplishment." It is wrong to declare forthwith that such an opinion is false, for it contains a certain kernel of truth. It is a quarter-truth that must be supplemented by the other three-quarters belonging to it, and a person who sees the one-quarter very well, but who has no conception of the other three-quarters, will only be made distrustful by our combatting the true one-quarter.— It must, in fact, be acknowledged without question that a consideration of what lies concealed in sleep and death is unhealthy if it leads to a weakening, to an estrangement from real life, and we must admit that much that has called itself occult science in the world from time immemorial, and is practiced also today under that name, bears a character unhealthy and hostile to life. But this unsound element does not spring from *true* supersensible knowledge. On the contrary, the real fact is the following. Just as man cannot always be awake, he also cannot, in regard to the real conditions of life in its widest sense, get along without what the supersensible is able to offer. Life continues during sleep, and the forces that are active and creative during the waking state receive their strength and renewal from what is given to them by sleep. Thus it is with what can be observed in the manifest world. The domain of the world is greater than the field of *this* observation, and what is known about the visible universe *must* be supplemented and fructified by what can be known about the invisible. A human being who does not continually draw strength for his weakened forces from sleep must of necessity destroy

48

his life. Likewise, a world concept that is not fructified by a knowledge of the hidden world must lead to desolation. It is similar with death. Living beings succumb to death in order that new life may arise. It is precisely the knowledge of the supersensible that can shed clear light upon the beautiful words of Goethe: "Nature has invented death that she might have abundant life." Just as there could be no life in the ordinary sense of the word without death, so can there be no true knowledge of the visible world without insight into the supersensible. All knowledge of what is visible must plunge again and again into the invisible in order to evolve. Thus it is evident that the science of the supersensible alone makes the life of revealed knowledge possible. It never weakens life when it appears in its true form. When, having been left to itself, life becomes weak and sickly, supersensible knowledge strengthens it and makes it, ever and again, fresh and healthy.

When man sinks into sleep, there is a change in the relationship of his members. That part of the sleeping man that lies in bed contains the physical and ether bodies, but not the astral body and not the ego. Because the ether body remains united with the physical body in sleep, the life-activities continue; for, the moment the physical body were left to itself, it would have to crumble to dust. What, however, is extinguished in sleep includes the mental images, pain and pleasure, joy and sorrow, the capacity to express a conscious will, and similar facts of existence. The astral body is the bearer of all this. An unbiased point of view can naturally never entertain the thought that in sleep the astral body is destroyed along with all pleasure and pain and the world of ideas and will. It simply exists in an-

49

other state. In order that the human ego and astral body not only be filled with joy and sorrow and all the other facts of existence mentioned above, but also have a conscious perception of them, it is necessary that the astral body be united with the physical and ether bodies. In the waking state, all three are united; in the sleeping state, the astral body withdraws from the physical and ether bodies. It assumes a different kind of existence from the one that falls to its lot during its union with the physical and ether bodies. It is the task of supersensible knowledge to consider this other kind of existence in the astral body. Observed from the standpoint of the outer world, the astral body disappears in sleep; supersensible perception must follow its life until it again takes possession of the physical and ether bodies on awakening. Just as in all cases where it is a matter of knowledge of the hidden things and events of the world, so supersensible observation is necessary for the discovery of the facts of the sleeping state in their particular form. If, however, what can be discovered by means of supersensible observation has once been uttered, it is comprehensible to truly unbiased thinking, for the processes of the hidden world reveal themselves in their effects in the manifest world. If it is seen how the revelations of supersensible perception make the sensory processes comprehensible, such a corroboration by means of life itself is the proof that can be required for such things. Anyone not desiring to employ the means for acquiring supersensible perception, indicated later on in this book, can have the following experience. He may at first accept the evidence of supersensible perception and then apply it to the manifest facts of his experience. He may, in this way, find that life has thereby become clear and comprehensible, and the more exact and thorough his observations of ordinary life are, the more readily will he come to this conviction.

Although the astral body, during sleep, experiences no mental pictures and also no pleasure and pain, it does not remain inactive. On the contrary, it is just in the sleep state that a lively activity is incumbent upon it. It is an activity into which it must again and again enter in rhythmical succession, if it has been for a time active in connection with the physical and ether bodies. Just as the pendulum of a clock, after having swung to the left and returned again to the center, must swing to the right because of the momentum gathered in its left swing, so the astral body and the ego living within it, after having been active for a time in the physical and ether bodies must, as a result of this, unfold a subsequent activity, body-free, in a surrounding world of soul and spirit. For the ordinary conditions of human life, unconsciousness occurs during this body-free condition of the astral body and ego because it presents the antithesis of the state of consciousness developed in the waking state through union with the physical and ether bodies, just as the swing of the pendulum to the right is the antithesis of the swing to the left. The necessity of entering into this state of unconsciousness is experienced by the soul-spirit nature of man as fatigue. But this fatigue is the expression of the fact that the astral body and ego, during sleep, prepare themselves to transform, during the following waking state, what has arisen in the physical and ether bodies through purely organic formative activity when freed from the presence of the spirit and soul elements. This unconscious formative activity and what takes

51

place in the human being during and by means of consciousness are antitheses that must alternate in rhythmic succession.—The physical body can retain the form and stature suitable for man only by means of the human ether body, which in turn receives its proper forces from the astral body. The ether body is the builder, the architect, of the physical body, but it can only build in the right way if it receives the impulse for this purpose from the astral body. In the astral body reside the *prototypes* according to which the ether body gives form to the physical body. During the waking state, the astral body is not filled with these prototypes of the physical body, or at least only to a certain degree, for, during the waking state, the soul puts its own images in the place of these prototypes. When man directs the senses toward his environment he forms, by means of perception, thought images that are likenesses of the world about him. These likenesses are at first disturbances for the images that stimulate the ether body to maintain the physical body. Were the human being able, through his own activity, to bring to his astral body the images that are required to give the right impulse to the ether body, then there would be no such disturbance. This very disturbance, however, plays an important rôle in human existence. It expresses itself in the fact that the prototypes for the ether body do not act to the full extent of their power during waking life. The astral body carries on its waking activity within the physical body. In sleep, it works upon the physical body from without.[1]

---

[1] Concerning the nature of fatigue, see "Details from the Domain of Spiritual Science" at the end of this book, Chapter VII.

Just as the physical body, for example, needs the outer world, which is of like nature to itself, to supply it with the means of subsistence, something similar is also the case with the astral body. Just imagine a physical human body removed from its surrounding world. It would have to perish. This demonstrates that without the whole physical environment it is not possible for the physical body to exist. In fact, the entire earth must be as it is, if human physical bodies are to exist upon it. The whole human body is, in reality, only a part of the earth; indeed, in a wider sense, a part of the whole physical universe. In this respect its relationship is similar, for example, to that of a finger to the entire human body. If the finger is severed from the hand, it can no longer continue to be a finger; it withers. This would also happen to the human body were it removed from the organism of which it is a member, from the life conditions offered it by the earth. If we were to lift it a sufficient number of miles above the earth's surface, it would perish just as the finger perishes that has been severed from the hand. If less consideration has been given to this fact in respect of the physical body and the earth than in respect of the finger and the body, it is simply because the finger cannot stroll about on the body in the way that the human being walks about on the earth, and because in the former case the dependence is more obvious.

Just as the physical body belongs to the physical world in which it is embedded, so does the astral body belong to its own world; during waking life, however, it is torn out of this world of its own. What happens there may be illustrated by an analogy. Imagine a vessel filled with water. A drop within this whole mass of water is not something iso-

53

lated. Let us, however, take a little sponge and with it absorb a drop from the whole. Something similar occurs with the human astral body on awaking. During sleep it is in a world like itself; in a certain sense it constitutes something that belongs to this world. On awaking, the physical and ether bodies suck it up; they fill themselves with it. They contain the organs through which the astral body perceives the outer world. But in order that it may acquire this perception, it must separate itself from its own world. From this world it can only receive the prototypes that it needs for the ether body.—Just as the physical body receives its food, for example, from its environment, so during the sleep state the astral body receives the *images* from the world about it. It lives there actually in the universe, separated from the physical and ether bodies, in the same universe out of which the entire human being is born. The source of the images through which the human being receives his form lies in this universe. During sleep he is harmoniously inserted into it, and during the waking state he lifts himself out of this all-encompassing harmony in order to gain external perception. In sleep, his astral body returns to this cosmic harmony and on awaking again brings back to his bodies sufficient strength from it to enable him to dispense with his dwelling within the cosmic harmony for a certain length of time. The astral body, during sleep, returns to its home and on awaking brings back with it renewed forces into life. These forces that the astral body brings with it on awaking find outer expression in the refreshment that healthy sleep affords. Further descriptions of occult science will show that this home of the astral body is more encompassing than that which belongs to the

54

physical body of the physical environment in the narrower sense. Whereas the human being is physically a part of the earth, his astral body belongs to worlds in which still other cosmic bodies besides our earth are embedded. Therefore he enters, during sleep, into a world to which other worlds than the earth belong, a fact that will only become clear from later descriptions.

It ought to be superfluous to call attention to a misunderstanding that can easily arise in regard to these facts, but to do so is not out of place in our age in which certain materialistic modes of thought are prevalent. Those who hold such thoughts can naturally say that it is only scientific to investigate the physical conditions of such a thing as sleep. They maintain that although scholars are not yet in agreement concerning the physical causes of sleep, yet one fact is certain: that definite physical processes must be assumed as lying at the foundation of this phenomenon. Oh! if people would only acknowledge the fact that supersensible knowledge in no way contradicts this assertion! It agrees with everything that is said from this point of view just as one agrees that in the physical erection of a house one brick must be laid upon another, and when it is finished, its form and cohesion can be explained by purely mechanical laws. In order that the house may be built at all, however, the thought of the builder is necessary. This thought is not to be discovered when merely the physical laws are investigated.—Thus, just as the thoughts of the builder of the house lie behind the physical laws that make the house comprehensible, so behind what physical science presents in an absolutely correct way lies the spiritual content of which supersensible knowledge speaks. It is true, this comparison is often presented when it is a matter of justification of a spiritual background of the world and it may be considered trivial. But in these things the point is not whether there is a familiarity with certain concepts, but rather whether they are properly evaluated in arguing the question. Opposing theories can have so great an effect on the power of judgment that the possibility of arriving at a proper evaluation is entirely excluded.

Dreaming is an intermediate state between waking and sleeping. What dream experiences offer to thoughtful consideration is a multi-colored interweaving of a picture world that conceals within it certain rules and laws. This world of dreams seems to display an ebb and flow, often in confused succession. In his dream life, the human being is freed from the law of waking consciousness that fetters him to sense-perception and to the rules governing his power of reason. Yet dreams have certain mysterious laws that are fascinating and alluring to man's prescience, and that are the deeper reason why the beautiful play of fantasy underlying artistic feeling is readily likened to "dreaming." It is only necessary to call to mind certain characteristic dreams to find this corroborated. Someone dreams, for example, that he drives away a dog that is rushing upon him. He awakens and finds himself in the act of unconsciously throwing off a part of the bedclothes that had pressed upon an unaccustomed part of his body and had, therefore, become burdensome. What does dreaming here make out of the sense-perceptible process? What the senses would perceive in the waking state, the life of sleep allows to remain in complete unconsciousness. It retains, however, something essential, namely the fact that the sleeping person wishes to *ward off* something. Around this fact sleep weaves a pictorial process. The images, as such, are echoes of waking-day life. The manner in which they are borrowed from it has something arbitrary about it. Every person has the feeling that under the same external provocation, the dream could conjure up different pictures in his soul, but they express symbolically the feeling that the person has something he wishes to ward off. Dreams create symbols; they are symbol-makers. Inner processes, too, can transform themselves into such dream symbols. A person dreams that a fire is crackling near him; in his dream he sees the flames. He awakens and finds that he has been too heavily covered and has become too warm. The feeling of too much warmth is symbolically expressed in the dream picture. Quite dramatic experiences can be enacted in dream. For example, a person dreams that he is standing at an abyss. He sees a child running toward it. In his dream he experiences all the agony of the thought: Oh! if the child would only take heed, would only pay attention and not fall into the abyss! He sees it falling and hears the dull thud of its body below. He awakens and becomes aware that an object hanging on the wall of his room had become loosened and, in falling, has made a dull sound. Dream life expresses this simple occurrence in an event that is enacted in exciting pictures.—For the present we do not need to enter into a consideration of why, in the last example, the moment of the dull thud of the falling object should spread out into a series of events that seem to extend over a certain period of time. We need only keep in mind how the dream transforms into a *picture* what sense-perception would offer were we awake.

We see that as soon as the senses cease their activity, something creative asserts itself in man. This is the same creative element that is also present in completely dreamless sleep and there presents the soul state that appears as the antithesis of the soul's waking state. If this dreamless sleep is to take place, the astral body must be withdrawn from the ether and physical bodies. During the dream state, it is separated from the physical body in so far as it no longer has any connection with this body's sense organs, but it still retains a certain connection with the ether body. That the processes of the astral body can be perceived in pictures is due to this connection with the ether body. The moment this connection ceases, the pictures sink down into the darkness of unconsciousness, and we have dreamless sleep. The arbitrary and often absurd character of dream pictures rests upon the fact that the astral body, because of its separation from the sense organs of the physical body, cannot relate its pictures to the proper objects and events of the external environment. This fact becomes especially clear if we consider a dream in which the ego is, as it were, split up; when, for example, a person dreams that, as a pupil, he cannot answer a question put to him by his teacher, while directly afterwards the teacher, himself, answers the question. Because the dreamer cannot make use of the organs of perception of his physical body he is unable to relate the two occurrences to himself, as the same individual. Thus, in order to recognize himself as an enduring ego, he must be equipped with the external organs of perception. Only if a person had acquired the capacity of becoming conscious of his ego otherwise than through these organs of perception, would the enduring ego become perceptible to him outside his physical body. Supersensible consciousness must acquire these capacities, and the means of accomplishing this will be considered later on in this book.

Even death occurs only because there is a change in the relationship of the members of man's being. What supersensible perception has to say about death can also be observed in its effects in the outer world, and by unbiased reason the communications of supersensible knowledge can be verified on this point also through observation of external life. The expression of the invisible within the visible is, however, less obvious in these facts. It is more difficult fully to feel the importance of what, in the events of external life, corroborates the communications of supersensible knowledge in this realm. Even more than in the case of many things already mentioned in this book it would be quite natural here to declare that these communications are simply figments of the imagination, if no heed is paid to the knowledge of *how* a clear indication of the supersensible is contained in the sensory.

In passing over into sleep, the astral body only severs its connection with the ether and physical bodies, the latter remaining bound together; in death, the physical body, however, is severed from the ether body. The physical body is left to its own forces and must, for that reason, disintegrate as a corpse. When death occurs, the ether body enters into a state that it never experienced during the time between birth and death, except under rare conditions that will be spoken of later. It is now united with its astral body, without the presence of the physical body, for the ether body and astral body do not separate immediately after death. For a time they remain together by means of a force whose existence is easily to be understood. If it did not exist, the ether body could not sever itself from the physical body, for it is bound to it. This is seen in sleep when the astral body is unable to tear these two members of the human organism apart. This force begins its activity at death. It severs the ether body from the physical, with the result that the ether body is now united with the astral body. Supersensible observation shows that after death this union varies in different people. Its duration is measured by days. For the present this duration is only mentioned by way of information.—Later the astral body separates from its ether body also and continues on its way bereft of it. During the union of the two bodies man is in a condition that enables him to perceive the experiences of his astral body. As long as the physical body is present, the work of refreshing the worn out organs must begin from outside the moment the astral body is severed from it. With the severance of the physical body this work ceases. The force that is employed for this work when the human being sleeps remains after death and can now be used to make the astral body's own processes perceptible.

An observation that clings to the externals of life may say that these are statements that are clear to those endowed with supersensible perception, but there is no possibility of anyone else ascertaining the truth about them. This is not a fact. What supersensible perception observes in this realm, removed from ordinary perception, can be comprehended by ordinary thought power *after it has once been discovered.* This thought power must consider in the right way the relationships of life that are present in the manifested world. Thinking, feeling, and willing stand in such a relationship to each other and to the experiences of man in the outer world, that they remain incomprehensible if the manner of their *revealed* activity is not considered as the expression of an unrevealed activity. This manifest activity becomes clear to the judgment only when it can be looked upon, in its course within physical human life, as the result of what supersensible knowledge establishes for the non-physical. In regard to this activity we are, without supersensible knowledge, much like a man in a dark room without light. Just as the physical objects around us are perceived only in the light, so will what takes place through the soul-life of man be explicable only by means of supersensible knowledge.

During the union of the human being with his physical body, the outer world enters his consciousness in images; after casting off this body, what the astral body experiences when it is not bound to the outer world by means of physical sense organs becomes perceptible. It has at first no new experiences. Union with the ether body prevents it from experiencing anything new. What it does possess, however, is a *memory* of the past life. The still present ether body allows this memory to appear as a comprehensive, living picture. This is the first experience of the human being after death. He perceives the life between birth and death in a series of *pictures* spread out before him. During physical life, memory exists only during the waking state when man is united with his physical body. Memory is present only to the extent allowed by this body. Nothing is lost to the soul that makes an impression upon it during life. Were the physical body a perfect instrument for this, it would be possible at every moment of life to conjure up before the soul the whole of life's past. This hindrance disappears at death. As long as the human being retains the ether body, a certain perfection of memory exists, and it disappears to the degree that the ether body loses the form it had during its sojourn in the physical body, when it resembled the physical body. This is also the reason why the astral body after a time separates from the ether body. It can remain united with the latter only as long as the ether form, which corresponds to the physical body, endures.— During life between birth and death, a separation of the ether body from the physical body takes place only in exceptional cases, and then only for a short time. If, for example, a person presses heavily upon one of his limbs, a part of the ether body may separate from the physical. When this occurs we may say that the limb has "gone to sleep." The peculiar feeling one has at that time comes from the severance of the ether body. (Naturally, here also a materialistic mode of thought may deny the existence of the invisible within the visible and say that all this simply comes from the physical disturbance caused by the pressure.) In such a case, supersensible perception is able to observe how the corresponding part of the ether body passes out of the physical. If a person experiences an unusual shock, or something of the kind, a separation of the ether body from a large part of the physical body may result for a short time. This happens if a person for one reason or another sees himself suddenly near death; if, for example, he is on the verge of drowning, or if, on a mountaineering trip, he is in danger of a precipitous fall. What is told by people who have experienced such things comes very near the truth and may be corroborated by supersensible observation. They state that in such moments their entire life passed before the soul in a great memory-picture. Of the many examples that could be cited here, only one will be referred to because it originates with a person to whose mode of thinking all that has been said here about these experiences must appear as idle fancy. For anyone who takes a few steps in supersensible observation, it is always useful to become acquainted with the statements of those who consider this science as something fantastic. Such statements cannot be so lightly attributed to the prejudice of the observer of the supersensible. (Spiritual scientists may well learn a great deal from those who consider their endeavors nonsense, and they need not be disconcerted if there is no reciprocal "affection" in this respect on the part of the critics. To be sure, for supersensible perception itself there is no need of *verification* of its results through such experiences. It does not desire to *prove* anything by these references, but to elucidate its findings.) The eminent criminologist and well known researcher in many other fields of natural science, Moritz Benedict, relates a personal experience in his memoirs. Once, when he was near being drowned while bathing, he saw in memory his whole life before him as though in a single picture.—If others describe differently the pictures experienced under similar circumstances, even in a way that lets them appear to have little to do with the events of their past, this does not contradict what has been said. For the pictures that occur in the quite unusual condition of the separation of the ether body from the physical are often not readily explicable in regard to their relation to life. Proper consideration will always recognize this relationship. Neither is it an objection if someone, for example, once came near drowning and did not have the experience described. It must be remembered that this can *only* occur when the ether body is actually separated from the physical and at the same time remains united with the astral body. If through the shock a loosening of the ether and astral bodies also takes place, then the experience does not occur, because there exists complete unconsciousness, as in dreamless sleep.

In the period immediately following death the experiences of the past appear summarized in a memory-picture. After the separation of the ether body and the astral body, the latter is left to itself in its further journey. It is not difficult to see that, within the astral body, everything remains that it has made its own through its own activity during its sojourn in the physical body. To a certain degree, the ego has developed spirit self, life spirit, and spirit man. As far as they are developed, they receive their existence, not from what exists as organs in the bodies, but from the ego. The ego is the very member that needs no external organs for self-perception; it also needs none in order to remain in possession of what it has united with itself. The objection can be made, "Why, then, is there no perception in sleep of this spirit self, life spirit, and spirit man, which have been developed?" There is none, because the ego is fettered to the physical body between birth and death. Even though in sleep the ego, united with the astral body, is outside the physical body, it remains, nevertheless, in close union with the latter, for the activity of the astral body is directed toward this physical body. Thus the ego with its perception is relegated to the external sense world and cannot therefore receive the revelations of the spirit in its direct form. Only at death does the ego receive these revelations because, at death, the ego is freed from its connection with the physical and ether bodies. Another world can flash up for the soul the moment it is withdrawn from the physical world that chains the soul's activity to itself during life— There are reasons why even at this moment all connections between man and the external sense world do not cease. Certain desires remain that maintain this connection. These are desires that the human being creates because he is conscious of his ego, the fourth member of his being. Those desires and wishes arising out of the nature of the three lower bodies can only be active within the external world, and when these bodies are laid aside the desires cease. Hunger is caused by the external body; it is silenced as soon as this outer body is no longer united with the ego. If the ego possessed no other desires than those arising from its own spiritual nature, it could at death draw complete satisfaction from the spiritual world into which it is translated. But life has given it still other desires. It has enkindled in the ego a longing for enjoyments that can only be satisfied through physical organs, although the desires do not have their origin in these organs themselves. Not only do the three bodies demand their satisfaction through the physical world, but the ego itself finds enjoyments within this world for which the spiritual world offers no means of satisfaction. For the ego there are two kinds of desires in life: the desires that have their source in the bodies, and therefore must be satisfied within these bodies, ceasing with the disintegration of these bodies, and the desires that have their source in the spiritual nature of the ego. As long as the ego is within the bodies, these desires also are satisfied by means of bodily organs, for in the manifestations of the bodily organs the hidden spirit is at work, and in all that the senses perceive they receive at the same time something spiritual. This spiritual element exists also after death, although in another form. All spiritual desires of the ego within the sense world exist also when the senses are no longer present. If a third kind of desire were not added to these two, death would signify merely a transition from desires that can be satisfied by means of the senses to those that find their realization in the revelation of the spiritual world. This third type of desire is produced by the ego during its life in the sense world because it finds pleasure in this world also in so far as there is no spirit manifest in it.—The basest enjoyments can be a manifestation of the spirit. The gratification that the hungry being experiences in taking food is a manifestation of spirit because through the eating of food something is brought about without which, in a certain sense, the spirit could not evolve. The ego can, however, transcend the enjoyment that this fact of necessity offers. It may long for good tasting food, quite apart from the service rendered the spirit by eating. The same is true of other things in the sense world. Desires are created thereby that would never have come into being in the sense world had the human ego not been incorporated in it. But neither do these desires spring from the spiritual nature of the ego. The ego *must* have sense enjoyments as long as it lives in the body, also in so far as it is spiritual; for the spirit manifests in the sense world and the ego enjoys nothing but spirit when, in this world, it surrenders itself to that medium through which the light of the

66

spirit radiates. It will continue to enjoy this light even when the sense world is no longer the medium through which the rays of the spirit pass. In the spirit world, however, there is no gratification for desires in which the spirit has not already manifested itself in the sense world. When death takes place, the possibility for the gratification of *these* desires is cut off. The enjoyment of appetizing food can come only through the physical organs that are used for taking in food: the palate, tongue, and so forth. After throwing off the physical body man no longer possesses these organs. But if the ego still has a longing for these pleasures, this longing must remain ungratified. In so far as this enjoyment is in accord with the spirit, it exists only as long as the physical organs are present. If it has been produced by the ego, without serving the spirit, it continues after death as desire, which thirsts in vain for satisfaction. We can only form an idea of what now takes place in the human being if we think of a person suffering from burning thirst in a region in which water is nowhere to be found. This, then, is the state of the ego, in so far as it harbors, after death, the unextinguished desires for the pleasures of the outer world and has no organs with which to satisfy them. Naturally, we must imagine the burning thirst that serves as an analogy for the conditions of the ego after death to be increased immeasurably, and imagine it spread out over all the other still existing desires for which *all possibility* of satisfaction is lacking. The next task of the ego consists in freeing itself from this bond of attraction to the outer world. In this respect the ego has to bring about a purification and emancipation within itself. All desires that have been created by it within the body and that have no inherent rights within the spiritual world must be rooted out.—Just as an object takes fire and is consumed, so is the world of desires, described above, consumed and destroyed after death. This affords us a glimpse into the world that supersensible knowledge designates as the "consuming fire of the spirit." All desires of a sensual nature, in which the sensual is *not* an expression of the spirit, are seized upon by this "fire." The ideas that supersensible knowledge must give in regard to these processes might be found to be hopeless and awful. It might appear terrifying that a hope, for whose realization sense organs are necessary, must change into hopelessness after death; that a desire, which only the physical world can satisfy, must turn into consuming deprivation. Such a point of view is possible only as long as one does not consider the fact that all wishes and desires, which after death are seized by the "consuming fire," in a higher sense represent not beneficial but destroying forces in life. By means of such destructive forces, the ego tightens the bond with the sense world more strongly than is necessary in order to absorb from this very sense world what is beneficial to it. This sense world is a manifestation of the spirit hidden behind it. The ego would never be able to enjoy the spirit in the form in which it is able to manifest through bodily senses alone, did it not want to use these senses for the enjoyment of the spiritual within the sense world. Yet the ego deprives itself of the true spiritual reality in the world to the degree that it desires the sense world without the spirit. If the enjoyment of the senses, as an expression of the spirit, signifies an elevation and development of the ego, then an enjoyment that is not an expression of the spirit signifies the impoverishing,

68

the desolation of the ego. If a desire of this kind is satisfied in the sense world, its desolating effect upon the ego nevertheless remains. Before death, however, this destructive effect upon the ego is not apparent. Therefore the satisfaction of such desires can produce similar desires during life, and man is not at all aware that he is enveloping himself, through himself, in a "consuming fire." After death, what has surrounded him in life becomes visible, and by becoming visible it appears in its healing, beneficial consequences. A person who loves another is certainly not attracted only to that in him which can be experienced through the physical organs. But only of what can thus be experienced may it be said that it is withdrawn from perception at death; just that part of the loved one then becomes visible for the perception of which the physical organs were only the means. Moreover, the only thing that then hinders that part from becoming completely visible is the presence of the desire that can only be satisfied through physical organs. If this desire were not extirpated, the conscious perception of the beloved person could not arise after death. Considered in this way, the picture of frightfulness and despair that might arise in the human being concerning the events after death, as depicted by supersensible knowledge, must change into one of deep satisfaction and consolation.

The first experiences after death are different in still another respect from those during life. During the time of purification man, as it were, lives his life in reverse order. He passes again through all that he has experienced in life since his birth. He begins with the events that immediately preceded death and experiences everything in reverse order back to childhood. During this process, everything that has not arisen out of the spiritual nature of the ego during life passes spiritually before his eyes, only he experiences all this now inversely. For example, a person who died in his sixtieth year and who in his fortieth year had done someone a bodily or soul injury in an outburst of anger will experience this event again when, in passing through his life's journey in reverse order after death, he reaches the place of his fortieth year. He now experiences, not the satisfaction he had in life from his attack upon the other person, however, but the pain he gave him. From what has been said above, it is at the same time also possible to see that only that part of such an event can be experienced painfully after death that has arisen from passions of the ego having their source only in the outer physical world. In reality, the ego not only damages the other person through the gratification of such a passion, but itself as well; only the damage to itself is not apparent to it during life. After death this whole, damaging world of passion becomes perceptible to the ego, and the ego then feels itself drawn to every being and every thing that has enkindled such a passion, in order that this passion may again be destroyed in the "consuming fire" in the same way it was created. Only when man in his backward journey has reached the point of his birth have all the passions of this kind passed through the fire of purification, and, from then on, nothing hinders him from a complete surrender to the spiritual world. He enters upon a new stage of existence. Just as, at death, he threw off the physical body, then, soon after, the ether body, so now that part of the astral body falls away that can live only in the consciousness of the

70

outer physical world. For supersensible perception there are, thus, three corpses: the physical, the etheric, and the astral corpse. The point of time when the latter is thrown off by man is at the end of the period of purification, which lasts about a third of the time that passed between birth and death. The reason why this is so can only become clear later on, when we shall consider the course of human life from the standpoint of occult science. For supersensible observation, astral corpses are constantly present in the environment of man, which have been discarded by human beings who are passing over from the state of purification into a higher existence, just as for physical perception there are physical corpses in the world in which men dwell.

After purification an entirely new state of consciousness begins for the ego. While before death the outer perceptions had to flow toward the ego in order that the light of consciousness might fall upon them, now, as it were, a world flows from within of which it acquires consciousness. The ego lives in this world also between birth and death. There, however, this world is clothed in the manifestations of the senses, and only there where the ego, taking no heed of all sense-perceptions, perceives itself in its innermost sanctuary is what otherwise appears veiled by the sense world revealed in its real form. Just as before death the self-perception of the ego takes place in its inner being, so after death and after purification the world of spirit in its plenitude is revealed from within. This revelation, in fact, takes place immediately after the stripping off of the ether body. But, like a darkening cloud, the world of desires, which are still turned toward the outer world, spreads out before it. It is as though dark demoniacal shadows, arising out of the passions "consuming themselves in fire," intermingled with a blissful world of spiritual experience. Indeed, these passions are now not mere shadows, but actual entities. This becomes at once apparent when the physical organs are removed from the ego and it, therefore, can perceive what is of a spiritual nature. These creatures appear like distortions and caricatures of what the human being previously knew through sense-perception. Supersensible perception says about the world of the purifying fire that it is inhabited by beings whose appearance for the spiritual eye can be horrible and painful, whose pleasure seems to be destruction and whose passion is bent upon a spiritual evil, in comparison with which the evil of the sense world appears insignificant. The passions indicated, which human beings bring into this world, appear to these creatures as food by means of which their power receives constant strengthening. The picture thus drawn of a world imperceptible to the senses can appear less incredible if one for a moment observes a part of the animal world with unprejudiced eyes. For the spiritual gaze, what is a cruel, prowling wolf? What manifests itself in what the senses perceive in it? Nothing but a soul that lives in passions and acts through them. One can call the external form of the wolf an embodiment of these passions, and even if a person had no organs with which to perceive this form, he would still have to acknowledge the existence of the being in question, if its passions showed invisibly in their effects; that is, if a power, invisible to the eye, were prowling around by means of which everything could happen that occurs through the visible wolf. To be sure, the beings of

72

the purifying fire do not exist for sensory, but for supersensible consciousness only; their effects, however, are clearly manifest: they consist in the destruction of the ego when it gives them nourishment. These effects become clearly visible when a well-founded pleasure increases to lack of moderation and excess, for what is perceptible to the senses would also attract the ego only in so far as the pleasure is founded in its own nature. The animal is impelled to desire only by means of that in the outer world for which its three bodies are craving. Man possesses nobler pleasures because a fourth member, the ego, is added to the three bodily members. But if the ego seeks for a gratification that serves to destroy its own nature, not to maintain and further it, then such craving can be neither the effect of its three bodies, nor that of its own nature. It can only be the effect of beings who, in their true form, remain hidden from the senses, beings who can set to work on the higher nature of the ego and arouse in it passions that have no relationship to sense existence, but can only be satisfied through it. Beings exist who are nourished by desires and passions that are worse than any animal passions, because they do not have their being in the sense world, but seize upon the spiritual and drag it down into the realm of the senses. For that reason the forms of such beings are, for supersensible perception, more hideous and gruesome than the forms of the wildest animals, in which only passions are embodied that originate in the sense world. The destructive forces of these beings exceed immeasurably all destructive fury existing in the visible animal world. Supersensible knowledge must, in this way, enlarge the human horizon to include a world of beings that, in a certain re-

73

spect, stand lower than the visible world of destructive animals.

When man, after death, has passed through this world, he finds himself confronted by a world that contains the spirit, producing a longing within him that finds its satisfaction only in the spirit. Now too, however, he distinguishes between what belongs to *his* ego and what forms the environment of this ego, that is, its spiritual outer world. Only, what he experiences of this environment streams toward him in the way the perception of his own ego streams toward him during his sojourn in the body. While in the life between birth and death his environment speaks to him through his bodily organs, after all bodies have been laid aside the language of the new environment penetrates directly into the "innermost sanctuary" of his ego. The entire environment of the human being is filled with beings of like nature with his ego, for only an ego has access to another ego. Just as minerals, plants, and animals surround him in the sense world and compose that world, so after death he is surrounded by a world that is composed of beings of a spiritual nature.—Yet he brings with him into this world something that does not belong to his environment there, namely, what the ego has experienced within the sense world. Immediately after death, and as long as the ether body was still united with the ego, the sum of these experiences appeared in the form of a comprehensive memory picture. The ether body itself is then, to be sure, cast off, but something from this memory picture remains as an imperishable possession of the ego. What has thus been retained appears as an extract, an essence made from all the experiences that the human being

74

has passed through between birth and death. This is life's spiritual yield, its fruit. This yield contains everything of a spiritual character that has been revealed through the senses. Without life in the sense world, however, it could not have come into existence. After death the ego feels this spiritual fruit of the sense world as its own inner world with which it enters a world composed of beings who manifest themselves as only his ego can manifest itself in its innermost depths. Just as the plant seed, which is an extract of the entire plant, develops only when it is inserted into another world—the earth, so what the ego brings with it out of the sense world unfolds like a seed upon which the spiritual environment acts that has now received it. If the science of the supersensible is to describe what occurs in this "land of the spirits," it can indeed only do so by portraying it in pictures. Still, these pictures appear as absolute reality to supersensible consciousness when it investigates the corresponding occurrences imperceptible to the physical eye. What is to be described here may be illustrated by means of comparisons with the sense world, for although it is wholly of a spiritual nature, it has, in a certain respect, a similarity to the sense world. For example, just as in the world of the senses a color appears when an object impresses the eye, in the "land of the spirits," when a spiritual being acts upon the ego, an experience is produced similar to one made by a color. But this experience is produced in the way in which, in the life between birth and death, only the perception of the ego can be produced in the soul's inner being. It is not as though the light struck the human inner being from without, but as though another being were acting directly upon the ego, causing it to portray this activity in a colored picture. Thus all beings of the spiritual environment of the ego express themselves in a world of radiating colors. Since their origin is of a different kind, these color experiences of the spirit world are, naturally, of a character somewhat different from the experiences of physical color. The same thing can be said of other impressions that the human being receives from the sense world. The impressions that resemble most those of the sense world are the tones of the spiritual world, and the more the human being becomes familiar with this world, the more will it become for him an inwardly pulsating life that may be likened to tones and their harmonies in sensory reality. These tones, however, are not experienced as something reaching an organ from outside, but as a force streaming through the ego out into the world. The human being feels the tone as he feels his own speaking or singing in the sense world, but he knows that in the spiritual world these tones streaming out from him are at the same time manifestations of other beings poured out into the world through him. A still higher manifestation takes place in the land of spirit beings when the tone becomes "spiritual speech." Then not only the *pulsing life* of another spirit being streams through the ego, but a being of this kind imparts its own inner nature to this ego. Without that separation which all companionship must experience in the physical world, two beings live in each other when the ego is thus permeated by "spiritual speech." The companionship of the ego with other spirit beings after death is really of this kind.

Three realms of the land of spirits appear before supersensible consciousness that may be compared with three

76

regions of the physical sense world. The first region is the "solid land" of the spiritual world, the second, the "region of oceans and rivers," the third, the "atmospheric region." —What assumes physical form on earth so that it may be perceived by means of physical organs is perceived in its spiritual nature in the first realm of the land of spirit beings. For example, the force that gives the crystal its form may be perceived there, but what thus appears is the antithesis of the form it assumes in the sense world. The space, which in the physical world is filled with the stone mass, appears to spiritual vision as a kind of cavity. Around this cavity, however, the force is visible that gives form to the stone. The color the stone possesses in the physical world is experienced in the spiritual world as the complementary color. Thus a red stone appears greenish in the spirit land and a green stone, reddish. The other characteristics also appear in their complementary forms. Just as stones, earth masses, and so forth, make up the solid land—the continental regions—of the physical world, so the structures described above compose "the solid land" of the spirit world.—Everything that is life within the sense world is the oceanic region in the spirit world. Life to the physical eye is manifest in its effects in plants, animals, and men. Life to spiritual vision is a flowing entity that permeates the land of spirits like seas and rivers. A still better analogy is that of the circulation of the blood in the body, for whereas oceans and rivers appear irregularly distributed within the physical world, there is a certain regularity, like that of the circulation of the blood, in the distribution of this streaming life of the land of spirit beings. This flowing life is heard simultaneously as a spiritual enton-

77

ing.—The third realm of the spirit land is its "atmosphere."
What appears in the sense world as sensation exists in the
spiritual realm as an all-pervading presence like the earth's
air. Here we must imagine a sea of flowing feeling. Sorrow
and pain, joy and delight flow through this realm like wind
or a raging tempest in the atmosphere of the sense world.
Imagine a battle raging upon earth. Not only human forms
confront each other there, forms that can be seen with the
physical eyes, but feelings stand forth opposing feelings,
passions opposing passions. The battlefield is filled with
pain as well as with human forms. Everything that is experienced there of the nature of passion, pain, joy of conquest, is present not alone in its effects perceptible to the
senses, but the spiritual sense becomes conscious of it as
atmospheric processes in the land of spirits. Such an event
in the spirit is like a thunder storm in the physical world,
and the perception of these events may be likened to the
hearing of words in the physical world. Therefore it is said
that just as the air surrounds and permeates the earth
beings, so do "wafting spiritual words" enclose the beings
and processes of the spirit land.

There are still other perceptions possible in this spiritual
world. What may be compared to warmth and light of the
physical world is also present. What permeates everything
in the spirit land, like warmth permeating earthly things,
is the thought world itself, only here, thoughts must be
imagined as living, independent entities. What is appre-
hended as thoughts in the physical world is like the shadow
of what exists in the land of spirits as thought beings. If we
imagine thought, as it exists in human beings, withdrawn
from man and endowed as an active entity with its own

78

inner life, then we have a feeble illustration of what permeates the fourth region of the spirit land. What man perceives as thoughts in his physical world between birth and
death is only the manifestation of the thought world as it is
able to express itself through the instrumentality of the
bodies. But all such thoughts entertained by human
beings, which signify an *enrichment* of the physical world,
have their origin in this region. One need not think here
merely of the ideas of the great inventors, of the geniuses.
It can be seen how every person has sudden ideas that he
does not owe merely to the outer world, but with which he
transforms this outer world itself. Feelings and passions
whose causes lie in the outer world have to be placed in the
third region of the spirit land. But everything that can so
live in the human soul as to make him a creator, causing
him to transform and fructify his surroundings, is perceptible in its primeval, essential form in the fourth sphere of
the spiritual world.—What exists in the fifth region may be
compared with physical *light*. It is *wisdom* revealing itself
in its innermost form. Beings belonging to this region shed
wisdom upon their environment, just as the sun sheds light
upon physical beings. What is illuminated by this wisdom
appears in its true significance and meaning for the spiritual world, just as a physical object displays its color when
it is shone upon by the light.—There exist still higher regions of the land of the spirits, descriptions of which will
be found in a later part of this work.

After death, the ego is immersed in this world, together
with the harvest that it brings with it from its life in the
sense world. This harvest is still united with that part of the
astral body that has not been thrown off at the end of the

period of purification. Only that part falls away which after death was inclined with its desires and longings toward physical life. The immersion of the ego in the spiritual world, together with what it has acquired in the sense world, may be compared with the insertion of a seed into the ripening earth. Just as this seed draws substances and forces from its environment in order to develop into a new plant, so, too, unfolding and growth is the very essence of the ego being embedded in the world of spirit.—Within what an organ perceives lies hidden the force by means of which the organ itself is created. The eye perceives the light, but without the light there would be no eye. Beings that pass their lives in darkness develop no organs of sight. In this manner the whole bodily organism of the human being is created out of the hidden forces lying within what is perceived with these bodily members. The physical body is built up by the forces of the physical world, the ether body by those of the life world, and the astral body is formed out of the astral world. When the ego is now transplanted into the spirit land, it encounters those forces that remain hidden to physical perception. In the first region of the spirit land the spiritual beings are perceptible who always surround the human being and who have also fashioned his physical body. Thus in the physical world, man perceives nothing but the manifestations of those spiritual forces that have also formed his own physical body. After death, he is himself in the midst of these formative forces that now appear to him in their own, previously concealed, form. Likewise, in the second region he is in the midst of the forces composing his ether body. In the third region, forces stream toward him out of which his astral body has been organized. The higher regions of the spirit land also now impart to him what composes his form in his life between birth and death.

These beings of the spirit world now co-operate with what man has brought with him as fruit from the former life and what now becomes a seed. By means of this co-operation man is built up anew as a spiritual being. In sleep the physical and ether bodies continue their existence; the astral body and ego are, to be sure, outside of these two bodies, but still united with them. Whatever influences the astral body and the ego receive in this state from the spiritual world can only serve to restore the forces exhausted during the waking period. When the physical and ether bodies have been laid aside, however, and when, after the period of purification, those parts of the astral body that are still connected with the physical world through their desires are also laid aside, all that streams toward the ego from the spirit world now becomes not only a perfector, but a recreator. After a certain length of time, which will be discussed in later parts of this work, an astral body has formed itself around the ego; the former can again dwell in ether and physical bodies befitting the human being between birth and death. He can again pass through birth and appear in a new earth existence into which the fruit of the previous life has been incorporated. Up to the time of re-forming a new astral body, man is a witness of his own re-creation. Since the powers of the spirit land do not reveal themselves to him by means of outer organs, but from within, like his own ego in self-consciousness, he is able to perceive this revelation as long as his mind is not yet directed to an outwardly perceptible world. The moment, however, the astral body is newly formed, his attention turns outward. The astral body once more requires an external ether and physical body. It therefore turns away from the revelations of the inner world. For this reason an intermediate state now begins, during which man sinks into unconsciousness. Consciousness can only reappear in the physical world when the necessary organs for physical perception have been formed. During this period in which consciousness, illuminated by inner perception, ceases, the new ether body begins to attach itself to the astral body and the human being can then again enter into a physical body. Only an ego that has of itself produced life spirit and spirit man, the hidden, creative forces in the ether and physical bodies, would be able to take part consciously in the attachment of these two members. As long as man is not developed to this point, beings who are further advanced than he in their evolution must direct the attachment of these members. The astral body is led by such beings to certain parents, so that he may be endowed with the proper ether and physical bodies.—Before the attachment of the ether body is completed, something extraordinarily significant occurs for the human being who is re-entering physical existence. He has, in his previous life, created destructive forces that became evident when he experienced his life in reverse order after death. Let us take again the example suggested above. A person had caused someone pain in an outburst of anger in the fortieth year of his previous life. After death, he met this pain of the other person in the form of a force destructive to the development of his own ego. So it is with all such occurrences of his previous life. On re-entering physi-

82

cal life, these hindrances to evolution confront the ego anew. Just as at death a kind of memory picture of the *past* life arose before the human ego, now a pre-vision of the *coming* life presents itself. Again he sees a tableau, which this time displays all the hindrances he must remove if his evolution is to make further progress. What he thus sees becomes the starting point of forces that he must carry with him into a new life. The picture of the pain that he has caused another person becomes the force impelling the ego, on re-entering life, to make reparation for this pain. Thus the previous life has a determining effect upon the new life. The actions of this new life are in a certain way caused by those of the previous life. This orderly connection between a former and a later existence must be considered as the *law of destiny*. It has become the custom to designate this law by the name *karma*, a term borrowed from oriental wisdom.

The fashioning of a new corporeal organization is not the only activity that is required of the human being between death and a new birth. While this building up is taking place, man lives outside the physical world. But during this time the earth proceeds in its evolution. Within relatively short periods of time the earth changes its countenance. How did those regions, which at present are occupied by Germany, appear a few millennia ago? When man reappears in a new life, the earth as a rule presents quite a different appearance from the one it had in his previous life. While he was absent from the earth all sorts of changes have occurred. Hidden forces also are at work in this transformation of the face of the earth. Their activities proceed from the same world in which man dwells after death, and he himself must co-operate in this transformation of the earth. He can do so only under the guidance of higher beings, as long as he has not acquired, through the development of life spirit and spirit man, a clear consciousness concerning the relationship between the spirit and its expression in the physical. But he helps to transform the earthly conditions. It can be said that human beings, during the period between death and a new birth, transform the earth in such a way that its conditions harmonize with their own development. If we observe a particular spot on the earth at a definite point of time and observe it again after a long span, finding it in a fully changed condition, the forces that have wrought this change are the forces of the human dead. In this way men have a relationship with the earth also during the period between death and a new birth. Supersensible consciousness sees in all physical existence the manifestation of a hidden spirituality. For physical observation, it is the light of the sun, climatic changes, and similar phenomena that bring about the transformation of the earth. For supersensible observation, the forces of the human dead are active in the rays of light that fall upon the plants from the sun. By observing supersensibly one becomes aware of how human souls hover above the plants, how they change the surface of the earth, and so forth. The attention of the human being is not only turned upon himself and upon the preparation for his own new earth life; indeed, he is called upon to work spiritually upon the outer world, just as he is called upon to work physically in the life between birth and death.

Not only from the land of spirit beings does human life affect the conditions of the physical world, however, but, vice versa, all activity in physical existence has its effects in the spiritual world. An example will illustrate what happens in this respect. A bond of love exists between mother and child. This love arises out of an attraction between the two that has its roots in the forces of the sense world. But it changes in the course of time; a spiritual bond is formed more and more out of the sensory, and this spiritual link is fashioned not merely for the physical world, but also for the land of spirits. This is also true for other relationships. What has been spun in the physical world through spiritual beings remains in the spiritual world. Friends who have become closely united in life belong together also in the land of spirits and, after laying aside their bodies, they are in much more intimate communion than in physical life. For as spirits they exist for each other through the manifestation of their inner nature in the same way that the higher spiritual beings manifest their existence to one another through their inner nature, as we have described above, and a tie that has been woven between two people brings them together again in a new life. Therefore, in the truest sense of the word, we must speak of people finding each other again after death.

What has once taken place with a person, during the period from birth to death and then from death to a re-birth, repeats itself. Man returns to earth again and again when the fruit that he has acquired in one physical life has reached maturity in the land of the spirits. Yet, we must not think here of repetition without beginning and end, for the human being passed, at some time, from other forms of existence into those that take place in the manner described, and he will in the future pass on to others. A picture of these transitional stages will be presented when, subsequently, the evolution of the cosmos—in relation to man—is described from the standpoint of supersensible consciousness.

The processes that occur between death and a new birth are, naturally, still more concealed for outer sensory observation than the spiritual element that underlies manifest existence between birth and death. This sensory observation can see the effects of this part of the concealed world only where they enter into physical existence. The question for sensory observation is, whether the human being who passes through birth into life brings with him something of the processes described by supersensible cognition as taking place between a previous death and birth. If someone finds a snail shell in which no trace of an animal is to be seen, he will nevertheless acknowledge that this snail shell has come into existence through the activity of some animal and will not believe that it has been constructed in its form purely by means of physical forces. Likewise, a person who observes a living human being and finds something that cannot have its origin in *this* life, can admit with reason that it originates in what the science of the supersensible described, if thereby a clarifying light is thrown upon what is otherwise inexplicable. Thus intelligent sensory observation would be able to find that the invisible causes are comprehensible through their visible effects, and to anyone who observes this physical life entirely without prejudice, the above will appear—with every new observation—more and more convincing. It is only a question of finding the right standpoint for observing the effects in outer life. For example, where are the effects of what supersensible cognition describes as processes of the time of purification? How do the effects of the experiences that man undergoes manifest themselves after this time of purification in the purely spiritual realm, according to the evidence of spiritual research?

Problems enough force themselves into every earnest and deep consideration of life in this field. We see one person born in need and misery, equipped with only meager ability, and he appears to be predestined to a pitiable existence because of the conditions prevailing at his birth. Another will, from the first moment of his life, be cherished and cared for by solicitous hands and hearts; brilliant capacities unfold in him, he is cut out for a fruitful, satisfactory existence. Two contrasting points of view can be asserted in respect of such problems. The one adheres to what the senses perceive and what the intellect, bound to the senses, can grasp. This point of view sees no problem in the fact that one person is born to good fortune, the other to misfortune. Although such a point of view may not wish to use the word "chance," still those who hold it are not ready to assume an interrelated web of laws that causes such diversities, and with respect to aptitudes and talents, this way of thinking adheres to what is said to be "inherited" from parents, grandparents, and other ancestors. It will refuse to seek the causes in spiritual events that man himself has experienced before his birth, and through which he has formed his capacities and talents, quite apart from the hereditary descent from his ancestors.—Another point of view will not feel satisfied with such an interpretation. It will hold that even in the outer world nothing occurs at a definite place or in definite surroundings without the necessity of presupposing a reason for the cause of it. Although in many instances these causes have not yet been investigated, yet they exist. An Alpine flower does not grow in the lowlands; there is something in its nature that unites it with the Alpine regions. Likewise, there must be something in a human being that causes him to be born in a definite environment. This is not to be explained by causes that lie merely in the physical world. To a serious thinker this must appear as though a blow dealt another should be explained not by the feelings of the aggressor, but rather by the physical mechanism of his hand.—Those who have this point of view must also be dissatisfied with all explanations of aptitude and talents as mere inheritance. Yet it may be said in this connection that obviously certain aptitudes continue to be inherited in families. During two and a half centuries musical aptitudes were inherited by the members of the Bach family. Eight mathematicians, some of whom in their childhood were destined for quite different professions, have appeared in the Bernoulli family. The "inherited" talents have always impelled them to take up the family profession. Furthermore, it can be shown through exact investigation of the line of ancestry of an individual that, in one way or another, the talents of this individual have appeared in the ancestors and that they present only a summation of inherited tendencies.— The one having the second point of view mentioned will certainly not disregard such facts, but they cannot mean the same thing to him as to the other who rests his explanations solely upon the processes of the sense world. The former will point out that it is just as impossible for the inherited traits to sum themselves up into an entire personality as it is for the metal parts of a clock to form themselves into a clock. If the objection is made that the united activity of the parents can bring about the combination of traits and that this, as it were, takes the place of the clock-maker, he will reply, "Just look with impartiality at the completely new element in every child's personality; this cannot come from the parents for the simple reason that it does not exist in them."

Unclear thinking can cause great confusion in this realm. The worst is if those having the first point of view previously stated look on those having the second as opponents of what is based upon "sure facts." But these latter may not even think of denying the truth or the value of these facts. They also see quite clearly, for example, that a definite spiritual predisposition, even a spiritual direction, is "inherited" in a family, and that certain capacities summarized and combined in one descendant result in a remarkable personality. They are ready to admit that the most illustrious name seldom stands at the beginning, but at the end of a blood relationship. But those holding this view should not be blamed if they are forced to draw conclusions from these findings quite different from those of the persons who merely hold to the facts of the senses. The latter may be countered by saying that the human being certainly displays the attributes of his ancestors, for the soul-spirit element, which enters into physical existence through birth, takes its physical form from what heredity gives it. But by this, nothing else is said than that a being bears the qualities of the medium in which it is immersed. The following is certainly a strange and trivial comparison, but the unprejudiced mind will not deny its justification when it is said that the fact that a human being appears clothed in the traits of his forebears gives no more evidence of the origin of his personal characteristics than the fact that he is wet because he fell into the water gives evidence of his inner nature. It can be said further that if the most illustrious name stands at the end of a blood relationship covering many generations, it shows that the bearer of this name needed this blood relationship in order to form the body required for the development of his entire personality. It is, however, no proof whatsoever of the "inheritance" of the personal element itself; in fact, for a healthy logic, this fact proves just the opposite. If indeed the personal gifts were inherited, they would have to stand at the beginning of this series of generations and be transmitted to the descendants. But the appearance of a great endowment at the end of a human series proves that it is *not* inherited.

It is not to be denied that those who speak of spiritual causation in life often add to the confusion. They often speak too much in general, indefinite terms. When it is declared that the inherited attributes are summed up into the personality of a human being, this can certainly be compared with the statement that the metal parts of a clock have assembled themselves. But it must also be admitted that many statements about the spiritual world are similar to the declaration that the metal parts of a clock cannot assemble themselves so that the hands move forward; therefore something spiritual must be present that takes care of the forward movement of the hands. In respect of such an assertion, he builds on a firmer foundation who says, "Oh, I shall not trouble about such 'mystical beings' who advance the hands of the clock; I am trying to learn to understand the mechanical relationships that bring about this forward movement of the hands." For it is not a question of merely knowing that behind such a mechanism as the clock, for example, there stands something spiritual—the clock-maker—but it is of significance only to learn to know the thoughts in the mind of the clock-maker that have *preceded* the construction of the clock. These thoughts can be found again in the mechanism.

All mere dreaming and imagining about the supersensible brings only confusion for they are incapable of satisfying the opponents. The latter are right when they say that such general references to supersensible beings are not an aid to the understanding of the facts. These opponents, it is true, may say the same thing about the *definite* indications of spiritual science. In this case, however, it can be shown how the effects of hidden spiritual causes appear in outer life. The following can be maintained: Suppose that what spiritual research has established by means of observation is true, namely, that man after death has passed through a period of purification and that he has *experienced* psychically during that time how a definite act, which has been performed in a previous life, is a hindrance to further evolution. While he was experiencing this, the impulse developed in him to rectify the consequences of this act. He brings this impulse with him into a new life, and it then forms the trait of character that places him in a position where this rectification is possible. Consider the totality of such impulses, and you have a reason for the destined environment in which a person is born.—The same may apply to another supposition. Again assume that what spir-

91

itual science says is true, namely, that the fruits of a past life are incorporated in the spiritual human seed, and that the land of the spirits in which this seed exists between death and rebirth is the realm in which these fruits ripen in order to appear again in a new life changed into talents and capacities, and to form the personality in such a way that it appears as the effect of what has been gained in a former life.—Anyone who makes these assumptions and, with them, observes life without prejudice will see that through them all facts of the sense world can be acknowledged in their full significance and truth, while at the same time everything becomes comprehensible that must remain forever incomprehensible to the one who, while relying only on physical facts, directs his attitude of mind toward the spiritual world. Above all, every illogical assumption will disappear, for instance the one mentioned above, that because the most important name stands at the end of a blood relationship series, the bearer of that name must have inherited his talents. Life becomes logically comprehensible by means of the supersensible facts communicated by spiritual science.

The conscientious truth-seeker who, without personal experiences in the supersensible world, wishes to find his way within the facts will, however, still be able to raise an important objection. For it can be asserted that it is inadmissible to assume the existence of any fact whatever simply for the reason that something that otherwise is inexplicable can thereby be explained. Such an objection is surely wholly without meaning for the one who knows the corresponding facts from supersensible experience. In the subsequent chapters of this work, the path will be indicated that can be traveled for the purpose of becoming acquainted, not only with other spiritual facts to be described here, but also with the law of spiritual causation as an individual experience. However, the above objection can, indeed, have significance for the person who is not willing to tread this path, but what can be said in refutation of this objection is also valuable for the one who has decided to take this path. For a person who accepts this in the right way has made the *best* initial step that can be taken on the path.—It is absolutely true that we should not accept something, the existence of which we do not otherwise know, simply because something, which otherwise remains incomprehensible, can be explained by it. In the case of the spiritual facts mentioned, however, the matter is quite different. If they are accepted, this has not only the intellectual consequence that life becomes comprehensible through them, but by the admission of these assumptions into our thoughts something else is experienced. Imagine the following case. Something happens to a person that arouses in him a feeling of distress. He can take this in two different ways. He can experience distress over the occurrence and yield himself to its disturbing aspects, even perhaps sink into grief. He can, however, take it in another way. He can say, "In reality, I have in a past life developed in myself the force that has confronted me with this event; I have, in fact, brought this thing upon myself," and he can arouse in himself all the feelings that can result from such a thought. Naturally, the thought must be experienced with the utmost sincerity and all possible force if it is to have such a result for the life of feeling and sensation. Whoever achieves this will have an experience that can best be illustrated by a comparison. Let us suppose that two men get hold of a stick of sealing wax. One makes intellectual observations concerning its "inner nature." These observations may be very clever; if there is nothing to show this "inner nature," one might easily reply that this is pure fantasy. The other, however, rubs the sealing wax with a cloth and then shows that it attracts small particles. There is a tremendous difference between the thoughts that have passed through the head of the first man, arousing his observations, and those of the second man. The thoughts of the first have no actual results; those of the second, however, have aroused a force, that is, something actual, from its concealment.—This is also the case with the thoughts of the human being who imagines that, through a former life, he has implanted into himself the power to encounter an event. This mere thought arouses in him a real force by means of which he can meet the event quite differently from the way he would have met it had he not entertained this thought. The inherent necessity of this event, which otherwise he might have considered merely due to chance, dawns upon him, and he will at once understand that he has had the right thought, for it had the force to disclose to him the facts. If a person repeats such inner processes, they become the means of an inner supply of strength and thus they prove their truth through their fruitfulness, and this truth becomes manifest gradually and powerfully. These processes have a healthy effect in regard to spirit, soul, and body; indeed, in every respect they act beneficially upon life. Man becomes aware that in this way he enters in the right manner into the relationships of life, whereas he is on the wrong path when he considers only the one life between birth and death. His soul becomes stronger because of this knowledge.—Such purely inner proof of spiritual causation can only be produced by each person himself in his own intimate soul life, but everyone can have such proof. Anyone who has not produced this proof cannot, of course, judge its power. Anyone who has produced it can no longer have any doubt about it. It is not surprising that this is so, for it is only natural that what is so intimately connected with man's innermost nature, his personality, can also be satisfactorily proved only by means of the most intimate experience.—The objection cannot be made, however, that each person must deal personally with such matters since they have to do with an inner experience of this kind, and that they cannot be the concern of spiritual science. It is true that each person must have the experience himself, just as each person must himself understand the proof of a mathematical problem. The means by which the experience can be attained, however, holds good for everyone, just as the method of proving a mathematical problem holds good for everyone.

It should not be denied that—aside from supersensible observations, of course—the proof by means of the force-producing power of the corresponding thoughts just referred to, is the only one that holds its own if viewed with impartial logic. All other considerations are certainly important, but they all will possess something that offers a point of attack. To be sure, anyone who has acquired a sufficiently unprejudiced point of view will find something in the possibility and actuality of the education of man that has logically effective power of proof for the fact that a spiritual being is struggling for existence within the bodily sheath. He will compare the animal with the human being and say to himself that in the former, its normal characteristics and capacities appear at birth as something definite, which shows clearly how it is predestined by heredity and how it will develop in the outer world. See how the tiny chick from birth carries out vital functions in a definite way. In the human being, however, something enters into relationship with his inner life, through education, that can exist without any connection whatsoever with heredity, and he can make the effects of such outer influences his own. Anyone who teaches knows that forces from the inner being must come to meet such influences. If this is not the case, then all schooling, all education is meaningless. For the unprejudiced educator, there exists a clearcut boundary between inherited characteristics and those inner human forces that shine through these characteristics originating in former earth lives. True, it is impossible to adduce "weighty" proofs for these things in the same way that certain physical facts may be demonstrated by means of the scales. But then, these things are the intimacies of life, and for the person who has a sense for such things, these impalpable evidences are likewise conclusive, even more conclusive than the obvious reality. That animals can be trained, that is, that they acquire qualities and faculties through education, offers no objection for the one who is able to see the essential thing. Aside from the fact that everywhere in the world transitions are to be found, the results of animal training do not fuse in like manner with the animal's personal nature, as is the case with human beings. It is even emphasized that the abilities the domestic animal acquires through training during its life with man, are inheritable, that is, that they have their effects in the species, not in the individual. Darwin describes how dogs fetch and carry without having learned to do so or having seen it done. Who would assert a similar thing in regard to human education?

There are thinkers who through their observation pass beyond the opinion that the human being is constructed from without purely through the forces of heredity. They rise to the idea that a spiritual being, an individuality, precedes physical existence and forms it. Many of them do not find it possible to comprehend that there are repeated earth lives, and that in the intervening existence between lives the fruits of the previous ones act cooperatively as formative forces. Let us mention one out of the list of such thinkers. Immanuel Hermann Fichte, son of the great Fichte, in his work *Anthropology*,[1] cites his observations that bring him to the following comprehensive conclusion:

"The parents are not the producers of the child in the fullest sense of the word. They offer the organic substance, and not alone that, but at the same time the median, sensory soul element that expresses itself in temperament, in special soul coloring, in definite specification of impulses, and the like, the general source of which is 'fantasy' in that broader sense already proved by us. In all these elements of personality the mixture and peculiar union of the parent souls is unmistakable; there are good reasons, therefore, to

[1] Immanuel Hermann Fichte, *Anthropologie,* p. 528. Brockhaus, Leipzig, 1860.

explain these as purely a product of procreation; all the more so, if procreation is understood to be an actual soul process. We had to come to this conclusion. But the actual conclusive central point of the personality is lacking just here. For by means of a deeper, more penetrating observation we see that even those characteristics of mind and soul are only vestures and *instruments* for embracing the real spiritual, ideal aptitudes of man, capable of furthering or retarding them in their development, but in no way capable of bringing them into existence out of themselves."

And we read further:

"*Each person* existed previously in accordance with his spiritual fundamental form, for spiritually considered, no individual resembles another any more than one *species of animal* resembles another." [2]

These thoughts only go so far as to permit a spiritual being to enter the physical corporeality of man. Since, however, this spiritual being's formative forces are not derived from the causes of a former life, each time that a personality comes into existence a spiritual being of this kind would have to emerge out of a divine primal fount. Assuming this to be true, there would be no possibility of explaining the relationship that exists between the aptitudes struggling forth out of the human inner being and what approaches this inner being in the course of life from the outer earthly

---

[2] Immanuel Hermann Fichte, *Anthropologie*, p. 532.

environment. The human inner being, which in every individual would have to spring from a divine primal source, would have to stand as a complete stranger before what confronts it in earth life. Only then will this not be the case—and so it is indeed—if this human inner nature had already been united with the external world—in other words, if it is not living in this world for the first time. The unbiased educator can clearly make the observation, "I bring something to my pupil from the results of earth life that is indeed foreign to his merely inherited characteristics, yet is something that makes him feel as if he had already been connected with the work in which these results of earth life have their source." Only repeated earth lives, in connection with the facts in the spiritual realm between these earth lives as presented by spiritual research, can give a satisfactory explanation of the life of present day humanity, considered from every point of view.—The expression, "present day" humanity, was intentionally used here, for spiritual research finds that there was a time when the cycle of earth lives began, and that at that time conditions different from those of the present existed for the spiritual being of man as it entered into the corporeal sheath. In the following chapters we shall go back to this primeval state of the human being. When it will have to be shown, from the results of spiritual science, how this human being has attained his present form in relation to the evolution of the earth, we shall then be able to point out still more exactly how the spiritual essential core of man penetrates into the physical body from supersensible worlds, and how the spiritual law of causation—"human destiny"—is developed.

IV

THE EVOLUTION OF
THE COSMOS AND MAN

FROM the foregoing considerations it may be seen that the being of man is composed of four members: physical body, life body, astral body, and the vehicle of the ego. The ego is active within the three other members and transforms them. Out of this transformation, at a lower level, are developed sentient soul, intellectual soul, and consciousness soul. At a higher stage of human existence, spirit self, life spirit, and spirit man are formed. These members of the human being stand in the most manifold relationships to the whole cosmos and their evolution is bound up with cosmic evolution. By considering this cosmic evolution, an insight may be gained into the deeper mysteries of man's being.

It is evident that human life is related in the most diverse ways to its environment, to the dwelling place in which it evolves. By means of existing facts even external science has been forced to the opinion that the earth itself, this dwelling place of man in the most comprehensive sense, has undergone an evolution. It points to the conditions of earth existence in which the human being, in his present form, did not yet exist upon our planet. It shows how mankind has slowly and gradually evolved from simple states of civilization to the present conditions. Thus, science also has come to the opinion that a relationship exists between the evolution of man and that of his heavenly body, the earth.

Spiritual science[1] traces this relationship by means of knowledge that gathers its facts from perception sharpened by spiritual organs. It traces back the process of human development, and it becomes clear to it that the real inner spiritual being of man has passed through a series of lives upon this earth. Spiritual science thus reaches a point of time, lying far back in the remote past, when for the first time this inner being of man enters an external life in the present sense of the word. It was in this first earthly incarnation that the ego began to be active within the three bodies, astral body, life body, and physical body, and it then carried with it the fruits of this activity into the succeeding life.

If one goes back in one's consideration to this point of time, in the manner indicated, one then becomes aware that the ego meets with an earth condition in which the three bodies, physical body, life body, and astral body, are already developed and have already a certain connection.

---

[1] The term "spiritual science," as is apparent from the context, is here synonymous with the terms "occult science" and "supersensible knowledge."

The ego unites for the first time with the being composed of these three bodies. From now on, it takes part in the further evolution of the three bodies. Heretofore, these bodies developed without this human ego up to the stage at which the ego came in touch with them.

Spiritual science must go still further back in its research, if it wishes to answer the following questions: How did the three bodies reach the stage of evolution at which they were able to receive an ego into themselves, and how did this ego itself come into existence and acquire the capacity to be active within these bodies?

An answer to these questions is only possible if one traces out the development of the earth planet itself, in the sense of spiritual science. By means of such research one arrives at the beginning of this earth planet. The mode of observation that relies merely upon the facts of the physical senses cannot come to conclusions that have anything to do with this beginning of the earth. A certain point of view, which makes use of such final conclusions, decides that all earthly substance has been formed out of a primeval mist. It cannot be the task of this work to enter into these ideas because for spiritual research it is a question of not merely considering the material processes of the earth's evolution, but chiefly of taking into account the spiritual causes lying behind matter. If we have before us a man who raises his hand, this raising of the hand can suggest two different ways of considering the act. We may investigate the mechanism of the arm and the rest of the organism and describe the process as it takes place purely in the realm of the physical. On the other hand, we may turn our spiritual attention to what is taking place in the human soul, to what constitutes the inner impulse of raising the hand. In a similar way the researcher, schooled by means of spiritual perception, sees spiritual processes behind all processes of the physical sense-world. For him, all transformations in the substances of the earth planet are manifestations of spiritual forces lying behind these substances. If, however, this spiritual observation of the life of the earth goes further and further back, it comes to a point in evolution where all matter has its primal beginnings. Matter evolves out of the spiritual. Prior to this, only the spiritual exists. By means of this spiritual insight, the spiritual is perceived, and on further investigation it can be seen how this spiritual element in part condenses, so to speak, into matter. Here we have before us, on a higher level, a process that may be likened to what would take place if we were observing a container of water in which lumps of ice were gradually forming by means of ingeniously controlled refrigeration. Just as we see here ice condensing from what was formerly water, so also, through spiritual observation, we are able to trace out the manner in which material things, processes, and beings are condensed from an element that was formerly spiritual.—In this way the physical earth planet has evolved out of a spiritual cosmic being, and everything material connected with this earth planet has condensed out of what was spiritually bound up with it previously. We must not imagine, however, that at any time *all* that exists of a spiritual nature is transformed into matter, but in matter we have before us transformed parts only of the primeval spiritual substance. Moreover, also during the period of evolution of matter, the spiritual remains the directing and guiding principle.

103

It is obvious that the mode of thought that restricts itself to the processes of the physical sense-world, and to what the intellect is able to infer from them, is incapable of giving information concerning the spiritual element in question. Let us imagine a being having only the senses that can perceive ice, not, however, the finer condition of water, out of which ice is formed by means of refrigeration. For such a being, water would be non-existent, and only when parts of this water had been transformed into ice would the water be at all perceptible to it. Thus the spiritual part lying behind the earth processes remains concealed to anyone who admits only what exists for the physical senses. If, from the physical facts he observes now in the present, he forms a correct conclusion concerning earlier conditions of the earth planet, he merely arrives at that point in evolution where a part of the preceding spiritual element condensed into matter. This method of observation perceives just as little of the preceding spiritual element as it does of the spiritual element that holds sway, also at the present time, invisibly behind the world of matter.

Only in the last chapters of this work shall we be able to speak of the paths upon which man must travel to acquire the capacity for looking back, with spiritual perception, at those earlier conditions of the earth under discussion here. Here we only wish to indicate that for spiritual research the facts even of the remote past have not disappeared. When a being reaches corporeal existence, the substance of his body disappears with his physical death. The spiritual forces that have expelled these corporeal elements from themselves do not "disappear" in the same way. They leave their impressions, their exact counterparts, behind in the spiritual foundations of the world, and he who, penetrating the visible world, is able to lift his perception into the invisible, is finally able to have before him something that might be compared with a mighty spiritual panorama, in which all past world-processes are recorded. These imperishable impressions of all that is spiritual may be called the "Akashic Record," thus designating as the Akashic essence the spiritually permanent element in universal occurrences, in contradistinction to the transient forms of these occurrences. It must be repeated, once more, that research in the supersensible realms of existence can only be carried on with the help of spiritual perception, that is, in the realm with which we are now dealing, only by reading the above-mentioned "Akashic Record." Yet what has already been said in earlier parts of this work in a similar connection applies here also. Supersensible facts can be *investigated* only by means of supersensible perception; if, however, they have been investigated and are communicated through the science of the supersensible, they may then be *comprehended* by ordinary thinking, provided this thinking is really unprejudiced. In the following pages, information concerning the evolution of the earth will be imparted from the standpoint of supersensible cognition. The transformations of our planet will be traced down to the condition of life in which we find it today. If a person observes what he has actually before him in pure sense-perception, and then grasps what supersensible cognition has to say in regard to the way in which what exists at the present time has been evolving since time immemorial, he is then able to say, if he really thinks impartially: in the first place, the information imparted by this form of cognition is thor-

105

oughly logical; in the second place, I can understand that things have become what they now are, if I admit the truth of what has been communicated through supersensible research. Naturally, when we speak of logic in this connection, we do not infer thereby that it is impossible for errors in logic to be contained in some presentation of supersensible research. We shall here speak of logic only as that word is used in the ordinary life of the physical world. Just as logical presentation is demanded in the physical world, even though the individual person presenting a range of facts may fall into logical error, so it is also the case in supersensible research. It may even happen that a researcher who has the power of perception in supersensible realms may fall into error in his logical presentation, and that someone who has no supersensible perception, but who has the capacity for sound thinking, may correct him. Essentially, however, there can be no objection to the logic employed in supersensible research. Moreover, it should be quite unnecessary to emphasize the fact that nothing can be charged against the facts themselves on purely logical grounds. Just as in the realm of the physical world it is never possible to prove logically the existence of a whale except by seeing one, so also the supersensible facts can be known only by means of spiritual perception.—It cannot, however, be sufficiently emphasized that it is necessary for the observer of supersensible realms first to acquire a view by means of the above-mentioned logic, before he tries to approach the spiritual world through his own perception. He must also recognize how comprehensible the manifest world of the senses appears when it is assumed that the communications of spiritual science are correct. All experience in the supersensible world remains an insecure, even dangerous, groping, if the above-mentioned preparatory path is ignored. Therefore in this work the supersensible facts of earth evolution are first communicated, before the path to supersensible knowledge itself is dealt with.—We must also consider the fact that anyone who finds his way purely through thinking into what supersensible cognition has to impart is not at all in the same position as someone who listens to the description of a physical process that he himself is unable to observe, since pure thinking is itself a supersensible activity. Thinking, as a sensory activity, cannot of itself lead to supersensible occurrences. If, however, this thinking be applied to the supersensible occurrences described by supersensible perception, it then grows *through itself* into the spiritual world. In fact, one of the best ways of acquiring one's own perception in the supersensible realm is to grow into the higher world by thinking about the communications of supersensible congnition, for, entrance into the higher realms in this way is accompanied by the greatest clarity of perception. For this reason a certain school of spiritual-scientific investigation considers *this* thinking the most excellent first stage of all spiritual-scientific training.—It should be quite comprehensible that in this book the way in which the supersensible finds its verification in the outer world is not described in all the details of earth evolution as it is perceived in spirit. That is not what was meant when it was said that the hidden is everywhere demonstrable by its visible effects. The idea is, rather, that whatever is encountered *can* become entirely clear and comprehensible to man, if the manifest processes are placed into the light afforded by spiritual science. Only

107

in a few characteristic instances will reference be made in the following pages to a verification of the concealed by means of the manifest, in order to show how it can be done at any point in the course of practical life.

If we trace back the evolution of the *Earth* by means of the spiritual-scientific method of research mentioned above, we come to a spiritual state of our planet. If we continue still further back on our path of research, we find that this spiritual element previously existed in a sort of physical embodiment. Thus we come upon a past physical planetary state that later became spiritualized and then, later still, through repeated materialization, became transformed into our *Earth*. Our *Earth* appears, therefore, as a reincarnation of an ancient planet. But spiritual science is able to go still further back and it then discovers the whole process repeated twice more. This *Earth* of ours passed through three preceding planetary stages, and in between these stages there lie intermediate stages of spiritualization. The physical element appears ever more subtle, the further back we trace the *Earth's* incarnations.

One may ask: How can a sound power of thought accept the existence of world stages lying so far back in the past, such as these that are spoken of here? This is a natural objection to the descriptions that are to follow. Our reply is that for anyone who with understanding is able to see the *present* hidden spiritual element in what is revealed to the senses, an insight into the earlier evolutionary states, however remote, presents no impossibility. Only for someone who does not acknowledge this hidden spiritual element finds that, in his perception of the present stage, the earlier ones are also contained, just as in his perception of a man of fifty the one-year-old child is still contained. But, you may say, in the latter case you have before you, besides the man of fifty, one-year-old children and all the possible intermediate stages. That is true, but it is also true for the evolution of the spirit as it is meant here. Whoever has come to an objective understanding in this field sees also that in a comprehensive survey of the present, which includes the spiritual, the past evolutionary stages have really survived, alongside the perfected stages of present-day evolution, just as alongside a man of fifty, one-year-old children are present. Within the earthly events of the present, the primeval happenings of the past may be seen if we are but able to distinguish between these different successive stages of evolution.

In the form in which he is evolving at present man appears for the first time during the fourth of the planetary incarnations characterized above, the actual *Earth* itself. The essential nature of this form shows the human being to be composed of the four members: physical body, life body, astral body, and ego. Yet this form would not have been able to appear had it not been prepared through the preceding processes of evolution. This preparation took place because within the previous planetary incarnation there were beings evolving who already possessed three of the present four human members—the physical body, life body, and astral body. These beings, who in a certain sense may be called our human ancestors, did not yet possess an ego, but they developed these three other members and their inter-relationships to the degree that made them mature enough later on to receive the ego. Thus the human ancestor, in the previous planetary incarnation, reached a certain stage of maturity in his three members. This state passed over into a spiritual one and out of it a new physical planetary state developed, that of the *Earth.* Within this *Earth,* the matured human ancestors were present, as it were, in a germinal state. Because the entire planet had passed over into a spiritualized condition and had reappeared in a new form, it offered to the embryonic human entities contained within it, with their physical, life, and astral bodies, the opportunity not only of developing again to their previous level, but also the further possibility, after having attained this point, of reaching out beyond it through the reception of the ego. The *Earth* evolution, therefore, falls into two parts. In the first period, the *Earth* itself appears as a reincarnation of the previous planetary stage. This recapitulatory stage, however, stands at a higher level than that of the previous incarnation because of the intervening stage of spiritualization. The *Earth* now contains within itself the germinal nuclei of the human ancestors from the previous planet. These at first develop to their previous level; then, when they have attained this point, the first period is concluded, but because of its own higher stage of evolution, the *Earth* can now develop the nuclei still further, namely, by making them fit to receive the ego. The unfoldment of the ego within the physical, life, and astral bodies is characteristic of the second period of *Earth* evolution.

In this way, by means of the evolution of the *Earth,* man is brought a stage higher. This was also the case in the previous planetary incarnations, for even in the first of these incarnations some element of the human being was pres-

110

ent. Therefore, light is shed upon the human being of the present if his evolution is traced back to the distant past of the very first of the planetary incarnations mentioned.—In supersensible research, the first of these planetary incarnations may be named *Saturn,* the second may be designated *Sun,* the third, *Moon,* and the fourth, *Earth.* It must be clearly understood, however, that these designations must not, at the outset, be associated with the same names that are used for the members of our present solar system. *Saturn, Sun,* and *Moon* are to be names for *bygone* evolutionary forms through which the *Earth* has passed.[1] The relationship that these worlds of the ancient past hold to the heavenly bodies constituting the present solar system will appear in the course of the subsequent descriptions. It will then become clear why these names have been chosen.

The conditions of the four planetary incarnations mentioned can be described only in outline, because the processes and the beings and their destinies upon *Saturn, Sun,* and *Moon* are truly as manifold as upon the *Earth* itself. Therefore in our descriptions of these states only single

---

[1] In order to make clear the difference between the designations of the Planetary Evolutions and our present planetary bodies, which bear the same names, the following system has been worked out. *Saturn, Sun, Moon, Earth, Jupiter, Venus, Vulcan* printed in italics with initial capitals designate the great cosmic planetary cycles of evolution. In the *Sun* evolution, after the separation of the main cosmic body into two parts, the designation is Sun and Saturn, spelt with initial capitals, but not with italics. In the *Moon* evolution, when a separation takes place, the remaining main body is spelt Moon, with an initial capital, the separating planetary sun is spelt with small letter. In the *Earth* evolution, the separated planetary bodies are spelt as is customary, that is, the planets Saturn, Jupiter, Mars, Venus, Mercury with initial capitals; sun, moon, earth with small letters. (Tr.)

characteristic points will be brought out that illustrate how the *Earth's* states have developed out of earlier ones. We must also consider the fact that the further back we go, the more do these states become dissimilar to those of the present. Yet in characterizing them, they can only be described by employing mental representations borrowed from present earthly relationships. When, for instance, we speak of light, heat, or other phenomena, in connection with these earlier states, we should not overlook the fact that we do not mean exactly what is meant by these words, light and heat, at the present time, and yet this terminology is correct, because for the observer of supersensible realms something appears in these earlier stages of evolution out of which the light and heat of the present have evolved. Those who follow the descriptions given here will indeed be well able to gather—from the connection in which these things are placed—what mental pictures are to be made in order to have characteristic images and symbols for things that have occurred in the distant, primeval past.

To be sure, these difficulties become especially significant for the planetary conditions that preceded the *Moon* incarnation, for, during this latter period, conditions prevailed that still show a certain similarity to earthly conditions. He who attempts to describe these conditions has in this similarity to the present a certain starting point for expressing in clear mental pictures the supersensibly acquired perceptions. It is a different matter when the evolution of *Saturn* and *Sun* are to be described. What presents itself there to clairvoyant observation is very different from the objects and beings belonging at present to the sphere of human life, and this dissimilarity makes it difficult to the

112

highest degree to bring the ancient matters in question within the scope of supersensible consciousness. Since, however, the present being of man cannot be understood unless we go back as far as the *Saturn* state, the description must nevertheless be given. Surely such a description will not be misunderstood by the one who holds the existence of such difficulties in mind and who remembers that much of what is said must of necessity be considered more in the light of an allusion and a reference to the corresponding facts than as an exact description of them.

A contradiction might be found between what is given here and in the following pages, and what is said on page 109 concerning the continuation of the past into the present. One might imagine that nowhere does there exist, alongside the present *Earth* state, a previous *Saturn, Sun,* and *Moon* state, or even a human form such as is described in this exposition as having existed in these earlier stages. It is true that *Saturn* human beings, *Sun* and *Moon* human beings do not move about side by side with *Earth* humanity in the same way as three-year-old children move about alongside fifty-year-old men and women, but *within* the earthly human being the previous states of humanity are supersensibly perceptible. In order to know this we must have acquired the power of discrimination and extend it to include the full scope of the conditions of life. The three-year-old child exists alongside the fifty-year-old man; similarly, the corpse, the sleeping, and the dreaming human being exist alongside the living, waking *Earth* man. Although these various forms of existence of the being of man—as they are at present—do not *directly* correspond to the various stages of evolution, nevertheless a genuine perception sees in such forms of manifestation these various evolutionary stages.

*   *   *

Of the present four members of the being of man, the physical body is the oldest. It is also the member that, in its own way, has attained the greatest perfection. Supersensible research shows that this human member was already in existence during the *Saturn* evolution. It will be seen in the course of this description that the form, however, which this physical body possessed upon *Saturn* was something quite different from the present human physical body. This earthly human physical body can only maintain its existence by reason of its connection with the life body, astral body, and ego, described in the preceding parts of this book. Such a connection did not yet exist upon *Saturn*. At that time the physical body passed through its first stage of evolution without having a human life body, astral body, or ego inserted into it. During the *Saturn* evolution it gradually matured so as to be able to receive a life body. To this end, *Saturn* had first to pass over into a spiritual state and then reincarnate as the *Sun*. During the *Sun* incarnation, what had become the physical body on *Saturn* unfolded again, as though from a germ of a past evolution, and only then could it draw into itself an etheric body. Through this insertion of an etheric body, the physical body changed its character. It was raised to a second degree of perfection. A similar thing occurred during the *Moon* evolution. The human ancestor, having evolved from the *Sun* to the *Moon*, received into himself the astral body, and thus the physical body became changed a third time; that is, it was raised to the third degree of its perfection. Moreover, the life body was likewise changed, and it stood now in the second stage of its perfection. Upon the *Earth* the ego was added to the human ancestor consisting of physical body, life body, and astral body. The physical body thereby reached its fourth degree of perfection, the life body its third, the astral body its second; the ego stands only in its first stage of existence.

If we give ourselves up to an unprejudiced examination of the human being, there will be no difficulty in correctly picturing these various degrees of perfection of the individual members. We need only in this connection compare the physical body with the astral. Certainly it is true that the astral body, as a soul member, stands at a higher stage of evolution than the physical body, and when, in the future, the astral body will have perfected itself, it will have a much greater significance for the entire being of man than the present physical body. Still *in its own way* the physical body has reached a certain climax of evolution. In this connection one need but think of the structure of the heart, organized in accordance with the greatest wisdom, the marvellous structure of the brain and other organs, even that of an individual portion of a bone, for example, that of the upper part of the thigh bone, the great trochanter. There is within the end of this bone a net-like or trestle-like structure of delicate bony fibers, formed in harmony with the laws of mechanics. The whole is fitted together in such a manner that, with the least amount of material, the most advantageous effect on the articular surfaces is attained, for example, the most suitable distribution of friction and as a result a proper kind of mobility. Thus in the various

115

parts of the human body structures are to be found full of wisdom, and if we consider further the harmonious co-operation between the parts and the whole, we shall certainly find that it is correct to speak of the particular perfection of this member of the human being. In this connection, the fact that in certain parts of the physical body seemingly inadequate phenomena may appear, or that disturbances may arise either in the structure or in the functions, is of no importance. We shall even be able to discover that these disturbances are, in a certain sense, only the necessary shadow side of the wisdom-filled light that is shed over the entire physical organism. Now compare with this the astral body as the bearer of joy and sorrow, of desire and passion. Oh, what insecurity reigns in this body in respect of joy and sorrow, what desires and passions are enacted within it, often meaningless and running counter to higher human purposes! The astral body is only in process of acquiring the harmony and inner completeness that we already find in the physical body. In like manner it is possible to show that the ether body, in its way, appears more perfect than the astral body, but less perfect than the physical body, and an adequate consideration will prove that the essential kernel of the human being, the ego, stands at present only at the beginning of its evolutions. For how much has this ego already accomplished of its task of transforming the other members of man's being in such a manner that they be a manifestation of its own nature?— What results from external observation in this direction is made more acute for those who understand spiritual science by means of something else. One may quote the fact that the physical body can be overtaken by sickness. Spiritual science is in the position to show that a great part of all sicknesses originates from the fact that the perversity and mistakes of the astral body are transmitted to the etheric body, and in a roundabout way through the latter destroy the complete harmony of the physical body. The deeper connection which can only be touched upon here, and the actual cause of many disease processes elude the scientific mode of observation that confines itself only to physical sensory facts. In most cases it happens that the damaging of the astral body does not produce pathological tendencies of the physical body in the same life in which the damage has occurred, but only in a subsequent one. Therefore, the laws that apply here have a meaning only for those who are able to acknowledge the repetition of human life on earth, but even if there is no desire to gain such deeper knowledge, yet the ordinary view of life shows that the human being indulges himself altogether too much in enjoyments and desires that undermine the harmony of the physical body. Pleasure, desire, passion do not reside in the physical, but in the astral body, and this is in many respects still so imperfect that it can destroy the perfection of the physical body.—We wish to call attention to the fact that no attempt is made here to prove by such arguments the statements of spiritual science concerning the evolution of the four members of man's being. The proofs are taken from spiritual research, and this shows that the physical body has passed through a fourfold metamorphosis on to higher degrees of perfection, and that the other human members, as already described, have undergone fewer transformations. We only wished to point out that these communications of spiritual research relate to facts the effects of which show also in the outwardly observable degrees of perfection of the physical, life, and astral bodies.

* * *

If we wish to form an approximately accurate pictorial idea of the conditions during the *Saturn* evolution, we must take into consideration the fact that during that period essentially nothing existed of the things and creatures that belong at present to the earth, and are counted among the mineral, plant, and animal kingdoms. The beings of these three kingdoms only came into existence in later periods of evolution. Of the present physically visible earth beings, only man existed at that time, and only that part of him, the physical body, as already described. At the present time, not only do these beings of the mineral, plant, animal, and human kingdoms belong to the earth, but there are also other beings who do not manifest in a physical body. These beings were also present during the *Saturn* evolution, and their activity on *Saturn* as a sphere of action resulted in the subsequent evolution of man.

If one directs the spiritual organs of perception, not to the beginning and the end, but to the middle evolutionary period of this *Saturn* incarnation, a state appears consisting chiefly of "heat." No gaseous, fluid, or solid elements are to be found there. All these conditions only appear in later cosmic incarnations. Let us imagine a human being with his present sense organs approaching this *Saturn* world as an observer. He would then experience none of the sense-impressions of which he is capable, except the sensation of heat. On reaching the space occupied by *Saturn,* he would only perceive that it had a condition of heat different from the rest of the surrounding space. He would not find this space uniformly warm throughout, but would find hot and cold regions alternating in the most varied manner. Heat would be perceived radiating according to certain lines, not straight lines, but in irregular forms, produced by the variations in heat. He would have before him something like an organized cosmic being, appearing in ever changing states, consisting only of heat.

For man of the present day it must be difficult to imagine something that consists only of heat, since he is not accustomed to recognize heat as something in itself, but to perceive it only in connection with hot or cold gaseous, fluid, or solid bodies. Especially the man who has acquired the ideas of modern physics will look upon the above way of speaking about heat as pure nonsense. He will perhaps say that there are solid, fluid, and gaseous bodies; heat, however, denotes only the condition in which any one of these three bodily forms finds itself. When the smallest particles of a gas are in motion, this motion is perceived as heat. Where there is no gas, there can be no such motion, therefore also no heat.—The matter appears quite different to the researcher in spiritual science. For him, heat is something about which he can speak in the same sense he can speak of a gas, of a fluid, or of a solid body; it is for him only a substance still finer than gas, and gas is to him nothing else than condensed heat, in the same sense that a fluid is a condensed vapor, or a solid body a condensed fluid. Thus the spiritual scientist speaks of heat bodies just as he speaks of gaseous and vaporous bodies.—If someone wishes to follow the spiritual researcher into this realm, it is only necessary to grant that there exists spiritual perception. In the given world of the physical senses, heat exists entirely as a state of a solid, a fluid, or gaseous body. This condition, however, is only the external aspect of heat, or its effect. The physicists speak only of this effect of heat, not of its inner nature. Let us try to disregard all effects of heat that we receive through external objects, and picture to ourselves only our inner experience when we say, "I feel warm," "I feel cold." This inner experience can alone give us an idea of the *Saturn* state at the period of its development described above. It would have been possible to pass through the whole of the space occupied by *Saturn* without finding any sort of gas that could exert pressure, or any sort of solid or fluid body from which we could receive an impression of light. But in every point in space, without any impression from outside, we would have had the inner feeling that here there exists this or that degree of heat.

In a cosmic body of such a character there are no conditions suitable for the animals, plants, and minerals of the present time. (It is, therefore, hardly necessary to state that what has just been described could never occur. A man of today, as such, cannot confront ancient *Saturn* as an observer. The exposition was only to serve as an illustration.) The beings of whom supersensible cognition becomes conscious while observing *Saturn,* were at a stage of evolution quite different from the present, sensorily-perceptible earth beings. Before this faculty of cognition beings appear who did not possess a physical body like that of present-day man. When we speak here of "physical body," we must be careful not to think of the physical corporeality as it exists today. Rather, we must differentiate carefully between the physical body and the mineral body. A physical body is

120

one that is ruled by physical laws observed today in the mineral kingdom. The present human physical body is not only ruled by these physical laws, but it is also permeated by mineral substance. It is impossible to speak of a physical-mineral body of this kind on ancient *Saturn*. At that time there existed only a physical corporeality governed by physical laws, but these physical laws manifested themselves only through heat effects. Thus the physical body was a fine, attenuated, etheric heat body, and the whole of *Saturn* consisted of these heat bodies. They were the first germinal beginnings of the present physical-mineral body of man. The latter fashioned itself out of the heat body as a result of the insertion into it of gaseous, fluid, and solid matter, which only came into existence later on. Among the beings perceived by supersensible consciousness when it becomes aware of the *Saturn* state and who, besides man, may be called inhabitants of *Saturn,* are those, for example, who have no need at all of a physical body. The lowest vehicle of these beings was an ether body; they had, however, besides this a higher member that transcended all the human vehicles. Man has as highest member spirit man. These beings have a still higher member, and between the ether body and spirit man they have all the members described in this book as belonging also to human beings: astral body, ego, spirit self, and life spirit. Just as our earth is surrounded by a sphere of air—an atmosphere—so was it also on *Saturn,* only this "atmosphere" was of a spiritual character.[1] It consisted of the

---

[1] Instead of saying, "*Saturn* was surrounded by an atmosphere," a precise mode of speech, in order to express exactly the inner experience of spiritual research, would have to say, "In becoming conscious of *Saturn* by

beings just mentioned and still others. Between the heat bodies of *Saturn* and these beings there was a constant reciprocal action. The latter submerged the members of their being into the physical heat bodies of *Saturn* and, although there was no life in these heat bodies themselves, the life of the beings in their environment was expressed in them. They might be compared to mirrors, only it was not the *images* of the beings in question that were mirrored, but their *life-conditions.* Nothing living could have been discovered on *Saturn* itself, but through its activity *Saturn* vitalized the surrounding heavenly space by reflecting back, like an echo, the life sent down to it. The whole of *Saturn* appeared like a mirror of celestial life. Certain exalted beings whose life was radiated back by *Saturn* may be called "Spirits of Wisdom." (In Christian Esotericism they bear the name "Kyriotetes" or "Dominions.") Their activity on *Saturn* does not begin with the middle period of its evolution just described; in fact, it had then already ceased. Before they had reached the ability to become conscious of the reflection of their own life from the heat bodies of *Saturn,* they had to develop these bodies to the point of being able to effect this reflection. Therefore their activity began soon after the beginning of the *Saturn* evolution. At that time the bodily nature of *Saturn* still consisted of chaotic substance that was unable to reflect anything.—By

means of supersensible cognition, this consciousness is confronted by a *Saturn* atmosphere," or, "by beings of this or that sort." The use of the expression: "this or that is present," must be permitted, for this is also the usage employed for the actual soul experience in sensory perception, but we are obliged to keep this in mind in the following exposition; it already follows from the context.

122

considering this chaotic substance, one has transplanted oneself through spiritual perception to the beginning of the *Saturn* evolution. What is observable there does not yet bear the subsequent heat character. If we wish to characterize it, it is only possible to speak of a quality that may be compared with the human will. It is will, through and through. Thus we have to do here entirely with a soul state. If we wish to trace back the source of this will, we find that it originates from the emanations of exalted beings who brought their development, in stages that can only be divined, to such a height that they were able, when the evolution of *Saturn* began, to pour forth the will from their own being. After this emanation had lasted for a time, the activity of the already mentioned Spirits of Wisdom unites with the will. Thus will, previously wholly without attributes, now gradually acquires the ability to reflect life back into cosmic space.—These beings, who experience their supreme bliss in pouring forth will out of themselves at the beginning of the *Saturn* evolution, may be called the "Spirits of Will." (In Christian esotericism they are called "Thrones.")—After a certain stage of the *Saturn* evolution has been reached through the co-operation of will and life, there begins the activity of other beings who are likewise present in the environment of *Saturn*. They may be called the "Spirits of Motion." (In Christian esotericism, "Dynameis," or "Powers.") They have no physical or ether body, but their lowest vehicle is the astral body. When the *Saturn* bodies have acquired the ability to reflect life, this reflected life is in a condition to be permeated with the qualities that reside in the astral bodies of the Spirits of Motion. The result of this is that it appears as though the

123

manifestations of sensation and feeling and similar soul activities were flung out into celestial space from *Saturn.* The whole of *Saturn* appears like an ensouled being, manifesting sympathies and antipathies. These manifestations of soul-qualities, however, are in no way its own, but only the flung-back soul activities of the Spirits of Motion.—After this state has lasted a certain length of time, there begins the activity of still other beings that may be called the "Spirits of Form." Their lowest member is also an astral body, but it stands at a stage of development different from that of the Spirits of Motion. Whereas these latter communicate only general expressions of feeling to the reflected life, the activity of the astral body of the Spirits of Form (in Christian esotericism, "Exusiai," or "Authorities,") is of such a nature that the expressions of feeling are flung back into cosmic space as though from individual beings. One might say that the Spirits of Motion cause *Saturn* as a whole to appear like an ensouled being. The Spirits of Form divide this life into individual living beings, so that *Saturn* now appears like an agglomeration of such soul beings.—In order to have a picture of this state, imagine a mulberry or a blackberry, and note how it is composed of small individual parts. For the observer of the spiritual world, *Saturn,* in the period of evolution just described, is similarly composed of a number of *Saturn* entities that, to be sure, do not possess a life and soul of their own, but that reflect the life and soul of the beings dwelling in them.—In this state of *Saturn,* beings now intervene who likewise have the astral body as their lowest member, but who have developed it to such a stage that it has the effect of a present-day human ego. Through these beings, the ego looks down upon *Saturn* from its environment and communicates its nature to the individual living beings of *Saturn*. Thus something is sent out into cosmic space from *Saturn* that appears similar to the activity of the human personality in the present cycle of life. The beings who bring this about may be called the "Spirits of Personality," ("Archai," "Primal Beginnings" in Christian Esotericism). They confer upon the small *Saturn* bodies the appearance of the character of personality. Personality does not exist on *Saturn* itself, however, but only its reflection, as it were, the shell of personality. The Spirits of Personality have their real personality on the periphery of *Saturn*. Just because these Spirits of Personality let their being be reflected back by the *Saturn* bodies in the manner indicated, the fine substance just described as "heat" is imparted to the latter.—In the whole of *Saturn* there is no inner life, but the Spirits of Personality recognize the image of their own inner life as it streams back to them from *Saturn* in the form of heat.

When all this occurs, the Spirits of Personality stand at the stage at which the human being is at present. At that time they pass through their human epoch. If we wish to look at these facts with an unprejudiced eye, we must imagine that a being can be "man" not merely in the form borne by man at the present time. The Spirits of Personality are "human beings" on *Saturn*. They do not have the physical body as their lowest principle, but the astral body with the ego. Therefore they are not able to express the experiences of this astral body in a physical and ether body like that of the present-day man; yet they not only *possess* an ego, but are fully *aware* of it, because the heat substance

125

of *Saturn* brings it to their consciousness in reflecting it back to them. They are "human beings" under conditions different from the earth state.

In the further course of the *Saturn* evolution, events ensue that are different in character from anything existing heretofore. While up to the present time everything was a reflection of external life and sensation, now a kind of inner life begins. Here and there within the *Saturn* world a life of light begins, now flaring up, now darkening. Flickering glimmers of light appear in certain places, and in others something occurs like flashes of lightning. The *Saturn* heat bodies begin to glimmer, to sparkle, even to radiate. Because this stage of evolution has been reached, again certain beings have the possibility of becoming active. These are beings who may be called "Spirits of Fire," (in Christian esotericism, "Archangeloi," or "Archangels"). Although these beings have an astral body of their own, they are unable, at this stage of their existence, to stimulate it; they would not be able to awake any feeling or sensation if they could not work upon the heat bodies that had reached the *Saturn* stage already described. This activity exerted by them gives them the possibility of becoming aware of their own existence. They cannot say to themselves, "I exist," but rather, "My environment permits me to exist." They perceive, and their perceptions consist in the activities of light described as taking place on *Saturn*. These activities are in a certain sense their ego. This gives them a certain kind of consciousness that may be designated as picture consciousness. It can be thought of as a kind of human dream consciousness, only we must think of the degree of intensity of this dream consciousness as being much greater than in human dreaming, and we must realize that we are concerned not with unreal dream pictures surging up and down, but with dream pictures that have an actual relationship to the play of light on *Saturn.*—Within this reciprocal activity taking place between the Spirits of Fire and the *Saturn* heat bodies, the germinal human organs of sense are started on the path of evolution. The organs through which the human being at present perceives the physical world flash up in their first etheric inceptions. Human phantoms, as yet manifesting nothing but the primal light images of the sense organs, can be recognized within *Saturn* by means of clairvoyant perception.—These sense organs thus are the fruit of the activity of the Spirits of Fire, but the Spirits of Fire are not the only beings who participate in the formation of these organs. Together with these Spirits of Fire, other beings enter the field of *Saturn,* beings who are so far advanced in their evolution as to be able to employ these germinal senses to perceive the cosmic processes taking place in the life of *Saturn.* These beings may be called "Spirits of Love," (in Christian esotericism, "Seraphim"). Were they not present, the Spirits of Fire could not have the consciousness described above. They behold the *Saturn* processes with a consciousness enabling them to convey these processes to the Spirits of Fire in the form of images. They forego all benefit they themselves might reap by perceiving the *Saturn* events; they renounce all enjoyment, all pleasure; they sacrifice all this in order that the Spirits of Fire might have it.

A new *Saturn* period follows these occurrences. Something else is added to the play of light. It may seem madness to many when we speak of what here presents itself to

127

supersensible cognition. The interior of *Saturn* appears like a billowing and surging of sensations of taste; sweet, bitter, sour may be observed at various points within *Saturn*, and outwardly, into cosmic space, this all appears as tone, as a kind of music.—Within these processes certain beings again find the possibility of developing an activity upon *Saturn*. They may be called the "Sons of Twilight, or Life," (in Christian Esotericism, "Angeloi," "Angels"). They enter into reciprocal activity with the surging forces of taste present within *Saturn,* and through it their ether or life body takes on an activity somewhat similar to metabolism. They bring life into the interior of *Saturn*. As a result, processes of nutrition and elimination take place. They do not *directly* produce these processes, but through their activities the processes *indirectly* come into existence. This internal life makes it possible for still other beings to enter the sphere of this cosmic body, beings who may be designated "Spirits of Harmony," (in Christian Esotericism, "Cherubim"). They bestow upon the Sons of Life a dull kind of consciousness, duller and vaguer than the dream consciousness of the present-day human being, a consciousness similar to that he possesses in dreamless sleep. This consciousness is of such a low order that man is not aware of it. It is present, however, and differs from day consciousness in degree and also in kind. Plant life at present also has this "dreamless sleep consciousness." Even though this consciousness does not excite perceptions of an outer world as they are understood today, nevertheless, it regulates the life-processes and brings them into harmony with the outer cosmic processes. At the *Saturn* stage under consideration, the Sons of Life cannot perceive this

128

regulating process; the Spirits of Harmony, however, perceive it and are therefore the actual regulators.—All this life-activity takes place in the human phantoms, already characterized. These phantoms therefore appear to spiritual perception as though endowed with life, but their life is only a semblance. It is actually the life of the Sons of Life. These Sons of Life make use of the human phantoms, in order, as it were, to unfold themselves.

Now let us consider these human phantoms with their semblance of life. During the *Saturn* period described, these phantoms have ever-changing forms, sometimes resembling this shape, sometimes that. During the further course of evolution these forms become more defined; occasionally they become permanent. The reason for this is that they are now permeated by the activities of the spirits who have to be taken into account already at the beginning of *Saturn* evolution, namely, the Spirits of Will (Thrones). As a result, the human phantom itself appears with the simplest, dullest form of consciousness. We must picture this form of consciousness as duller than that of dreamless sleep. Under present conditions, the minerals have this consciousness. It brings the inner being into harmony with the outer physical world. Upon *Saturn,* the Spirits of Will are the regulators of this harmony, and the human being appears like a small counterpart of the life of *Saturn* itself. What constitutes the *Saturn* life on a large scale, constitutes man, at this stage, on a small scale. This is the primary nucleus of what even in the modern human being exists only in a germinal state, namely, spirit man (atma). Within *Saturn,* this dull human will manifests itself to supersensible perception through effects that may be compared with "scents," or "odors." Toward the outside, toward celestial space, something is to be perceived like the manifestation of a personality that is, however, not controlled by an inner ego, but is regulated from without like a machine. The regulators are the Spirits of Will.

If we survey the preceding description, it becomes apparent that, starting from the middle stage of *Saturn* evolution described at the very beginning, the stages of this evolution might be characterized by comparing their various effects with sense-impressions of the present. It was said that the *Saturn* evolution manifests as heat, then a play of light begins, followed by a play of taste and tone; finally, something arises that manifests within the interior of *Saturn* like the sensation of smell, and externally like a mechanically acting human ego.

One might ask what the manifestations of the *Saturn* evolution prior to this state of heat are. What existed before cannot in any way be compared with anything that is accessible to an outer sense-impression. Prior to the state of heat, a state existed that the human being can experience at the present time only in his inner nature. If he gives himself up to ideas that he himself forms in his soul without the impelling impulse of an external impression, he has something within himself that physical senses cannot perceive; on the contrary, it is only accessible to higher perception. The manifestations that preceded the state of heat of *Saturn* can be present only for him who possesses supersensible perception. Three such states may be mentioned: pure soul heat, which is outwardly imperceptible; pure spiritual light, which is external darkness; finally, a spiritual state of being that is complete within itself and needs no external being in order to become conscious of itself. Pure inner heat accompanies the appearance of the Spirits of Motion; pure spiritual light, that of the Spirits of Wisdom; pure inner being is bound up with the first emanation of the Spirits of Will.

With the appearance of the *Saturn* heat, our evolution for the first time passes over from a purely spiritual, inner existence into one manifesting externally. It will be especially difficult for the present-day consciousness to accept the statement that with the *Saturn* state of heat what is called "time" first makes its appearance, for the preceding states are not at all temporal. They belong to the region that in spiritual science may be called "duration." For this reason it must be understood that in all that is said in this work about such states in the "region of duration," expressions referring to temporal relationships are only used by way of comparison and explanation. What precedes "time," as it were, can only be characterized in human language by expressions containing the idea of time, for we must also be conscious of the fact that although the first, second, and third states of *Saturn* did not take place one after the other in the present sense of the word, we cannot do otherwise than describe them one after the other. Indeed, in spite of their duration or simultaneity, they are so inter-dependent that this dependence may be compared with a sequence in time.

By thus pointing to these earliest evolutionary states of *Saturn,* light is also thrown upon all other questions about the "whence" of these states. From the purely intellectual standpoint it is naturally quite possible, in regard to any origin, to continue asking about the "origin of this origin."

But this is not permissible in the face of facts. We only need to make this clear by a comparison. If we find traces in a road, we may ask what has caused them. The answer may be: a wagon. We can then ask further: whence came the wagon and whither has it gone? An answer founded upon facts is again possible. We might then ask further: who was sitting in it? What was the intention of the person who was using it? What was he doing? Finally, however, we shall come to a point where the questioning through the very facts comes to an end. Whoever continues to question, deviates from the original intention of the question. He continues the questioning mechanically. We can easily see in cases like the one just cited for the sake of comparison where the nature of facts brings an end to the questioning. In respect of the great questions of the cosmos this is not so easily seen. By really exact observation, however, we shall notice that all questions concerning the "whence" must end at the above described *Saturn* states. For we have come to a sphere in which the beings and processes no longer justify themselves through their origin, but through themselves.

The result of *Saturn* evolution is the development of the human germ to a certain stage; it has reached that low, dim consciousness spoken of above. It must not be imagined that the latter's development begins only in the last stage of *Saturn*. The Spirits of Will are active throughout all conditions of *Saturn,* but to supersensible perception the result in the last stage is most conspicuous. There exists no definite boundary line between the activities of the individual groups of beings. If it is said that in the beginning the Spirits of Will are active, then the Spirits of Wisdom, then another group of spiritual beings, it is not intended to mean that they were *only* active at that time. They are active throughout the whole of the *Saturn* evolution, but in the periods mentioned their activity can best be observed. The individual beings have then, as it were, the leadership.

Thus the whole of the *Saturn* evolution appears like a fashioning, a working over of what has streamed out of the Spirits of Will by the Spirits of Wisdom, Motion, Form, and so forth. At the same time, these spiritual beings themselves undergo an evolution. For example, after having received their life reflected back to them from *Saturn,* the Spirits of Wisdom stand at a different stage from that at which they previously stood. The fruit of this activity enhances the capacities of their own being. The result is that after the completion of such activity something happens to them similar to what happens to man in sleep. After their periods of activity on *Saturn* follow other periods during which they live, so to speak, in other worlds. Their activity is then turned away from Saturn. Therefore, clairvoyant perception observes in the described evolution of *Saturn* an ascent and a descent. The ascent continues until the formation of the state of heat; then with the play of light an ebb tide sets in, and when the human phantoms have assumed a form through the activity of the Spirits of Will, the spiritual beings have gradually withdrawn. The *Saturn* evolution slowly dies and as such disappears. A period of rest then occurs. The germinal human being passes over into a condition of dissolution, not, however, one in which it entirely disappears, but one that is similar to that of a plant seed resting in the earth, preparing to grow into a new plant. In a similar manner the human germ rests in the

133

bosom of the cosmos, awaiting a new awakening, and when the moment of this awakening comes, the above described spiritual beings have acquired, under other conditions, capacities for working further upon the germinal human being. The Spirits of Wisdom have acquired the capacity in their ether bodies not only of enjoying the reflection of life, as they did on *Saturn,* but also the ability of letting life stream forth from themselves and of endowing other beings with it. The Spirits of Motion are now as far advanced as were the Spirits of Wisdom on *Saturn.* The lowest principle of their being was then the astral body; now they possess an ether or life body. The other spiritual beings have correspondingly advanced to a higher stage of their evolution. All these spiritual beings, therefore, are able to work upon the further evolution of the germinal human being in another way than on *Saturn.*—But at the end of the *Saturn* evolution the germinal human being was dissolved. In order that the more evolved spiritual beings may continue from the point where they ended their previous activities, this germinal human being has briefly to recapitulate the stages through which it passed on *Saturn.* This is to be seen by supersensible perception. The germinal human being emerges from its concealment and, through the forces that have been implanted within it on *Saturn,* it begins to develop through its own power. It emerges out of the darkness as a being of will; it advances itself to a being possessed of a semblance of life, of a soul-like nature and other characteristics, until it reaches the stage of automatic manifestation of personality that it possessed at the end of the *Saturn* evolution.

* * *

The second of the great evolutionary periods alluded to, the "*Sun* stage," effects the raising of man to a condition of consciousness higher than that which he attained on *Saturn*. Compared with the present consciousness of man, this *Sun* stage could, to be sure, be designated as "unconsciousness," for it closely approximates the state in which the human being now exists during completely dreamless sleep. It might also be compared with the low degree of consciousness in which our plant world is at present slumbering. For supersensible perception there is no such thing as "unconsciousness," but only varying degrees of consciousness. Everything in the world possesses consciousness.—The human being attains a higher degree of consciousness in the course of the *Sun* evolution because at that time his nature is invested with the etheric or life body. Before this can occur, however, the *Saturn* conditions must be recapitulated, as described above. This recapitulation has a quite definite significance. When the period of rest, of which we have spoken in the previous description, has come to an end, what was formerly *Saturn* issues forth out of "cosmic sleep" as a new cosmic being, the *Sun*. But as a result, the conditions of evolution are changed. The spiritual beings, whose activities on *Saturn* have been described, have now advanced to other conditions. The germinal human being, however, first appears on the newly formed *Sun* just as it was at the end of the *Saturn* evolution. It must first transform the various evolutionary stages that it had reached on *Saturn*, so that they conform with the conditions on the *Sun*. The *Sun* epoch, therefore, begins with a recapitulation of the occurrences on *Saturn*, but adjusted to the changed conditions of the

135

life of the *Sun*. When the human being has developed to the point where the stage of his evolution acquired on *Saturn* conforms to the conditions of the *Sun,* the already mentioned Spirits of Wisdom, the Kyriotetes, begin to let the ether or life body flow into the human physical body. The more advanced stage that man attains on the *Sun* may be characterized by saying that the physical body, germinally formed already on *Saturn,* is raised to a second stage of perfection by becoming the bearer of an ether or life body. This ether or life body itself attains the first degree of its perfection during the *Sun* evolution. In order, however, that this second degree of perfection of the physical body and the first degree of perfection of the life body be attained, it is necessary in the further course of the life of the *Sun* that yet other spiritual beings interpose themselves in a way similar to what was already described for the *Saturn* stage.

When the Spirits of Wisdom begin to pour the life body into man, the *Sun,* previously dark, now begins to radiate. At the same time the first signs of an inner activity appear in the germinal human being; life begins. What on *Saturn* had to be characterized as an appearance of life, now becomes actual life. This pouring in of the life body continues for a certain length of time, after which an important change takes place in the human germ, namely, it divides into two parts. Whereas previously the physical body and life body formed one closely-bound whole, the physical body now begins to detach itself as a separate part. This detached physical body, however, continues also to be permeated by the life body. We have now before us a twofold human being. One part is a physical body worked

136

upon by a life body, the other part is pure life body. This separation takes place during an interval of rest in the life of the *Sun*. During this interval, the radiation that had already begun is again extinguished. The separation takes place, as it were, during a "cosmic night." This interval of rest is much shorter than the interval of rest between the *Saturn* and *Sun* evolutions, of which we have spoken previously. After the expiration of this interval, the Spirits of Wisdom continue to work for a time upon the twofold human being just as they had worked before on the single-membered human being. The Spirits of Motion then begin their activity. They let their own astral body surge through the human life body. As a result, it acquires the capacity to carry on certain inner movements within the physical body. These movements may be likened to the movements of sap in our present-day plants.

The *Saturn* body consisted solely of heat substance. During the *Sun* evolution this heat substance condenses to a state that may be compared with the present state of gas or vapor. It is the state that may be designated by the word "air." The first appearance of such a state manifests itself after the Spirits of Motion have begun their activity. The following spectacle presents itself to supersensible consciousness. Within the heat substance something appears like delicate structures that are set into regular motion by means of the forces of the life body. These structures represent the human physical body at that stage of evolution. They are completely permeated by heat and enclosed by a mantle of heat. Physically speaking, this human being may be said to consist of heat structures into which air forms are articulated that are in regular motion. If we wish to

137

keep to the above comparison with the plants of the present day, we must remain conscious of the fact that we are not dealing with a compact plant formation, but with a gaseous or aeroform structure, the movements of which may be compared with the movements of the sap in present-day plants. The gas appears to supersensible consciousness through the effect of light, which the gas permits to stream forth from itself. We might thus also speak of light structures that are perceptible to spiritual vision.— This evolution then proceeds further. After a certain length of time a pause again ensues, after which the Spirits of Motion continue their activities until these are supplemented by the activities of the Spirits of Form, the effect of which produces permanency in the previously continuously changing gaseous forms. This, too, takes place through the fact that the Spirits of Form permit their forces to flow in and out of the human life body. Previously, when only the Spirits of Motion were acting upon them, these gaseous structures were in ceaseless motion, holding their form only momentarily. Now, however, they assume temporarily distinguishable shapes.—Again after a certain length of time there ensues a period of rest, at the end of which the Spirits of Form continue their activities. Then entirely new conditions arise within the *Sun* evolution.

We have reached the point where the *Sun* evolution has arrived at the central stage of its development. It is at this time that the Spirits of Personality—who had reached their human stage on *Saturn*—rise to a still higher stage of perfection. They surpass their human stage and acquire a consciousness that our present earthly humanity has not yet attained in the regular course of its evolution. It will reach

138

this stage of consciousness when the *Earth*—that is to say, the fourth planetary evolutionary stage—shall have reached its goal and passed over into the subsequent planetary period. Man will then not only be able to perceive in his environment what at present is transmitted to him by the physical senses, but he will be able to observe in pictorial images the inner soul states of the beings in his environment. He will possess a picture consciousness, but at the same time retain full self-consciousness. His pictorial perception will not be dreamy and dull. He will perceive the soul pictorially, yet at the same time these soul pictures will be the expression of realities just as now physical colors and tones are expressions of realities. At the present time, a human being can only develop such perception in himself through spiritual-scientific training. The nature of this training will be dealt with in a later part of this book. —During the *Sun* stage, the Spirits of Personality acquire this perception as a normal part of their evolution. Because of this they become, during the *Sun* evolution, capable of working upon the newly formed human life body just as they worked upon the physical body on *Saturn*. Just as at that time heat reflected back to them their own personality, so now the gaseous shapes reflect back to them in resplendent light the pictures of their perceiving consciousness. They behold supersensibly what takes place upon the *Sun,* and this perception is by no means mere observation. It is as though something of the force that on earth is called love were making itself felt in the images that stream forth from the *Sun.* If we observe more closely with our soul powers, the reason for this phenomenon may be discovered. Exalted beings are now working actively in the

139

light radiating from the *Sun.* These beings are the already designated Spirits of Love—Seraphim. They work, henceforth, on the human ether or life body in co-operation with the Spirits of Personality. By means of this activity, the life body itself advances a stage on its evolutionary journey. It acquires the capacity, not only to transform the gaseous structures within it, but to fashion them in such a way that the first indications of a reproduction of the living human being appear. Exudations are driven out, sweated out of these gaseous structures, which assume shapes similar to their maternal forms.

In order to characterize the further evolution of the *Sun,* it is necessary to draw attention to the important fact of cosmic history, that in the course of an epoch all the beings involved do not by any means reach the goal of their evolution. There are some who fall short of it. Thus during the *Saturn* evolution not all of the Spirits of Personality actually reach the human stage for which they were originally destined in the manner described. Likewise, not all of the human physical bodies, formed on *Saturn,* attain the degree of maturity that would have made them capable of becoming bearers of an independent life body on the *Sun.* The result is that upon the *Sun* there exist beings and formations that do not fit into its conditions. These have to retrieve, during the *Sun* evolution, what they failed to attain upon *Saturn.* Hence, during the *Sun* stage the following can be observed. When the Spirits of Wisdom begin to pour in the life body, the body of the *Sun,* as it were, becomes turbid—darkened. Structures are mingled with it that in reality would belong to *Saturn.* These are heat structures that are unable to condense properly to air.

These are the human beings who have remained behind at the *Saturn* stage. They are unable to become bearers of a regularly developed life body.—The heat substance of *Saturn,* which remained behind in this way, divides itself into two sections on the *Sun.* One section is absorbed, as it were, by the human bodies and forms a kind of lower nature within the human being. This human being at the *Sun* stage thus takes into his corporeality something actually corresponding to the *Saturn* stage. Just as the human body of *Saturn* made it possible for the Spirits of Personality to rise to their human stage, so now this *Saturn* part of the human being performs on the *Sun* the same task for the Spirits of Fire. These Spirits of Fire rise to the human stage by allowing their forces to surge in and out of this *Saturn* part of the human being, just as this was performed by the Spirits of Personality on *Saturn.* This, too, happens at the central stage of the *Sun* evolution. At that time the *Saturn* part of the human being is so far matured that with its help the Spirits of Fire—Archangels—are able to pass through their human stage.—Another section of the *Saturn* heat substance acquires an independent existence alongside and in the midst of the human beings on the *Sun.* This then forms a second kingdom alongside the human kingdom, a kingdom that develops upon the *Sun* a fully independent, but purely physical, body, a body of heat. The result is that the fully developed Spirits of Personality cannot exert their activity upon an independent life body in the manner described. There are, however, certain Spirits of Personality who have remained behind at the *Saturn* stage. These had not at that time reached the human stage. Between them and the second kingdom, which became independent on

141

the *Sun*, there exists a bond of attraction. Their behavior toward the retarded kingdom on the *Sun* must now be similar to the behavior of their advanced companions toward the human beings on *Saturn*. On the latter, the human physical body was alone developed. Upon the *Sun* itself, however, there is no possibility of a similar activity by the retarded Spirits of Personality. They, therefore, withdraw from the main body of the *Sun* and form an independent cosmic body outside of it. From it the retarded Spirits of Personality work back upon the beings of the *Sun's* second kingdom already described. Thus two cosmic bodies are formed out of the one that was formerly *Saturn*. The *Sun* has now in its environment a second cosmic body, one that represents a kind of rebirth of *Saturn*, a new Saturn. From this new Saturn, the character of personality is bestowed upon the second kingdom of the *Sun*. Hence in this second kingdom we are concerned with beings who have no personality of their own upon the Sun itself, but who reflect back to the retarded Spirits of Personality on new Saturn these spirits' own personality. By means of supersensible consciousness it is possible to observe the play of heat forces among the human beings on the Sun; these heat forces send their influence into the regular *Sun* evolution; in them may be seen the sway of the designated spirits of new Saturn.

During the middle part of the *Sun* evolution the human being is organized into a physical body and a life body. Within him there takes place the activity of the advanced Spirits of Personality and the Spirits of Love. A part of the retarded *Saturn* nature is mixed with the physical body, within which the Spirits of Fire are active. In the effects of the activity of the Spirits of Fire upon the retarded *Saturn*

142

nature the precursors of the sense organs of the present earth man can be seen. It has been shown how even on *Saturn* the Spirits of Fire were at work forming germinal sense organs in the heat substance. In what is accomplished by the Spirits of Personality in co-operation with the Spirits of Love we can discern the germinal beginnings of the present human glandular system.—The work of the Spirits of Personality dwelling upon the new Saturn is not exhausted in what has been described above. They extend their activity not only to the above-mentioned second Sun kingdom, but they effect a kind of connection between this kingdom and the human senses. The heat substances of this kingdom flow in and out through the germinal human sense organs. Through this fact the human being on the Sun acquires a mode of perceiving the lower kingdom existing outside himself. This perception is, of course, only a dull perception, corresponding wholly to the dull *Saturn* consciousness of which we have spoken above, and it consists essentially of various heat effects.

Everything that has been described as existing in the middle of the *Sun* evolution lasts for a certain time. Then another period of rest begins, following which evolution goes on for a time in the same way until it reaches a stage when the human ether body is sufficiently matured to permit the beginning of a united activity of the Sons of Life—Angels—and the Spirits of Harmony—Cherubim. To supersensible consciousness, manifestations appear within the human being that may be likened to the perceptions of taste, which express themselves outwardly as tones. Something similar had to be described already for the *Saturn* evolution. Only here on the *Sun* everything within the human

143

being is more individual, fuller of independent life.—The Sons of Life acquire, as a result, the dull picture consciousness that the Spirits of Fire had attained on *Saturn.* In this the Spirits of Harmony are their helpers. The Cherubim actually perceive spiritually what is now taking place within the *Sun* evolution, but they renounce all the fruits of this perception; they forego the feelings produced by these wisdom-filled images that arise there; they allow these to flow into the dreamy consciousness of the Sons of Life as magnificent, magic visions. These Sons of Life in turn work the imagery of their visions into the human ether body, thus enabling it to reach ever higher stages of evolution.—Again a pause sets in; again the whole cosmos arises out of a "universal sleep," and after a time the human being becomes mature enough to employ his own forces. These are the forces that streamed into him through the activity of the Thrones during the last part of the *Saturn* period. This human being now develops an inward life that manifests itself to consciousness in a way comparable to an inner perception of smell. Outwardly, however, toward cosmic space, this human being presents himself as a personality, yet as a personality not directed by an inner ego. It appears more like a plant giving the impression of personality. We have seen already at the end of the *Saturn* evolution that personality manifests itself like a machine. Just as at that time the first germ of spirit man (atma) was developed, which is still today only germinally present in man, so similarly here in the *Sun* period the primary nucleus of life spirit (buddhi) is formed.—At a certain time after this has occurred, another period of rest ensues; at its end, as in previous similar instances, human activity proceeds for a time. Then conditions arise that prove to be a new intervention of the Spirits of Wisdom, through which the human being becomes capable of experiencing the first traces of sympathy and antipathy toward his surroundings. In all this there is no actual sensation present, yet it is a forerunner of it, for the inner life-activity, which in its manifestation might be characterized as perceptions of smell, expresses itself outwardly as a kind of primitive language. If a pleasant scent, or taste, or glimmer of light is perceived inwardly, the human being expresses this outwardly by means of a tone, and this also occurs in regard to an inwardly antipathetic perception.—In fact, the actual meaning of the *Sun* evolution for the human being is gained by means of all the processes that have been described. This human being has now reached a higher stage of consciousness than on *Saturn*. This is the dreamless consciousness of sleep.

After a time, the point of evolution is also reached when the higher beings bound up with the *Sun* stage must pass on to other spheres in order to assimilate what they have acquired for themselves through their activities on the being of man. A major period of rest ensues, similar to that that took place between the *Saturn* and *Sun* evolutions. Everything that was fashioned on the *Sun* passes over into a condition that may be likened to that of the plant when its powers of growth lie dormant in the seed. But just as these forces of growth come to the light of day in a new plant, so, after the rest period, all life upon the *Sun* comes forth again out of the cosmic womb and a new planetary existence begins. The significance of such a pause, such a cosmic sleep, can be well understood if we direct our spirit-

145

ual gaze toward one of the orders of beings mentioned, for instance, toward the Spirits of Wisdom. On *Saturn,* they were not yet far enough advanced to be able to let an ether body flow out of themselves. Only through the experiences they passed through upon *Saturn* have they been prepared for this. During the pause, they transform into actual capacities what previously had only been prepared in their inner being. Thus upon the *Sun* they are so far advanced that they can let life flow out of themselves and endow the human entity with a life body of its own.

* * *

Following the pause in outer activity, what was previously the *Sun* emerges again out of cosmic sleep, becoming once more perceptible to the powers of spiritual observation. It was previously perceptible to these powers, but had disappeared from view during the period of rest. A twofold element now appears within the newly emerging planetary being that shall be called the *Moon.* This *Moon,* however, must not be confused with the part of it that is at present the earth's moon. The first thing to be noted is that that part of the world mass which, during the *Sun* period, had detached itself as a new Saturn, is once more within the totality of the new planetary organism. During the pause, this new Saturn had again united itself with the *Sun.* Everything that was within the original *Saturn* reappears at first as one cosmic formation. The second thing to be noted is that the human life bodies formed upon the *Sun* were absorbed during the pause by what, in a certain sense, forms the spiritual sheath of the planet. Thus these life bodies do not appear at this time as something united

146

with the corresponding physical human bodies, but these latter appear at first by themselves. They bear within their inner nature all that has been worked into them on both *Saturn* and *Sun,* but they lack an ether or life body. Moreover, they are unable to incorporate this ether body immediately into themselves, for during the pause the ether body itself has passed through a development to which the physical bodies are not yet adapted.—In order that this adjustment may be achieved, once more a recapitulation of the *Saturn* activities occurs at the beginning of the *Moon* evolution. The physical life of man recapitulates the stages of the *Saturn* evolution, but under quite changed conditions. On *Saturn,* only the forces of a heat body were active within the physical human being; now the forces of the acquired gaseous body are also active within him. The latter, however, do not appear at once at the beginning of the *Moon* evolution. At that time it is as though the human being consisted only of heat substance, while within the latter the gaseous forces slumbered. Then comes a time when the first indications of these gaseous forces make their appearance, and finally, in the last period of the *Moon* recapitulation of *Saturn* activities, the human being reappears as he was during his life-endowed state of the *Sun.* At this time, however, all life still appears as a semblance of life. Then a pause occurs similar to the short pauses occurring during the *Sun* evolution, after which the instreaming of the life body, for which the physical body has now become ripe, begins again. As in the case of the *Saturn* recapitulation, this influx takes place again in three distinctly separate epochs. During the second of these, the human being is so far adjusted to the new *Moon* conditions

147

that the Spirits of Motion are able to employ their acquired ability. It consists in allowing the astral body to flow forth from their own essential nature into the human being. They prepared themselves for this task during the *Sun* evolution and, during the pause between the *Sun* and *Moon* evolutions, they transformed what had thus been prepared into the ability alluded to above. This influx of the astral body lasts again for a time, then one of the shorter pauses ensues, after which the instreaming of the astral body of the Spirits of Motion continues until the Spirits of Form begin their activity. Because the Spirits of Motion allow their astral body to flow into the human being, he acquires his first soul qualities. As a result, he now begins to accompany the processes, which occur in him through the possession of a life body and which during the *Sun* evolution were still plantlike, with sensations and to feel pleasure and displeasure through them; this remains a changing inner ebb and flow of pleasure and displeasure, until the intervention of the Spirits of Form. Then these changing feelings become transformed in such a way that the first traces of longing and desire appear in the human being. He seeks to repeat what has caused pleasure and strives to avoid what has caused sensations of antipathy. Since, however, the Spirits of Form do not give up their own nature to him, but only allow their forces to flow in and out of him, the impulse of desire lacks inwardness and independence. It is guided by the Spirits of Form and bears an instinctive character.

On *Saturn*, the human physical body was composed of heat, which on the *Sun* was condensed to a gaseous state, or air. During the *Moon* evolution, when the astral flows

148

into the physical body, the latter attains a further degree of condensation at a definite time and reaches a state that may be compared with the density of a present-day fluid. This state may be called "water." We do not mean by this, however, our present water, but any fluid form of existence. The human physical body now gradually takes on a form composed of three substantial organisms. The densest is a water body. This is permeated by air currents, and all this is permeated by the activities of heat.

During the *Sun* stage, too, not all organisms attain their full and proper maturity. As a result, on the *Moon* there are organisms that stand only at the *Saturn* stage, while others have only attained the *Sun* stage. Because of this, two other kingdoms arise alongside the regularly developed human kingdom. One of these consists of beings who have remained behind at the *Saturn* stage and therefore possess only a physical body, which, even on the *Moon,* is unable to become the bearer of an independent life body. This is the lowest of the *Moon* kingdoms. A second kingdom consists of beings who have remained behind at the *Sun* stage and who, therefore, on the *Moon* are too immature to incorporate into themselves an independent astral body. These form a kingdom intermediate between the one just mentioned and the regularly advanced human kingdom.—But something else takes place. The substances composed merely of the forces of heat, and those composed merely of air also permeate the human beings. Thus it happens that on the *Moon* the latter bear within themselves a *Saturn* and a *Sun* nature. As a result, a kind of cleavage arises in human nature, and through this cleavage, after the Spirits of Form begin their activity, something significant is called into existence within the *Moon* evolution. A cleavage begins in the cosmic *Moon* body. A part of the *Moon's* substances and beings separates from the rest. Two cosmic bodies are thus formed from one. Certain higher beings who, prior to this, were closely linked with the unitary cosmic body, now take up their abode on one of these parts. The remaining part, in contrast, is occupied by the human beings, by the two lower kingdoms just characterized, and by certain higher beings who did not go over to the first cosmic body. This latter cosmic body, occupied by higher beings, appears like a reborn, but refined sun; the other is now the actually new formation, the ancient Moon, the third planetary embodiment of our *Earth* that follows after the *Saturn* and *Sun* evolutions. The separating, reborn sun carries away with it, from the substances arising on the Moon, only heat and air. Besides these two substances, the liquid, watery state is to be found on what remains over as Moon. The result of this separation is that the beings, departed with the re-emerging sun, are unhampered in their further development by the denser Moon beings. They are thus able to advance unhindered in their evolution. As a result they acquire a still greater degree of power with which to work down upon the Moon beings from their sun. These Moon beings likewise acquire new possibilities of evolution. The Spirits of Form, in particular, have remained united with them and have solidified the nature of passion and desire. This expresses itself gradually by a further condensation of the human physical body also. The former purely watery element of this body now takes on a viscous fluidic form, and the aeriform and heat formations condense corre-

150

spondingly. Similar processes take place also in the two lower kingdoms.

In consequence of the separation of the Moon from the sun body, the former has the same relationship to the latter that the *Saturn* body once had to the entire surrounding cosmic evolution. The *Saturn* body was formed from the body of the Spirits of Will—Thrones. From this *Saturn* substance everything was radiated back into cosmic space that the above-mentioned spiritual beings, living in the environment, experienced, and by means of the succeeding events, the reflecting radiation gradually awoke to independent life. The whole of evolution depends first upon the severance of independent being from surrounding life; the environment then imprints itself upon this severed being as though by reflection, and then this separated entity develops further independently.—In this way the Moon body severed itself from the sun body and then reflected back its life. Had nothing else happened, the following cosmic process would have to be described. There would be a sun body in which spiritual beings, adapted to it, would have their experiences in the heat and air element. Opposite this sun body there would be a Moon body in which other beings would evolve with heat, air, and water life. The progress from the *Sun* to the *Moon* embodiment would consist in the fact that the sun beings would have their own life before them, like a reflection, mirrored back to them from the Moon processes, and they would be able to enjoy it—an experience that during the *Sun* embodiment was still impossible for them.—But the processes of evolution did not stop here. Something occurred that was of the deepest significance for all subsequent evolution. Certain

151

beings, who were adapted to the Moon body, seized upon the will element—the heritage of the Thrones—that was then at their disposal, and by means of it developed their own life, which shaped itself independent of the life of the sun. Alongside the experiences of the Moon, which stand only under the sun influence, other independent Moon experiences occur—revolts or rebellions, as it were, against the sun beings. The various kingdoms that had come into existence on the sun and Moon, especially the kingdom of our human forebears, were drawn into these conditions. Thus the Moon body contained within itself, spiritually and materially, a twofold life: one that stood in close union with the life of the sun, and one that deserted it and went its own independent way. This division into a twofold life expresses itself in all subsequent events of the *Moon* embodiment.

What this evolutionary period presents to supersensible consciousness may be characterized in the following pictures. The entire fundamental mass of the Moon is fashioned out of a half-living substance that is at times in sluggish, at times in animated movement. A mineral mass of rocks and earth elements, like that upon which the present human being treads, does not yet exist. We might speak of a kingdom of plant-minerals, only we must imagine that the entire foundational mass of the Moon is composed of this plant-mineral substance, just as the earth today consists of rocks, soil, and other matter. Just as at present we have towering masses of rocks, so at that time harder portions were embedded in the Moon's mass. These may be compared with hard, woody structures, or with horny forms. Just as plants spring up at present out of the mineral soil, so on the Moon the second kingdom—a sort of plant-animal—sprang up, covering and permeating the Moon ground. The substance of this kingdom was softer than the ground mass and more mobile in itself. This kingdom spread itself out over the other like a viscous sea. The human being himself may be called a kind of animal-man. His nature contained the essential elements of the other two kingdoms, but his being was completely permeated by an ether and an astral body, upon which the forces of the higher beings emanating from the severed sun were active. His form was thus ennobled. Whereas the Spirits of Form gave him a shape through which he was adapted to Moon life, the sun spirits made of him a being lifted above that life. By means of the capacities bestowed upon him by these spirits he had the power to ennoble his own nature, indeed, to lift to a higher stage that part of it that was related to the lower kingdoms.

The processes that have to be taken into consideration here, perceived spiritually, may be described in the following manner. The human forebear had been ennobled by beings who had deserted the sun kingdom. This ennobling extended especially to everything that could be experienced in the water element. The sun beings, who were rulers of the elements of heat and air, had less influence upon this water element, with the result that two kinds of beings were active in the organism of the human ancestor. One part of this organism was wholly permeated by the activities of the sun beings; in the other part, the seceded Moon beings were active. Through this fact, the latter part was more independent than the former. In the sun-part, only states of consciousness could arise in which the sun

153

beings lived. In the Moon-part there existed a sort of cosmic consciousness, similar to the ancient *Saturn* state, only now at a higher stage. The human ancestor thus beheld himself as a copy of the cosmos, while his sun-part felt itself only as a copy of the sun.—These two kinds of beings began a sort of conflict within human nature, and through the influence of the sun beings an adjustment of this conflict was brought about by rendering the material organism, which made an independent cosmic consciousness possible, frail and perishable. It was necessary now for this part of the organism to be eliminated from time to time. During this elimination and for a certain time thereafter, the human ancestor was a being dependent only upon the influence of the sun. His consciousness became less independent; he lived in it in complete surrender to the life of the sun. The independent Moon part was then renewed. After a certain length of time, this process was repeated again and again. The human ancestor on the Moon thus lived in alternating conditions of clearer and duller consciousness, and this alternation was accompanied by a metamorphosis of the material aspect of his being. From time to time he discarded his Moon body and renewed it again later.

Seen physically, a great variation appears in the kingdoms of the Moon described here. The mineral-plants, the plant-animals, and the animal-men are differentiated according to groups. This will be understood if we bear in mind that, because certain organisms have remained behind at each of the earlier stages of evolution, these organisms have been embodied, endowed with the most varied qualities. There are organisms that still display the characteristics of the first epochs of the *Saturn* evolution, some those of the middle periods, and some those of its end. This is also true of all the stages of the *Sun* evolution.

Just as organisms connected with the progressively evolving cosmic body remain behind, so is this also the case with certain beings connected with this evolution. In the progressive development up to the appearance of the ancient *Moon*, several grades of such beings have already come into existence. There are, for instance, Spirits of Personality who, even on the *Sun*, have not yet attained their human stage; there are, however, others who, on the *Sun*, have retrieved their failure to rise to this stage. Many Fire Spirits, too, who should have become human on the *Sun*, have remained behind. Just as certain retarded Spirits of Personality withdrew during the *Sun* evolution from the body of the *Sun* and caused Saturn to arise again as a special cosmic body, so also in the course of the *Moon* evolution the beings described above withdrew to special cosmic bodies. Thus far we have spoken only of the separation into sun and Moon, but for the reasons given above, still other cosmic bodies detach themselves from the cosmic *Moon* body that made its appearance after the long pause between *Sun* and *Moon* evolutions. After a lapse of time there comes into existence a system of cosmic bodies, the most advanced of which, as may be easily seen, is the new sun. In much the same way that during the *Sun* evolution —as has already been described above—a bond of attraction was formed between the retarded *Saturn* kingdom and the Spirits of Personality on the new Saturn, now during the *Moon* evolution a bond is also formed between every such cosmic body and the corresponding *Moon* beings. It

155

would carry us much too far to follow up in detail all the cosmic bodies that come into existence. It must suffice to have indicated the reason why a series of cosmic bodies is detached by degrees from the undivided cosmic organism that appeared in the beginning of mankind's evolution as *Saturn.*

After the intervention of the Spirits of Form on the *Moon,* evolution proceeds for a time in the manner described. After this, another pause in outer activity ensues, during which the coarser parts of the three Moon kingdoms remain in a state of rest, but the finer parts—chiefly the human astral bodies—detach themselves from these coarser organisms. They enter a state in which the higher powers of the exalted sun beings can work upon them with special force.—After the rest period, they again permeate the parts of the human being composed of coarser substances. Through the fact that, during the pause, they have absorbed powerful forces in a free state, they are able to prepare these coarser substances for the influences that the regularly advanced Spirits of Personality and Spirits of Fire must, after a certain time, bring to bear upon them.

These Spirits of Personality have attained a stage at which they possess the consciousness of inspiration. Not only are they able to perceive the inner state of other beings in pictures—as was the case in their former picture consciousness—but they are able to perceive the inner nature of these beings as a spiritual tone language. The Spirits of Fire, however, have risen to the degree of consciousness possessed by the Spirits of Personality on the *Sun.* As a result, both kinds of spirits are able to intervene in the matured life of the human being. The Spirits of Personality work upon his astral body, the Fire Spirits upon his ether body. The astral body thus receives the character of personality. It experiences henceforth not only pleasure and pain within itself, but it relates them to itself. It has not yet attained a full ego consciousness that says to itself, "I exist," but it feels itself borne and sheltered by other beings in its environment. Looking up to them, as it were, it can say, "This, my environment, gives me existence."— The Fire Spirits work henceforth upon the ether body. Under their influence the movement of forces in this body becomes more and more an inner life activity. What thus comes into existence finds physical expression in a circulation of fluids and in phenomena of growth. The gaseous substances have condensed to a fluid. We can speak of a kind of nutrition in the sense that what is absorbed from without is transformed and worked over within. If we think perhaps of something midway between nutrition and breathing in the present day sense, then we shall have some idea of what happened at that time in this respect. The human being drew nutritive substances from the kingdom of the animal-plants. These animal-plants must be thought of as floating, swimming in—or even lightly attached to—a surrounding element in much the same way the present-day lower animals live in water or the land animals in the air. This element, however, is neither water nor air in the present sense of the word, but something midway between the two—a kind of thick vapor in which the most varied substances, as though dissolved, move hither and thither in the most varied currents. The animal-plants appear only as condensed, regular forms of this element, often differing physically very little from their environ-

157

ment. The process of respiration exists alongside the process of nutrition. It is not like what occurs on earth, but it is like an insucking and outpouring of heat. For supersensible observation it is as though, during these processes, organs opened and closed through which a warming stream flowed in and out. Through these organs the airy and watery substances are also drawn in and expelled, and because the human being at this stage of his evolution already possesses an astral body, this breathing and nutrition are accompanied by feelings, so that a kind of pleasure occurs when substances that are beneficial for the building up of the human being are drawn in from outside. Displeasure is excited when injurious substances flow in or even when they only approach the human being.—During the *Moon* evolution there was a kinship between the processes of breathing and nutrition, as described. Similarly the process of visualization was in close correspondence with the process of reproduction. Objects and beings in the environment of the humanity of the *Moon* did not produce immediate effects on any kind of senses. Visualization was of such a character that images were evoked in the dull dim consciousness by the presence of the things and beings in its neighborhood. These pictures had a much more intimate relationship with the actual nature of the environment than present-day sense perceptions which, through color, tone, and odor, only indicate the external aspects of things and beings. In order to have a clearer concept of this consciousness of the *Moon* humanity, let us imagine this humanity as being embedded in the above described vaporous environment. The most manifold processes occur within this mistlike element. Substances now unite, now separate. Certain parts condense, others become rarefied. All of this occurs in such a way that the human beings neither see nor hear it directly, but images are called forth by it in their consciousness. These may be compared to the images of present-day dream consciousness. For example, when an outer object falls to the ground and a sleeping man does not perceive the actual event itself, but instead experiences the rise of some kind of picture, he might, let us say, believe a shot was fired. The only difference is that the pictures of the *Moon* consciousness are not arbitrary as are the dream pictures of the present day. Although they are symbols, not copies, they correspond, nevertheless, to the outer events. A definite picture appears with a definite outer event. The *Moon* humanity is thus in the position to direct its actions in accordance with these pictures, just as present-day humanity directs its actions according to its perceptions. Notice, however, must be taken of the fact that conduct based on perception admits of freedom of choice, while action under the influence of the pictures indicated is impelled by a dull urge.—This picture consciousness is by no means one by which only outer physical processes are visualized, but through them the spiritual beings ruling behind the physical facts as well as their activities are imaginatively perceived. Thus the Spirits of Personality become, as it were, visible in the objects of the animal-plant kingdom; behind and within the mineral-plant beings the Fire Spirits appear. The Sons of Life appear as beings that the human being is able to picture mentally without connection with anything physical; he perceives them, as it were, as etheric soul forms.—Although these mental pictures of the *Moon* consciousness were not copies, but only symbols of the outer world, they did have a much more important effect upon the inner nature of the human being than the present visualizations of man transmitted through outer perception. They had the power to set the whole inner being in motion and activity. The inner processes shaped themselves in accordance with them. They were genuine formative forces. The human being took on the shape these formative forces gave him; he became, as it were, a copy of his processes of consciousness.

The further that evolution continues in this manner, the deeper and more incisive is the change that in consequence takes place in the human entity. The power that proceeds from these consciousness-images is gradually no longer able to extend over the entire human corporeality. The latter divides into two parts, two natures. Members are fashioned that are subject to the formative effect of the picture consciousness, and to a great degree they become a copy of the life of mental images in the sense of the above description. Other organs, however, withdraw from this influence. The human being, in one part of his nature is, as it were, too dense, too much determined by other laws to be able to conduct himself according to the consciousness-pictures. These withdraw from human influence, but they become subject to the influence of the exalted sun beings themselves. A rest period precedes this stage of evolution, during which the sun spirits gather the power to work upon the Moon beings under wholly new conditions.—After this pause the human being is distinctly split into two natures. One of these natures, not subject to the independent activity of the picture consciousness, takes on a more definite form and comes under the influence of forces that, to be sure, proceed from the Moon body, but within which they arise only through the influence of the sun beings. This part of the human being participates increasingly in the life that is inspired by the sun. The other part rises out of the former like a kind of head. It is in itself mobile, plastic, and becomes the expression and bearer of the dull life of consciousness of the human being. Yet the two parts are closely bound together. They send their fluids into one another, and their members stretch from one into the other.

A significant harmony is now achieved through the fact that, during the time in which all this happened, a relationship between sun and Moon has been developed that is in accord with the direction of this evolution.—It has already been pointed out in a previous paragraph (see page 150) how, as a result of their stage of evolution, the advancing beings sever their cosmic bodies from the general cosmic mass. They radiate the forces in accordance with which the substances form themselves. Sun and Moon have thus separated from one another in accordance with the necessity of establishing proper dwelling places for the corresponding beings. This conditioning of substance and its forces by means of the spirit, however, extends further. The beings themselves determine certain movements of cosmic bodies and their definite revolution around each other. In this way these bodies come into varying positions in relation to each other. If the location or position of one cosmic body in relation to another is changed, then the effects of their corresponding beings upon one another are also changed. This happened with the sun and the Moon. Through the movement begun by the Moon around the sun, the human beings come now under the influence of the sun activity, now they turn away from this influence and are then more dependent upon themselves. The movement is a result of the secession of certain Moon beings already described and the adjustment of the conflict brought about by it. It is only the physical expression of the spiritual relationship of forces created by this secession. The revolution of one body around the other resulted in the previously described changing states of consciousness in the beings dwelling on the cosmic bodies. It can be said that the Moon alternately turns its life toward and away from the sun. There is a sun period and a Moon period; during the latter, the Moon beings develop on the side of the Moon that is turned away from the sun. For the Moon, however, something else was added to the movement of the heavenly bodies. The retrospective supersensible consciousness is able to see how the Moon beings themselves revolve around their own cosmic body in quite regular periods. At certain times they seek out the places where they can expose themselves to the influence of the sun. At other epochs they migrate to the regions where they are not exposed to this influence and where they can, as it were, reflect upon themselves.

In order to complete the picture of these processes, we have also to consider that at this time the Sons of Life reach their human stage. The human being on the Moon cannot yet use his senses, the primal indications of which had come into existence already on *Saturn,* for his own perception of external objects. At the *Moon* stage of evolution, however, these senses become the instruments of the Sons of Life. The latter make use of these senses in order to perceive by means of them. These senses, which belong to the physical human body, enter in this way into reciprocal

162

relationship with the Sons of Life, who not only make use of them, but perfect them as well.

Through the changing relationships to the sun a change occurs, as described, in the conditions of life within the human being himself. Things shape themselves in such a way that each time the human being comes under the influence of the sun, he devotes himself more to the life of the sun and its phenomena than to himself. At such times he experiences the grandeur and majesty of the universe as this is expressed in the sun existence. He absorbs this. The exalted beings who have their habitation upon the sun exercise their power upon the Moon, which in turn has its effect upon the being of man. This effect does not extend to the entire human being; it affects particularly those parts of him that have withdrawn from the influence of his own picture consciousness. Thus the physical and ether bodies especially attain a certain size and form, but in order that this may occur, the phenomena of consciousness withdraw. When, now, the life of the human being is removed from the influence of the sun, he is occupied with his own nature. An inner vivacity begins chiefly in the astral body, but the external shape becomes less conspicuous, less perfect in form.—Thus during the *Moon* evolution there are these two clearly distinguishable, alternating states of consciousness—a duller state during the sun period and a clearer state during the period in which life is more dependent upon itself. The first state is, indeed, duller, but it is for that reason also more selfless. Man surrenders himself more to the outer world, to the universe mirrored in the sun. There is an alternation in the states of consciousness that may be compared with the alternation

163

of sleeping and waking in the present human being, as well as with his life between birth and death on the one hand, and with the more spiritual existence between death and a new birth, on the other. The awaking on the Moon, when the sun period gradually ceases, should be characterized as a state intermediate between our present waking every morning and our being born. Likewise, the gradual dimming of consciousness at the approach of the sun period may be likened to an intermediate state between going to sleep and dying, for a consciousness of birth and death similar to the one belonging to present-day man did not yet exist on the ancient *Moon*. In a kind of sun-life the human being surrendered himself to the enjoyment of this life. He was, during this time, withdrawn from his own life. He lived more spiritually. Only an approximate and comparative description of what the human entity experienced in these periods can be attempted. He felt as though the causative forces of the cosmos streamed into him, pulsated through him. He felt as though intoxicated with the harmonies of the universe of which he partook. At such times his astral body was as though freed from the physical body, and a part of the life body was likewise withdrawn from it. This organism composed of astral body and life body was like a marvelous, delicate musical instrument upon whose strings the mysteries of the universe resounded, and the members of that part of the human being upon which consciousness had but little influence took on forms in response to the universal harmonies, for in these harmonies the sun beings were active. Thus, through spiritual cosmic tones this human part was given form. The alternation between the brighter state of consciousness and

164

this duller one during the sun period was not as abrupt as is the alternation between waking and a completely dreamless sleep for man today. The picture consciousness, to be sure, was not as clear as the present waking consciousness; the other consciousness, in turn, was not as dull as the dreamless sleep of today. Thus the human being had a vague notion of the play of universal harmonies in his physical body and in that part of the ether body that had remained united with it. At the time during which the sun was not shining, as it were, for the human being, the imaginative thought pictures pervaded his consciousness instead of harmonies. Especially those members of the physical and ether bodies that were under the direct power of consciousness were then vivified. In contrast, however, the other parts of the human being, upon which the formative forces from the sun now had no influence, passed through a kind of hardening and drying out process. When the sun period again drew near, these old bodies disintegrated; they severed themselves from the human being and then, as though from the grave of his old corporeality, he arose, inwardly newly formed, although he was still insignificant in this new shape. A renewal of the life-processes had taken place. Through the activity of the sun beings and their harmonies the new-born body again reached its perfection and the process described above repeated itself. Man experienced this renewal as the donning of a new garment. The kernel of his being had not passed through an actual birth or death, it only had shed its skin, as it were, by passing over from a spiritual tone-consciousness in which it yielded itself up to the external world, to one in which it was turned more toward the inner life. The old body had become unusable; it was cast off and then renewed. This characterizes more exactly what was described above as a kind of reproduction, and of which it was said that it is closely related to visualizing activity. The human being has generated his kind with respect to certain parts of the physical and ether bodies. Yet there is no engendering of a daughter being completely distinguished from its parent, but the essential kernel of the latter passes over into the former. This kernel does not produce a new being, but brings itself forth in a new form. Thus the Moon human being experiences a change of consciousness. When the sun epoch approaches, his visualizations become duller and duller, and a state of blissful surrender pervades him. Within his quiet inner being resound cosmic harmonies. Toward the end of this period the images in the astral body begin to revive. Man begins to feel and experience himself. He experiences something like an awakening from the blissfulness and quiet into which he was immersed during the sun period. In this connection yet another important experience occurs. With the new awakening of the picture consciousness the individual man perceives himself as though enveloped in a cloud that had descended upon him like a being from the cosmos. He feels this being as something belonging to him, as a completion of his own nature. He feels it as something that gives him his own existence; he feels it as his ego. This being is one of the Sons of Life. He feels toward this being somewhat as follows, "I lived in this being even during the sun period of the Moon when I had surrendered myself to the glory of the cosmos, but at that time it was invisible to me. Now, however, it becomes visible to me." It is also from this same Son of Life that the power proceeds that produces the activity performed by man upon his own bodily nature during the sunless period. Then when the sun period again approaches, man feels as if he himself became one with the Son of Life. Even though he may not behold him, nevertheless he feels himself intimately united with the Son of Life.

The relationship to the Sons of Life was of such a character that not each individual human being had a Son of Life for himself, but a whole group of human beings felt that one of these beings belonged to it. Thus on the Moon the inhabitants lived divided into such groups, and every group looked up to a Son of Life as the common group ego. The difference between the groups became apparent through each group having a different form, especially in its ether bodies. But since the physical bodies are formed in accordance with the ether bodies, the differences in the latter were imprinted upon the former, and the various human groups appeared as so many different types of men. When the Sons of Life looked down upon the human groups belonging to them, they saw themselves, as it were, manifolded in the individual human beings. In this way they experienced their own egohood. They mirrored themselves in the human beings. This was also the task of the human senses at that time. We have seen that these did not yet transmit any external objective perceptions. But they reflected the being of the Sons of Life. What these Sons of Life perceived through this reflection gave to them their ego consciousness. It was, however, the images of the dull, vague Moon consciousness that were aroused in the human astral body by this reflection.—The effect of this activity of man, achieved in reciprocal relationship with the Sons of Life, brought into existence the first traces of the nervous system in the physical body. The nerves represent a sort of extension of the senses into the inner nature of the human body.

From this description it can be seen how the three categories of spirits, the Spirits of Personality, the Fire Spirits, and the Sons of Life, are active upon the Moon man. If the main period of the *Moon* evolution—the middle evolutionary period—is considered, we may say that it was then that the Spirits of Personality implanted independence, the character of personality, in the human astral body. It is due to this fact that during the time when the sun does not shine on the human being, as it were, he can turn in upon himself, is able to fashion himself. The Fire Spirits manifest themselves in the ether body to the degree that this body imprints upon itself the independent human structure. It is because of them that the human being feels himself to be again the same being each time after the renewal of his body. A kind of memory is thus given to the ether body through the Fire Spirits. The Sons of Life work upon the physical body in such a way that it is able to become the expression of the now independent astral body. They thus make it possible for this physical body to become a physiognomic copy of its astral body. On the other hand, higher spiritual beings, especially the Spirits of Form and the Spirits of Movement, intervene in the formation of physical and ether bodies insofar as these develop in the sun periods independent of the autonomous astral body. It is from the sun that their intervention occurs in the manner described above.

Under the influence of such facts the human being gradually matures in order to develop in itself the germ of spirit self, just as in the second half of the *Saturn* evolution the human being developed the germ of spirit man, and on the *Sun* the germ of life spirit. Through this, all relationships on the *Moon* change. Through the successive changes and renewals human beings have become ever more noble and delicate. They have also gained in strength. As a result, the picture consciousness was increasingly preserved also during the sun cycles. In this way it acquires an influence over the formation of the physical and ether bodies that formerly happened only through the activity of the sun beings. What happened on the Moon through the human beings and the spirits united with them became more and more like the former achievements of the sun with its higher beings. As a result, these sun beings could increasingly apply their forces for the sake of their own evolution and because of this the Moon became ready, after a certain length of time, to be reunited with the sun.—Spiritually perceived, these processes appear as follows. The revolting Moon beings have been gradually overcome by the sun beings and must now adjust themselves by becoming subject to them, so that the functions of both are in mutual harmony.—This happened only after long preceding epochs in which the Moon cycles became shorter and shorter and the sun cycles longer and longer. A cycle of evolution now begins during which sun and Moon are again a single cosmic organism. At this time the physical human body has become wholly etheric.—When this is said, it must not be imagined that under such conditions we cannot speak of a physical body. What has been formed as physical body during the *Saturn, Sun,* and *Moon* evolutions still remains present. It is important to recognize the physical not only where it manifests outwardly physically. The physical can also be present in such a way that it can show externally the form of the etheric, and indeed, even show the form of the astral. It is important to differentiate between external appearances and inner laws. A physical body can become etherized or astralized, yet at the same time retain its physical laws. This is the case when the human physical body on the Moon has reached a certain degree of perfection. It becomes ether-like. When, however, supersensible consciousness—able to observe things of this kind—turns its attention to such an ether-like body, it appears to it permeated not by the laws of the etheric but by the laws of the physical. The physical is taken up into the etheric in order to rest there and be fostered as in a maternal womb. Later it appears again in physical form but at a higher stage. Were the human Moon being to keep its physical body in the grossly physical form, the Moon would never be able to reunite itself with the sun. By the acquisition of an etheric form, the physical body becomes more related to the ether body and it can, moreover, be permeated again more inwardly by those parts of the ether and astral bodies that, during the sun periods of the *Moon* evolution, had to withdraw from it. The human entity, which appeared like a double being during the separation of sun and Moon, becomes again a unified being. The physical becomes more soul-like, and the soul in turn more closely united with the physical.—The sun spirits, into whose direct sphere this unitary human being has now come, are able to work upon him quite differently from the time when they worked from without, downward upon the

170

Moon. The human being is now more in a soul and spirit environment. Through this fact the Spirits of Wisdom can achieve a significant effect. They imprint wisdom in him. They ensoul him with wisdom. He becomes in this way in a certain sense an independent soul. To the influence of these beings is added that of the Spirits of Motion. They act especially upon the astral body in such a way that, under the influence of the beings described, it evolves a soul activity and a life of ether body filled with wisdom. The wisdom-filled ether body is the first germinal nucleus of what has been described in an earlier chapter as the intellectual soul in present-day humanity, whereas the astral body stimulated by the Spirits of Motion contains the germinal nucleus of the sentient soul. Because all this is brought about within the human entity in its increased state of independence, these germinal nuclei of the intellectual and sentient souls appear as the expression of spirit self. The mistake must not be made of thinking that, at this period of evolution, spirit self is something special, independent of the intellectual and sentient souls. These latter are only the expression of spirit self that signifies their higher unity and harmony.

It is of special significance that during this epoch the Spirits of Wisdom intervene in the manner described. They do this not alone in respect of the human being but also of the other kingdoms that have developed upon the Moon. When the sun and Moon again become united, these lower kingdoms are drawn within the sphere of the sun. All that was physical in them becomes etherized. Thus, just as human beings are to be found on the sun, so there are also to be found mineral-plants and plant-animals. These other

171

creatures, however, remain endowed with their own laws. They feel, therefore, like strangers in their new surroundings. They appear with a nature that has little in common with that of their environment. But since they have an etheric form, the activity of the Spirits of Wisdom can extend to them also. All that has come from the Moon into the sun is now permeated with the forces of the Spirits of Wisdom. Therefore what is fashioned from the sun-Moon organism within this evolutionary period may be called the "Cosmos of Wisdom."—When our *Earth* system, as a descendant of this Cosmos of Wisdom, appears after a rest period, all the beings coming to life again upon the *Earth,* springing forth from their *Moon* nuclei, show themselves filled with wisdom. Thus we see the reason why the present earth man, looking attentively at the things about him, can discover wisdom in the nature of their being. We can marvel at the wisdom in each plant leaf, in each animal and human bone, in the miraculous structure of the brain and heart. When man needs wisdom in order to understand things, that is, when he extracts wisdom from them, it shows that wisdom exists in the things themselves. For however much the human being might try to understand the things by means of ideas filled with wisdom, he would be unable to extract any wisdom from them were it not already embodied in the things themselves. Anyone who wishes by means of wisdom to comprehend things that, as he thinks, have not first received wisdom, may also imagine that he can take water out of a glass into which none has previously been poured. The *Earth,* as will be seen later on in this book, is the resurrected ancient *Moon.* It appears as a wisdom-filled organism because in the epoch

172

described it has become permeated by the forces of the Spirits of Wisdom.

It will, it is hoped, appear comprehensible that in this description of the *Moon* conditions only certain transitory forms of evolution could be concentrated upon. Certain things in the progress of events had to be selected and emphasized for the description. This kind of description offers, to be sure, only single pictures, and the preceding descriptions of evolution may therefore seem lacking through not being woven into a web of definitely fixed concepts. In regard to such an objection attention may perhaps be drawn to the fact that the description has intentionally been given in less concise concepts. For it is not so much a question here of the construction of speculative concepts and ideas, but rather of a mental picture of what can present itself to the spiritual eye through supersensible perception directed to these facts. These facts do not appear in such sharp and definite outlines in the *Moon* evolution as is the case with the perceptions on our earth. In the *Moon* epoch we are concerned with vacillating, changing impressions, with fluctuating, mobile pictures, and with their transitions. Besides this, we must consider the fact that we are concerned with an evolution covering long, long periods of time and that in describing this, only momentary pictures can be seized on and fixed.

At the point of time when the astral body implanted in the human being has advanced him so far in his evolution that his physical body gives the Sons of Life the possibility of attaining their human stage, the actual climax of the *Moon* epoch is reached. At that time the human being also has attained all that this epoch can give him for his inner

173

development on the forward path. The following cycle, that is, the second part of the *Moon* evolution, can be designated as one of ebb-tide. But it can be seen that with respect to the human environment and also to man himself something most important transpires just at this period. It is then that *wisdom* is implanted within the sun-Moon body. We have seen that during this ebb-tide the nuclei of the intellectual and sentient souls are engendered. Yet it is not until the *Earth* period that their unfolding and that of the consciousness soul occurs together with the birth of the ego, of independent self-consciousness. At the Moon stage, the intellectual and sentient souls do not yet appear as though the human being himself were able to express himself through them, but as though they were instruments for the Sons of Life belonging to the human being. If we wish to characterize the feeling that man had on the Moon in regard to this, we would have to say that he felt as follows. "The Son of Life lives in and through me; he beholds the Moon environment through me; he thinks in me about the things and beings in this environment." The Moon man feels overshadowed by his Son of Life, he experiences himself as the instrument of this higher being, and during the separation of sun and Moon, when the Moon was turned away from the sun, he had a feeling of greater independence. At the same time he also felt as if the ego belonging to him, which had disappeared from his picture-consciousness during the sun cycles, now became visible to him. This was for the Moon human being what we might call alternation in the states of consciousness. This gave him the feeling, "In the sun period my ego soars away with me up

174

into higher regions to sublime beings, and, when the sun disappears, it descends with me into lower worlds."

A preparatory period preceded the actual *Moon* evolution. A kind of repetition of the *Saturn* and *Sun* evolution occurred at that time. Then, after the reunion of the sun and Moon in the ebb-tide period, two epochs can likewise be distinguished during which there take place, to a certain degree, even physical condensations. The psycho-spiritual states of the sun-Moon organism alternate with physical states. In these physical epochs the human beings, and likewise the beings of the lower kingdoms, appear in stiff forms, lacking independence, forms that were forecasts of what they were to become as more independent shapes later on in the *Earth* evolution. Thus we can speak of two preparatory periods of the *Moon* evolution and of two others during the time of ebb-tide. Such epochs can be called cycles. In what follows the two preparatory cycles, and that precedes the two cycles of ebb-tide—that is, in the time of the Moon separation—three epochs can also be distinguished. It is in the middle epoch of these three that the Sons of Life reach their human status. Prior to this there is an epoch during which all conditions lead to a concentration on achieving this main event. Then another epoch follows that can be described as a condition in which the beings become familiar with and develop the new creations. Thus the middle period of the *Moon* evolution is divided into three epochs. Together with the two preparatory and the two ebb-tide epochs, they make seven *Moon* cycles. It may thus be said that the entire *Moon* evolution runs its course in seven cycles. Between these cycles

175

lie rest periods that have been mentioned previously. We shall arrive at a true conception of the situation only if we do not imagine abrupt transitions between periods of activity and those of rest. The sun beings, for example, withdraw, little by little, from their activity on the *Moon*. A time begins for them that, outwardly observed, appears like their period of rest, while upon the *Moon* itself, animated, independent activity reigns. Thus the period of activity of one kind of being extends into the rest period of other beings. If we take these things into account we can speak of a rhythmic rising and falling of forces in cycles. Indeed, similar divisions can also be observed within the seven *Moon* cycles described. We can then call the whole *Moon* evolution a great cycle, a planetary cycle; the seven divisions within one of these cycles, small cycles, and the divisions of these last again still smaller sub-cycles. This membering into seven times seven sections is already observable in the *Sun* evolution and is indicated also during the *Saturn* epoch. Yet we must consider the boundaries between the divisions as being blurred on the *Sun* and as being still more vague on *Saturn*. The boundary lines become more and more clearly defined the farther evolution proceeds toward *Earth*.

*   *   *

After the conclusion of the *Moon* evolution described in the foregoing sketch, all beings and forces concerned appear in a more spiritual form of existence, a form that stands at a quite different level from that of the *Moon* period and also from that of the subsequent *Earth* evolution. A being who possessed such highly developed capacities of

176

cognition that he could perceive all the details of the *Moon* and *Earth* evolutions would not necessarily be able also to perceive what happens between the two evolutions. For such an individual, the beings and forces at the end of the *Moon* period would disappear as though into nothingness and after the lapse of an interim make their appearance again out of the dim darkness of the cosmic womb. Only a being possessing still higher faculties could follow up the spiritual events that occur in this interim.

At the end of the interval of rest from outer activity, the beings who had taken part in the evolutionary processes on *Saturn, Sun,* and *Moon* appear with new abilities and faculties. The beings standing above men have acquired, through their previous acts, the capacity to develop the human being to such a point that, during the *Earth* period following the *Moon* period, he can unfold in himself a degree of consciousness that stands one stage higher than the picture-consciousness possessed by him during the *Moon* period. Man, however, must first be prepared to receive what is to be bestowed upon him. During the *Saturn, Sun,* and *Moon* evolutions he invested his being with a physical, life, and astral body, but these members of his being have received only the capacities and forces that enable them to live in a picture-consciousness; they still lack the organs and structure enabling them to perceive a world of outer sense objects as it is required for the *Earth* stage. Just as the new plant only develops what is inherent in the seed coming from the old plant, so in the beginning of the new stage of evolution the three members of human nature appear with structures and organs that make possible the development of picture-consciousness only. They must first

177

be prepared for the development of a higher stage of consciousness.—This takes place in three preliminary stages. In the first stage, the physical body is raised to a level where it is possible to make the necessary transformation that can be the basis for an objective consciousness. This is a preliminary stage of the *Earth* evolution, which may be termed a repetition of *Saturn* at a higher level, for during this period, just as during the *Saturn* evolution, higher beings work only upon the physical body. When the physical body has progressed far enough in its evolution, all beings must again pass over into a higher form of existence before the life or ether body can also advance. The physical body must be remodelled, as it were, in order to be able, when it unfolds again, to receive the more highly developed life body. After this intermediate period devoted to a higher form of existence, something like a repetition of the *Sun* evolution takes place on a higher level for the purpose of developing the life body. Again after an intermediate period something similar happens for the astral body in a repetition of the *Moon* evolution.

Let us now turn to the events of evolution after the completion of the third of the recapitulation periods just described. All beings and forces have again become spiritualized. During this spiritualization they have ascended into sublime worlds. The lowest of these worlds in which something of these beings and forces can still be perceived during this period of spiritualization, is the same world in which the present human being dwells between death and re-birth. These are the regions of the land of spirits. The beings and forces then gradually descend again to lower worlds. Before the physical *Earth* evolution begins, they

178

have descended so far that their lowest manifestations are to be perceived in the astral or soul world.

Everything human existing at this period still possesses its astral form. In order to understand this state of humanity, special attention should be given to the fact that man possesses a physical body, a life body, and an astral body, but that the physical body as well as the life body do not yet exist in a physical or etheric form, but in an astral form. What at that time makes the physical body physical is not its physical form but the physical laws that are present in it, although it has an astral form. It is a being ruled by physical laws appearing in soul form. This is also true of the life body.

At this stage of evolution the *Earth* stands before the spiritual eye as a cosmic being that is wholly soul and spirit, and in which the physical and life forces still appear in soul form. Within this cosmic structure everything that is to be transformed later into the creatures of the physical earth is contained in a germinal state. This cosmic *Earth* being is luminous, but its light is not one that physical eyes could perceive, even were they present, for it gleams with soul radiance only for the opened eye of the seer.

In this cosmic being something now takes place that may be called a condensation, which after a time results in a fire form appearing in the midst of this soul structure, a form similar to *Saturn* in its densest condition. This fire form is interwoven with the activities of the various beings who participate in evolution. What may be observed as a reciprocal activity between these beings and the celestial body is like an emerging from the *Earth* fire-ball and a re-immersing in it. Therefore the *Earth* fire-ball is by no means a uniform substance, but something like an organism permeated with soul and spirit. The beings who are destined to become human beings in our present form on the *Earth* are still in a condition in which they participate the least in the activity of immersion in the fire-body. They still remain almost wholly in the non-condensed environment. They still are within the bosom of the higher spiritual beings. At this stage they touch the fire *Earth* only with one point of their soul form, with the result that the heat causes a part of their astral form to condense. Through this fact, *Earth* life is enkindled within them, but the largest part of their being still belongs to the world of soul and spirit. Only through the contact with the *Earth* fire does the warmth of life play around them. If we wish to form a sensible-supersensible picture of this human being in the beginning of the physical *Earth* period, we must imagine an egg-shaped soul form, existing in the surroundings of the *Earth* enclosed by a cup at its lower end like an acorn. But the substance of the cup consists purely of heat or fire. The enkindling of life within the human being was not the only result of this enclosure in heat, but simultaneously with it a change in the astral body occurred. Inserted into it is the primal nucleus of what later becomes the sentient soul. Therefore, it may be said that at this stage of his existence man consists of sentient soul, astral body, life body, and physical body woven of fire. The spiritual beings who take part in human existence surge up and down in the astral body; through the sentient soul man feels himself bound to the body of the *Earth*. At this time, therefore, he has a preponderant picture-consciousness in which the spiritual beings manifest themselves. He lies within their bosom,

180

and the sensation of his own bodily existence appears only as a point within this consciousness. From the spiritual world he looks down, as it were, upon an earthly possession about which he feels, "That is mine."—The condensation of the *Earth* advances further and further and with it the characterized organizing of man becomes ever more distinct. At a definite point of time in its evolution the *Earth* becomes condensed to such a degree that only a part remains fiery. Another part has taken on a substantial form that may be represented as gas or air. A change now takes place also in man. Not only the *Earth* heat touches his organism, but air substance is drawn into his fire body. Just as heat has enkindled life in him, so air playing about him produces an effect that may be likened to spiritual tone; his life body resounds. At the same time the astral body detaches a part of itself; this becomes the primal nucleus of what appears later as the intellectual soul.—In order to form a picture of what is taking place at this time within the human soul, we must realize that beings higher than men surge up and down within the air-fire body of the *Earth.* In the fire *Earth* we have first the Spirits of Personality who are of importance to man, and when the latter is aroused to life by the *Earth* heat, his sentient soul says to itself, "These are the Spirits of Personality." Likewise, the beings who have been called Archangels—in the sense of Christian esotericism—proclaim themselves in the air body, and when the air plays about the human being it is their activities that he experiences in himself as tone; the intellectual soul says to itself, "These are the Archangels." Thus, at this stage man does not yet perceive through his connection with the *Earth* what might be called an aggre-

181

gation of physical objects, but he lives in sensations of heat arising in him and in sounding tone; in these heat streams and tone waves he perceives the Spirits of Personality and the Archangels. He cannot, however, perceive these beings directly; he can only sense them through the veil of heat and tone. While these perceptions coming from the *Earth* penetrate his soul, still rising and falling within it are the images of the higher beings in whose bosom he feels his existence.

The evolution of the *Earth* now advances further and its continuation expresses itself again in condensing. The *Earth* receives the watery substance into its body, which now consists of three members—the fiery, the airy, and the watery elements. Prior to this an important event takes place. An independent cosmic body severs itself from the fire-air *Earth*. This becomes in its subsequent evolution the present sun.[1] Previously, *Earth* and sun were one body. After the separation of the sun, the Earth[2] still contains within it all that comprises the present moon. The separation of the sun takes place because exalted beings can no longer endure the matter now condensed to water in their own evolution and in their task for the advancement of the *Earth*. They extract from the general *Earth* mass the substance alone suited to their purposes and withdraw in order to establish a new habitation in the present sun. They now send down their activities from the sun to the Earth. Man, however, needs for his further development a place of action in which substance continues to condense.

---

[1] The early stage of our present sun, now spelt with small s. (Tr.)

[2] Earth spelt thus, with a capital E, means the cosmic body containing the moon and other planets after the sun separation. (Tr.)

The incorporation of the watery substance into the Earth body is accompanied by a change in the human being. Not only does fire stream into him and air play about him, but watery substance is incorporated into his physical body. At the same time his etheric part undergoes a change and he perceives it now as a delicate body of light. Previously he felt the streams of heat arising from the *Earth,* he experienced air pressing upon him through tones. Now the watery element also penetrates his fire-air body, and he perceives its instreaming and outstreaming as a flashing up and dimming of light. In his soul also a change has taken place. To the germs of the sentient and intellectual souls is now added that of the consciousness soul. In the water element the Angels are active; they are also the actual producers of light. The human being feels as though they appeared to him in light.—Certain higher beings who were previously within the Earth body now work down upon it from the sun; through all this there is a change in the effects on the Earth. Man chained to the Earth would no longer be able to sense the effects of the sun beings within himself if his soul were constantly turned toward the Earth from which he has received his physical body. An alternation now takes place in the states of human consciousness. The sun beings tear the human soul away from the physical body at certain times so that man now lives alternately within the bosom of the sun beings, purely as a soul, and at other times in a condition where he is united with the body and receives the influences of the Earth. If he is in the physical body, the streams of heat surge up to him; the air masses sound around him; the waters flow in and out of him. If he is outside his body, his soul is then

183

permeated by the images of the higher beings in whose bosom he lives.—At this stage of its evolution the Earth experiences two alternating periods. During the one, it is permitted to weave its substances around the human souls and invest them with bodies; during the other, the souls desert it and only the bodies remain. It, together with the human beings, is in a sleeping state. It is entirely possible to say that at this time of the far distant past the Earth passes through a day and a night period. (This expresses itself physically and spatially in the movement of the Earth in relation to the sun as a result of the mutual action of the sun and Earth beings. In this way the alternation in the characterized day and night period is effected. The day period occurs when the Earth surface upon which man is evolving is turned toward the sun. The night period, that is, the time during which man leads a purely soul existence, occurs when this surface is turned away from the sun. It should not, however, be imagined that in that primeval epoch the Earth's movement around the sun was at all like that of the present. The conditions were then quite different. It is, however, useful to realize here that the movements of the heavenly bodies arise as a result of the relationships the spiritual beings inhabiting them bear to one another. The heavenly bodies are brought into such positions and movements through soul and spirit causes that the spiritual states are enabled to unfold themselves in the physical world.)

Were we to turn our glance toward the Earth during its night period we would see its body in a corpse-like state, for it consists in large part of the decaying bodies of human beings whose souls dwell in another state of existence. The organic, watery, and aeriform structures constituting the human bodies fall into decay and resolve themselves into the rest of the Earth mass. Only that part of the human body, which at the very beginning of the *Earth* evolution took form through the co-activity of fire and the human soul, and in consequence became continually denser, remains in existence like an outwardly inconspicuous germinal nucleus. What is said here about day and night should, therefore, not be taken to be at all similar to what is indicated by these terms at the present earth stage. If at the beginning of the day period the Earth again is a participant in the direct effect of the sun, then the human souls penetrate into the realm of physical life. They come in contact with the nuclei mentioned above and cause them to germinate so that the latter assume an external form that appears like a copy of the human soul nature. It is something like a gentle fructification that occurs between the human soul and the germinal human body. These souls thus embodied now begin also to draw in the surrounding air and water masses and to incorporate them into their bodies. The air is expelled from the organized body and then drawn in again; this is the first indication of what is later to become the breathing process. The water is also drawn in and then expelled; this is the origin of the process of nutrition. These processes are not yet externally perceived. A kind of outer perception occurs through the soul only in the already mentioned fructifying process. Then the soul feels dully its awakening into physical existence by coming in contact with the germinal body the Earth offers it. It hears something that may be expressed in the words, "That is my form!" and this feeling, which

185

might also be called a dawning of the ego-feeling, remains in the soul during its entire connection with the physical body. The process of assimilating air, however, is felt by the soul as something entirely of a soul-spirit nature, entirely pictorial. It appears in the form of an up and down undulating tone-configuration that gives shape to the developing embryonic body. The soul feels itself surrounded completely by undulating tone, and it is conscious of how it fashions its own body according to these tone forces. Thus, at that stage, human forms took shape that are not observable by present-day human consciousness in an external world. They fashion themselves in plant and flower-like structures of delicate substance that are inwardly mobile, appearing like fluttering flowers, and during the Earth period the human being experiences the blissful feeling of being fashioned into such forms. The absorption of the watery parts is felt in the soul as a source of power, as an inner strengthening. Seen from without it appears as growth of the physical human structure. With the waning of the direct effect of the sun the human soul also loses the power to control these processes. By degrees they are discarded. Only those parts remain that permit the above characterized germinal nucleus to ripen. The human being, however, forsakes his body and returns to the spiritual state of existence. (Since not all parts of the Earth body are used in fashioning human bodies, it should not be imagined that during the night period the Earth consists solely of decaying corpses and germinal nuclei awaiting to be wakened. All of these are embedded in other forms that take shape from the substances of the Earth. The condition of these will be shown later.)

The process of Earth-substance condensation now continues. The solid element, which may be called "earthy," is added to the watery element. With this the human being also begins to invest his body with the earthy element during his sojourn on Earth. As soon as this investing process begins, the forces that the soul brings with it from the time it is freed from the body no longer have the same power as previously. Formerly, the soul fashioned the body for itself from the fiery, airy, and watery element according to the tones sounding around it and the light shapes playing about it. The soul is unable to do this with the solidified form. Other powers now intervene in the fashioning process. In the part of the human being that remains when the soul abandons the body, now not only a germinal nucleus is present, which is quickened by the returning soul, but an organism is present that contains also the vivifying force itself. By its severance, the soul does not leave behind on Earth merely a likeness of itself, but it also implants a part of its vivifying power into the likeness. When the soul reappears on Earth, it can no longer only awaken the likeness to life, but the quickening must take place in the likeness itself. The spiritual beings who affect the Earth from the sun sustain the quickening force in the human body although man himself is not on Earth. By incarnating, the soul feels not only the resounding tones and light shapes in which it senses the presence of the beings standing next above it, but through the intake of the Earth element it feels the influence of the still higher beings who have established their field of activity on the sun. Previously man felt himself belonging to the beings of soul and spirit with whom he was united when body-free. His ego still existed within their bosom. This ego now confronts him during physical embodiment while at the same time the surrounding world encompasses him. Independent likenesses of the soul-spirit nature of the human being were now on Earth, likenesses that, when compared with the present human bodies, were structures composed of delicate substantiality, for the earthy parts mingled with them only in the finest state, in a way comparable to the modern human being's absorption of the finely diffused substances of an object with his organ of smell. Human bodies were like shadows. Since they were distributed over the whole Earth, however, they became subject to the Earth influences, which varied at different points of its surface. While previously the bodily likenesses corresponded to the soul-men who animated them and, for that reason, were essentially similar to one another over the whole Earth, now variations appear among human forms. In this way what later emerged as race differentiation was prepared.—Coincident with the growing independence of the human bodily being there was a loosening of the previous close connection between the earth man and the soul-spirit world. When the soul now left the body, the latter lived on in a sort of continuation of life.—If evolution had continued in this way, the Earth would have had to harden under the influence of its solid element. Supersensible knowledge, looking back upon these conditions, perceives how the human bodies abandoned by their souls solidify more and more. After a time the souls returning to Earth would have found no usable material with which they might unite. All the substances suitable for the human being would have been employed in filling the Earth with the woodlike remains of incarnations.

An event then occurred that gave a different direction to the whole process of evolution. Everything was eliminated that could contribute to permanent induration in the solid Earth substance. At that time our present moon[1] withdrew from the Earth, and what had previously contributed directly to the fashioning of permanent forms in the Earth worked now indirectly in a diminished way from the moon. The higher beings upon whom this fashioning of form depends had decided no longer to bestow their effects upon the Earth from within it, but to bestow them upon it from the outside. As a result there appeared a variation in the bodily human structure that must be regarded as the beginning of the separation into two sexes, male and female. The human structures composed of fine substance that previously inhabited the Earth, permitted—through the co-operation within themselves of both these forces, the germinal and the engendering force—the new human form, their descendant, to come into existence. These descendants now transformed themselves. In the one group of such descendants, the soul-spirit germ force was more effective; in the other group it was the life-giving, engendering force that was more effective. This was caused by the weakening of the power of the Earth element through the withdrawal of the moon from the Earth. The interworking of both forces became more delicate than it was previously when it occurred in a single living individual. As a result the descendant, too, was more delicate, finer.

[1] The early stage of our present moon, hereafter spelt with small m. (Tr.)

He entered the earth[1] existence in a delicately formed structure and only by degrees did the more solid substances pervade it. This gave the possibility for the soul—returning to earth—to unite itself again with the body. Now the soul quickened the body no longer from without, for this quickening occurred on the earth itself, but it united itself with it and caused it to grow. A certain limit, however, was set to this growth. As a result of the moon separation, the body had for a time become flexible, but the longer it continued to grow on the earth, the more the solidifying forces gained the upper hand. Finally, the soul was less and less able to participate in the organization of the body. The latter decomposed as the soul ascended to soul-spirit existence.

It is possible to trace how the forces that man gradually appropriated during the *Saturn, Sun* and *Moon* evolutions participate by degrees in human advancement during the fashioning of the earth just described. First, it is the astral body—which also contains both the life or ether body and physical body in a condition of dissolution within itself—that is enkindled by the earth fire. Then this astral body is organized into a rarefied astral part, the sentient soul, and into a coarser part, the etheric, which is now affected by the earth element. With this the previously formed ether or life body makes its appearance. While the intellectual and consciousness souls fashion themselves within the astral human being, the coarser parts of the ether body, which are susceptible to tone and light, organize themselves within it. It is at the time when the ether body condenses

[1] The early stage of our present earth, hereafter spelt with a small e. (Tr.)

itself still further, so that it is transformed from a light body into a fire or heat body, that the stage of evolution is reached in which, as described above, the parts of the solid earth element are incorporated into the human being. Because the ether body has condensed itself to the density of fire, it is now able through the forces of the physical body previously implanted in it to unite itself with the substances of the physical earth that have become attenuated to a condition of fire. It would, however, be unable by itself to infuse the body, which has become more dense in the meantime, also with the airy substances. Here, as indicated above, the higher beings dwelling on the sun interpose and breathe the air into it. Whereas man, by virtue of his past, has thus the power to infuse himself with earthly fire, higher beings guide the instreaming breath of air into his body. Before solidification, the human life body, as a receiver of tone, was the guide of the air stream. It permeated its physical body with life. This physical body now receives life from without. In consequence of this, this life becomes independent of the soul part of the human being who, by leaving the earth, not only leaves his germinal form behind, but also a living likeness of himself. The Spirits of Form remain united with this likeness; they lead the life bestowed by them upon the individual over to the descendants also after the human soul has left the body. Thus, what may be called heredity is developed. When the human soul appears again on earth, it feels itself in a body, the life of which has been transferred to it from the ancestors. It feels itself especially attracted to just such a body. As a result something is formed like a memory about the ancestor with whom the soul feels itself at one. Such a mem-

191

ory passes like a common consciousness through the line of descendants. The ego flows down through the generations.

At this stage of evolution, man felt himself during his earth existence as an independent being. He felt the inner fire of his life body united with the external fire of the earth. He was able to feel the heat streaming through him as his own ego. In these currents of heat, interwoven with life, the first tendency to form a blood circulation is to be found. The human being did not, however, quite feel his own being in what streamed into him as air. In this air the forces of the already described higher beings were active. But that part of the effective forces within the air streaming through him, which belonged to him already by virtue of his previously created ether forces, had remained. He was ruler in one part of these air currents and to the degree that this was so, not only did the higher beings operate in fashioning him, but he himself also assisted in his own formation. According to the images of his astral body he fashioned the air portions. While air thus streamed into the human being from without, becoming the basis of his breathing, a part of the air he contained developed into an organism that was then impressed into him; this became the foundation of the later nervous system. Thus man of that time was connected with the external world of the earth by warmth and air. On the other hand, he was unconscious of the introduction into his organism of the solid element of the earth; this element co-operated in bringing about his incarnation on earth, yet he was unable to perceive directly its infusion into himself, but could only perceive it in a dull state of consciousness in the pictures of higher beings who were active in this element. In such a picture form—as an expression of beings standing above him—man had previously perceived the introduction of the liquid earth elements into himself. As a result of the densification of his earth form, these pictures have now undergone a transformation in his consciousness. The liquid is admixed with the solid element. The infusion of this latter element also must thus be felt as something proceeding from higher beings acting from without. The human soul no longer possesses the power to infuse this element into itself, for this power must now serve the human body, which is built up from outside. Man would spoil its form were he to direct the introduction himself. What he infuses into himself from outside appears to him to be directed by the command of the higher beings who work on the fashioning of his bodily structure. Man feels himself as an ego, he has his intellectual soul within himself as a part of the astral body, through which he experiences inwardly in pictures what is taking place externally, and which permeates his delicate nervous system. He feels himself as the descendant of ancestors by virtue of the life flowing through generations. He breathes and feels it as the effect of the higher beings, described as Spirits of Form, and he accepts what is brought to him through their impulses from the external world as nourishment. What is most obscure to him is his own origin as an individual. In regard to this he is only aware of having experienced an influence from the Spirits of Form expressing themselves in the forces of the earth. He was directed and guided in his relationship to the external world. This is expressed by his possession of a consciousness of the activities of spirit and soul taking place behind his physical environment. He does not perceive the

spiritual beings in their own form, but in his soul he feels
the presence of tone, of color, and other manifestations,
and he knows that the deeds of spiritual beings live in this
world of mental images. What these beings communicate
to him, resounds to him; their manifestations are revealed
to him in pictures of light. Through mental images received
from fire and heat the earth man is most inwardly conscious of himself. He already distinguishes between his
inner heat and the heat radiations of the earthly environment. In the latter the Spirits of Personality manifest themselves. The human being, however, has only a dim consciousness of what exists behind the radiating outer heat.
He feels in these radiations the influence of the Spirits of
Form. When powerful heat effects appear in the human
environment, the soul feels within itself: "Now spiritual
beings are sending their glow around the earth; from this a
spark has been liberated, warming my inner being through
and through."—In the phenomena of light, the human
being does not yet differentiate in the same way between
the outer and inner worlds. When light images arise in the
surroundings, they do not always produce the same feeling
in his soul. There were times when he felt these pictures of
light as something external. This was at the time when he
had just descended from the body-free state into incarnation. It was his period of growth upon the earth. When the
time approached for the fashioning of the germ for the new
earth man, these pictures faded, and the human being only
retained something like memory pictures of them. In these
light pictures the deeds of the Fire Spirits, the Archangels,
were contained. The latter appeared to man as the servants
of the beings of heat who introduced a spark into his inner

194

nature. When their external manifestations were extinguished, he felt them as memory pictures in his inner nature. He felt himself united with their forces, and this was indeed the fact. For he was able to act upon the surrounding atmosphere through what he had received from them. The atmosphere began to shine through this influence. This was a time when nature forces and human forces were not yet separated as they were later. What occurred on the earth proceeded to a large degree from the forces of man himself. Anyone who might have observed the processes of nature on the earth from the outside would not have seen in them merely something that was independent of the human being; he would have perceived in them the effects of human activity. The perceptions of tone took place in a different way for the earth man. From the beginning of earth life they were perceived as outer tones. Whereas the air images were perceived from without right up to the middle period of human earth existence, the outer tones could still be heard after this middle period. Only toward the end of life was the earth man no longer sensitive to them. The tone memories remained with him. In them were contained the revelations of the Sons of Life, the Angels. If the human being toward the end of his life felt himself united inwardly with these forces, then he was able by means of imitation of these forces to produce powerful effects on the water element of the earth. The waters surged in and over the earth under his influence. The human being had notions of taste only during the first quarter of his life, and even then they appeared to the soul like a memory of the experiences passed through in the body-free state. As long as he possessed this memory, the

195

solidification of his body through absorption of outer substances continued. In the second quarter of earth life growth continued, although man's form was already completely developed. At this time he could perceive other living beings beside him only through their warmth, light, and tone effects, for he was not yet capable of visualizing the solid element. Only from the liquid element he obtained, in the first quarter of his life, the described effects of taste.

The external bodily form was an image of this inner soul condition of man. The parts that contained tendencies toward the subsequent head form were developed most perfectly. The other organs gave the impression of appendages. They were shadowy and unclear. The earth men, however, were varied in regard to form. In some the appendages were more or less developed according to the earthly conditions under which they lived. They were varied according to the earthly dwelling places of the human beings. Wherever the latter were entangled in the earth world to a greater degree, the appendages appeared more in the foreground. Those human beings who, as a result of their previous development, were the most mature at the beginning of physical earthly evolution, who right at the beginning—before the *Earth* had condensed to air—experienced the contact with the fire element, could now develop the head capacities most perfectly. These were the human beings who were most harmonious in their nature. Others were ready to come into contact with the element of fire only when the *Earth* had already developed the air element. These human beings were more dependent upon outer conditions than those described above who were able

196

to feel the Spirits of Form clearly by means of heat and who during their earth life felt—as though preserved in a memory—that they belonged to these spirits and were united with them in their body-free condition. The second type of human being had only a slight memory of the body-free state; this type felt its relationship to the spiritual world chiefly through the light activity of the Fire Spirits, the Archangels. A third type of human being was still more entangled in earth existence; it was the type that could be affected by the fire element only when the Earth was separated from the sun and had received the watery element into its composition. The feeling of relationship to the spiritual world was especially weak in human beings of this type at the beginning of earth life. Only when the effect of the activity of the Archangels, and chiefly of the Angels, made itself evident in the inner mental life, did they feel this connection. On the other hand, at the commencement of the earth epoch they were full of active impulses for deeds that can be carried out in earthly conditions. These human beings were especially strongly developed in their appended organs.

Prior to the separation of the moon from the Earth, when the latter, through the presence of the moon forces, tended more and more toward solidification, it happened that because of these forces there were some among the descendants of the abandoned germinal human beings left behind on earth, in which the human souls, returning from the body-free state of existence, could no longer incarnate. The form of such descendants was too solidified, and, because of the moon forces, had become too dissimilar to the human form to be able to receive a human soul. Certain

197

human souls, therefore, found it no longer possible under such circumstances to return to the Earth. Only the ripest and strongest souls were able to feel themselves equal to the task of remodeling the Earth body during its growth so that it blossomed forth bearing the form of a human being. Only a part of the bodily human descendants attained the ability to bear the earthly man. Another part, on account of the solidified form, was only able to receive souls of an order lower than the human being. A number of the human souls were compelled to forego Earth evolution at that time. They were, therefore, led to another course of life. There were souls who had been unable, even at the time when the sun separated from the Earth, to find a place in the latter. In order to develop further they were removed to a planet that, under the guidance of cosmic beings, had been severed from the common universal substance that at the beginning of physical *Earth* evolution was bound up with it, and from which the sun also had detached itself. This planet is the one whose physical expression is known to modern science as Jupiter. (We speak here of the celestial bodies, planets, and their names in exactly the same way as was the custom of a more ancient science. What is meant becomes clear from the context. Just as the physical earth is only the physical expression of a soul-spirit organism, so is that the case with every other celestial body. The supersensible observer does not intend to designate merely the physical planet by the name earth, not merely the physical fixed star by sun, but he has in mind a much wider spiritual connotation; this is also true when he speaks of Jupiter, Mars, and the other planets. The celestial bodies have changed essentially in regard to their configuration and task since the time spoken of here; in a certain respect, even their location in heavenly space has changed. Only someone who has traced back, with the penetration of supersensible knowledge, the evolution of these heavenly bodies right into the distant primeval past is capable of recognizing the connection between the present-day planets and their ancestors.) The souls described evolved further on Jupiter, and later on, as the earth showed an increasing tendency to become more solidified, still another dwelling place had to be fashioned for souls who, although they found it possible to inhabit these solidifying bodies for a certain length of time, could no longer do so when the solidification had advanced too far. For these a place on Mars was provided for their further evolution. Even at the time when the Earth was still bound to the sun and its air element had been inserted into its constitution, it became evident that certain souls proved to be unfit to participate in *Earth* evolution. They were too strongly affected by the earthly body configuration. Thus even at that time they had to be withdrawn from the direct influence of the sun forces. The latter had to act on them from without. For these souls, a place on Saturn was created for their further development. Thus in the course of Earth evolution the number of human shapes diminished; configurations appeared in whom human souls did not incarnate. They could receive only astral bodies in the same way the human physical and life bodies had received them on the ancient *Moon*. While the earth became a waste in regard to its human inhabitants, these beings colonized it. All human souls would have been compelled to forsake the earth finally, had not the withdrawal of the moon from the

199

earth made it possible for the human forms—in which human souls at that time were still able to incarnate—to withdraw the germinal human being during their earth life from the influence of the moon forces that came directly from the earth and to let it mature within themselves as long as necessary until it could be surrendered to these moon forces. As long as the germinal human being then shaped itself within the inner human nature, it came under the influence of the beings who had, under the guidance of their mightiest companion, separated the moon from the earth in order to carry the evolution of the latter over a critical point.

After the *Earth* had developed the air element within itself, there were astral beings, as described above, left over from the ancient *Moon,* who were greater laggards in evolution than the lowest human souls. These became the souls of the forms that had to be forsaken by human beings even before the separation of the sun from the *Earth.* These beings are the ancestors of the present animal kingdom. In the course of time, they developed the organs especially that were present in the human being only as appendages. Their astral body had to affect the physical and ether bodies in the same way that this was the case for human beings on the ancient *Moon.* The animals thus created had souls that could not reside in the individual animal. The soul extended its nature upon the inheritors of the forebear's form. The animals originating from a single configuration have a common soul. Only when the descendant under especial influences departs from the form of its forebear does a new animal soul commence its embodiment. We may speak in this sense in spiritual science in regard to animal souls of a species or group soul.

Something similar occurred at the time of the separation of the sun from the Earth. Forms emerged from the watery element that were no further evolved than the human being prior to evolution on the ancient *Moon*. They were able to receive the effect of the activity of an astral element only when this influenced them from outside. That could only occur after the separation of the sun from the Earth. With every repetition of the sun period of the Earth, the sun's astral element animated these forms in such a way that they constructed their life bodies from the Earth's etheric element. When the sun again turned away from the Earth, this life body dissolved into the common body of the Earth. As a result of the co-operation of the astral element of the sun with the ether element of the Earth there emerged from the watery element the physical structures that formed the ancestors of the present-day plant kingdom.

Upon the earth the human being has become an individualized soul-being. The astral body, which had flowed into him through the Spirits of Motion during the *Moon* evolution, became tripartite as sentient soul, intellectual soul, and consciousness soul upon the earth. When his consciousness soul had advanced far enough so that during earth life it could form a body fit to receive it, the Spirits of Form endowed the human being with a spark of their own fire. The ego, the I, was enkindled within him. Every time the human being left the physical body he found himself in the spirit world in which he encountered beings who had

201

given him his physical body, his life or ether body, and his astral body during the *Saturn, Sun,* and *Moon* evolutions and had brought them up to the level of the *Earth* evolution. Since the enkindling of the fire spark of the ego during earth life, a change had taken place also for the body-free life. Prior to this point in the evolution of his nature, man had no independence in regard to the spirit world. Within this spirit world he did not feel himself as an individual, but as a member of an exalted organism composed of the beings standing above him. The ego experience on earth now extends itself also into the spirit world. Man feels himself now to a certain degree as a unity in this world, but he feels also that he is constantly united with the same world. In the body-free state he finds again in a higher configuration the Spirits of Form whom he had perceived on earth in their manifestation through the spark of the ego.

With the separation of the moon from the earth, experiences that were connected with that separation developed also for the body-free soul in the spirit world. Only because a part of the shaping forces had been transferred from the earth to the moon was it possible to reproduce, on the earth, the human shapes that were able to receive the individuality of the soul. Through this fact the human individuality entered the sphere of the moon beings. The reflection of the earth individuality could only be effective in the body-free state through the fact that in this state also the soul remained in the sphere of the mighty spirits who had caused the moon separation. The process took place in such a way that immediately after the soul had forsaken the earth body it could perceive the exalted sun beings only in the reflected splendor of the moon beings. It was only after gazing at this splendor for a considerable length of time that the soul was sufficiently prepared to behold the sublime sun beings themselves.

The earth's mineral kingdom also came into existence through having been expelled from the general evolution of mankind. Its structures are what remained solidified when the moon separated from the earth. Only that part of soul nature felt itself attracted to these forms that had remained on the *Saturn* stage and is thus fit only to fashion physical forms. All events under consideration here and in the following pages occurred in the course of vast lengths of time. We cannot, however, enter here into a discussion of chronology.

The events described here present *Earth* evolution from the external side. When observed spiritually it can be said that the spiritual beings who withdrew the moon from the earth and united their own existence with it, thus becoming earth-moon beings, caused a certain configuration of the human organism to take place by sending forces from this cosmic body down upon the earth. Their activity was directed upon the ego acquired by the human being. This activity made itself felt in the interplay between this ego and the astral body, ether body, and physical body. As a result it became possible for man to reflect within himself consciously the wisely fashioned configuration of the world, to reflect it as though in a mirror of knowledge. It may be remembered in our description how, during the ancient *Moon* period, the human being acquired through the separation of the sun at that time a certain independence in his organism and a less restricted degree of conscious-

203

ness than could be derived directly from the sun beings. This free, independent consciousness reappeared during the characterized period of *Earth* evolution as a heritage of the ancient *Moon* evolution. But this very consciousness, brought again into harmony with the cosmos through the influence of the earth-moon beings referred to above, could be made into a copy of it. This would have happened had no other influence made itself felt. Without such an influence man would have become a being in whom the content of consciousness would not have reflected the cosmos in the images of cognitional life through his own free volition, but as a necessity of nature. This did not occur. Certain spiritual beings took an active part in the evolution of mankind just at the time of the moon separation, beings who had retained so much of their *Moon* nature that they could not participate in the separation of the sun from the earth; they were excluded also from the activity of the beings who, from the earth-moon, directed their activity upon the earth. These beings with the ancient *Moon* nature were confined with their irregular development to the earth. In their *Moon* nature lay the cause of their rebellion during the ancient *Moon* evolution against the sun spirits, a rebellion that was at that time beneficial to the human being by its having led him to an independent state of consciousness. The consequences of the peculiar development of these beings during the *Earth* epoch entailed their becoming—during that time—enemies of the beings who, from the moon, wished to turn human consciousness into a universal mirror of knowledge under the compulsion of necessity. What on the ancient *Moon* had helped man to a higher state proved to be in opposition to the possibilities that had developed through *Earth* evolution. The opposing powers had brought with them, out of their *Moon* nature, the force to work on the human astral body, namely, in the sense of the above descriptions, to make it independent. They exercised this force by giving the astral body a certain independence— now also for the earth period—in contrast to the compelled (unfree) state of consciousness that was caused by the beings of the earth-moon. It is difficult to express in current language how the activity of the characterized spiritual beings affected human beings in the indicated primeval period. We may neither think of this activity as something like a present-day nature force, nor as something like the action of one man upon another when with words the first man calls forth in the second inner forces of consciousness, through which the second learns to understand something or is stirred to perform a moral or immoral deed. The effect described as taking place in the primeval age was not a nature effect but a spiritual influence, having spiritual effects, transferring itself spiritually from the higher beings to the human being in accordance with his state of consciousness at that time. If we think of this matter as a nature activity then we miss entirely its true, essential character. If we say, on the other hand, the beings endowed with the ancient *Moon* nature approached the human being in order to "seduce" him for their own ends, we employ a symbolic expression that is good as long as we remain conscious of its symbolical character and are at the same time clear in our own minds that behind the symbol stands a spiritual fact, a spiritual reality.

The effect that proceeded from the spiritual beings who

had remained behind in their ancient *Moon* state had a twofold consequence for man. His consciousness was divested of the character of a mere reflector of the cosmos, because the possibility was aroused in the human astral body to regulate and control, by means of it, the images arising in the consciousness. Man became the master of his knowledge. On the other hand, it was just the astral body that became the starting point of this control, and the ego, set above this body, became thus steadily dependent upon it. As a result the future human being was exposed to the continuous influences of a lower element in his nature. It was possible for him during his life to sink below the height at which he had been placed by the earth-moon beings in the course of world events. The continuous influence of the characterized irregularly developed *Moon* beings remained with him throughout the subsequent periods. These moon beings, in contrast to the others who from the earth-moon satellite fashioned human consciousness into a cosmic mirror but gave no independent will, may be called Luciferic spirits. These spirits brought to the human being the possibility of unfolding a free activity in his consciousness, but at the same time also the possibility of error, of evil.

The consequence of these processes was that man came into quite a different relationship with the sun spirits from the one for which he was predestined by the earth-moon spirits. The latter wished to develop the mirror of his consciousness in such a way that the influence of the sun spirits would be the dominant one in the whole of human soul life. These processes were thwarted, and in the human being the contrast was created between the sun spirit influence and the influence of the spirits with an irregular *Moon* evolution. Through this contrast the human being became unable to recognize the physical sun activity as such; it remained concealed behind the earthly impressions of the outer world. The astral nature of man filled by these impressions was drawn into the sphere of the ego. This ego, which otherwise would have felt only the spark of fire bestowed on it by the Spirits of Form, and in everything that concerned the outer fire would have subordinated itself to the commands of these spirits, this ego now —because of the astral element injected into it—exerted its influence also upon the outer heat phenomena. Through creating a bond of attraction between itself and the earth fire, the ego entangled man in earthly matter more than was predestined for him. Whereas previously he had a physical body, which in its principal parts consisted of fire, air, and water, and to which was added only something like a shadowy semblance of earth substance, now the body became denser because of the presence of earth substance. Whereas man existed previously like a finely organized being swimming, hovering over the solid earth surface, he was compelled now to descend from the earth's environment down upon such parts of the earth as were already more or less solidified.

That such physical effects could result from the above described spiritual influences becomes comprehensible through the fact of their being of the sort described above. They were neither nature influences nor soul influences acting from one human being upon another. The latter do not extend their effects as far into the bodily nature as do the spiritual forces that are here under consideration.

207

Because the human being exposed himself to the influences of the outer world through his own visualizations subject to error, because he lived under the impulsion of desire and passion that did not permit of regulation by higher spiritual influences, the possibility of disease appeared. A special effect of the Luciferic influence, however, was that man could now no longer feel his single earth life as a continuation of the body-free existence. He received now earth impressions that could be experienced through the inoculated astral element and that united themselves with the forces destroying the physical body. Man felt this as the dying out of his earth life, and through it death, caused by human nature itself, made its appearance. With this a significant mystery in human nature is indicated, namely, the connection of the human astral body with sickness and death.

Special relationships now appeared for the human life body. It was placed in a relationship to the physical and astral bodies that, in a certain sense, deprived it of the faculties the human being had acquired through the Luciferic influence. A part of this life body remained outside the physical body, so that it could not be controlled by the human ego, but only by higher beings. These higher beings were the same who, at the time of the sun separation, had forsaken the earth under the leadership of one of their exalted companions in order to take up another dwelling place. If the characterized part of the life body had remained united with the astral body, man would have put supersensible forces to his own use that formerly were his own. He would have extended the Luciferic influence also to these forces. As a result man would have thus gradually separated himself entirely from the sun beings, and his ego would have become completely an earth-ego. Consequently, after the death of the physical body—indeed even during its deterioration—this earth-ego would have been obliged to inhabit another physical body—the body of a descendant—without going through a union with higher spiritual beings in a body-free condition. Man would have become conscious of his ego, but only as an earth-ego. This was averted by the above-mentioned event, involving the life body, caused by the earth-moon beings. The actual individual ego was released from the mere earth-ego to such a degree that man felt himself only partially as his own ego during earth life; at the same time he felt that his own earth-ego was an extension of the earth-ego of his forebears throughout the generations. In earth life the soul felt the existence of a sort of group ego right back to the earliest ancestor and man felt himself as a member of the group. Only in the body-free state was the individual ego able to feel itself as an independent being. But this state of separateness was impaired because the ego was afflicted with the memory of the earth consciousness, the earth-ego. This darkened the vision of the spirit world, which began to cover itself with a veil between death and birth as was the case for physical vision on earth.

The physical expression of all the changes that occurred in the spirit world while human evolution went through the described conditions was the gradual regulation of the reciprocal relationships of sun, moon, and earth, and in a broader sense also of the other heavenly bodies. The alternation of day and night can be emphasized as being one consequence of these relationships. (The movements of the

209

heavenly bodies are regulated by the beings inhabiting them. The movement of the earth through which day and night occur was caused by the reciprocal relationships of the various spirits standing above man. In like manner also the movement of the moon was caused, in order that after its separation from and the revolving around the earth the Spirits of Form could act in the right way, with the right rhythm, upon the physical human body.) During the day the human ego and astral body worked in the physical and life bodies. At night this activity ceased. The ego and astral body left the physical and life bodies. They entered during this period entirely into the realm of the Sons of Life (the Angels), of the Spirits of Fire (the Archangels), of the Spirits of Personality, and the Spirits of Form. Besides the Spirits of Form, the Spirits of Motion, the Spirits of Wisdom, and the Thrones included at that time the physical and life bodies in their sphere of action. It was thus possible that the injurious influences, which during the day were exercised upon the human being through the errors of the astral body, could be repaired.

As the human beings now multiplied again on earth, there was no longer any reason why human souls should not have incarnated in their descendants. The influence of the earth-moon forces of that time permitted human bodies to develop, that were thoroughly fit to embody human souls. The souls who previously were removed to Mars, to Jupiter, and to other planets, were led to the earth. There was in consequence a soul present for every human descendant born within the cycle of generations. This continued through long periods, so that the soul migrations to the earth corresponded to the increase in the number of human beings. The souls who left the body at death retained in the body-free state the echo of the earthly individuality like a memory. This memory acted in such a way that when bodies corresponding to the souls were born on earth, they reincarnated in them. As time went on, there were among the human offspring human beings who had souls coming from the outside, who had for the first time since the earliest ages of the Earth appeared again upon it, and there were others having earthly-reincarnated souls. In the subsequent period of the *Earth* evolution, there were fewer and fewer of the young souls appearing for the first time and more and more of the reincarnated souls. Nevertheless, for long ages the human race consisted of the two kinds of human beings resulting from these facts. On earth, man felt more united by a common group-ego with his forebears. The experience of the individual ego was, however, all the stronger in the body-free state between death and a new birth. The souls who came from celestial space and entered human bodies were in a different position from those who already had one or more earth lives behind them. The former brought along with them for the physical earth life only the conditions to which they were subjected by the higher spiritual world and by their experiences made outside the earth region. The others had themselves in previous lives added new conditions. The destiny of the former souls was determined only by facts that lay outside the new earth relationships. The destiny of the reincarnated souls was also determined by what they themselves had done in previous lives under earthly conditions. With reincarnation there appeared at the same time individual human karma.—Through the fact that the human life body was withdrawn from the influence of the astral body, in the manner indicated above, the conditions of reproduction also were not within the scope of human consciousness, but were subject to the dominion of the spiritual world. If a soul was to sink down to the sphere of the earth, the reproductive impulses of the human earth being appeared. To earthly consciousness the entire process was to a certain degree enveloped in a mysterious obscurity.—But the consequences of this partial separation of the life body from the physical appeared also during earth life. The capabilities of this life body could be easily increased by means of spiritual influence. In the life of the soul this expressed itself through an especial perfection of memory. Independent, logical thinking was at this period only in its very beginnings. The capacity of memory was, on the other hand, almost limitless. Externally, it was evident that the human being had direct knowledge—tinged with feeling—of the active forces of every living thing. He was able to employ in his service the forces of life and reproduction of animal nature, and chiefly those of plant nature. He could extract, for example, the force that causes plant growth and employ it in much the same way that the forces of inanimate nature are used at the present time, for example, the way the forces slumbering in coal are extracted and employed to set machines in motion.—Also the inner soul life of man was changed through the Luciferic influence in the most manifold way. Many examples of feelings and sensations due to it could be given. Only a few instances, however, will be described. Prior to the advent of the Luciferic influence, the human soul carried out all its activities in line with the intentions of higher spiritual beings. The plan of all that should be accomplished was determined from the beginning, and to the degree that human consciousness was developed it could foresee how, in the future, evolution would be compelled to proceed in accordance with the preconceived plan. This prophesying consciousness was lost when the veil of earthly perceptions was woven over the manifestation of higher spiritual beings and the real forces of the sun nature concealed themselves in these perceptions. The future now became uncertain. With this uncertainty, the possibility of the sense of fear implanted itself in the soul. Fear is the direct result of error.—But we also see how under the Luciferic influence man became independent of certain forces to which he previously submitted himself without will. Now he could make decisions by himself. Freedom is the result of this influence, and fear and similar feelings are only the accompanying phenomena of the progress of man to freedom.

Seen spiritually, the way fear appears indicates that within the earth forces—under the influence of which the human being had come through the Luciferic powers—other powers were active that had followed an irregular course in evolution much earlier than the Luciferic powers. With the earth forces man absorbed the influence of these powers into his being. They gave the character of fear to feelings that would have manifested quite differently without the presence of these powers. These beings may be called "Ahrimanic." They belong to the category called, in the Goethean sense, "Mephistophelean."

Although the Luciferic influence made itself felt at first only in the most advanced individuals, it soon spread out also to others. The descendants of these advanced human beings intermingled with the less advanced described above. By this means the Luciferic power injected itself also into the latter. But the ether body of the souls returning from the planets could not receive the same degree of protection enjoyed by the ether body of the descendants of those who had remained on earth. The protection of these latter life bodies came from an exalted Being in whose hands rested the leadership of the cosmos at the time the sun withdrew from the Earth. This Being appears in the realm here under consideration as ruler of the kingdom of the sun. With Him exalted spirits who through their cosmic evolution had attained the necessary maturity migrated to the sun abode. There were, however, other beings who had not, at the time of the sun separation, attained such heights. They were compelled to seek other abodes. It was through these very beings that Jupiter and the other planets broke loose from the common world substance that originally composed the physical *Earth* organism. Jupiter became the dwelling place of the beings who had not reached maturity enough to attain the heights of the sun. The most advanced of these became the leader of Jupiter. In just the same way that the leader of the sun development became the higher ego that was active in the life body of the descendants of the human beings who had remained on earth, this Jupiter leader became the higher ego that permeated, as a common consciousness, the human beings who had originated from an interbreeding of the offspring of those who had remained on the earth and those other human beings who, in the way described above, had appeared upon the *Earth* only at the time of the

214

advent of the air element and who had then gone over to Jupiter as a dwelling place. These human beings are designated by spiritual science as "Jupiter men." They were human descendants who in that ancient time still had received human souls into their nature, but who at the beginning of *Earth* evolution were not mature enough to come in contact with the fire. They were souls standing at the stage midway between the realm of human and animal souls. There were also beings who under the leadership of one of their most exalted members had separated Mars from the common world substance as a suitable dwelling place. They exerted their influence upon a third kind of man, who had come into existence through interbreeding, the "Mars man." (From this knowledge a light is thrown upon the origin of the planets of our solar system. For, all bodies of this system have originated through the various stages of maturity of the beings dwelling on them. It is, however, not possible here to enter into a discussion of all the details of cosmic organization.) The human beings who, in their life body, perceived the presence of the lofty Sun Being Himself may be designated "sun men." The Being Who lived in them as "Higher Ego"—naturally only in the whole race, not in the individual—is the One to Whom later, when man acquired a conscious knowledge of Him, various names were given. He is the Being in Whom the relationship that the Christ has to the cosmos manifests itself to the human beings of our time. We can, in addition, distinguish "Saturn men." With them there appeared a being as higher ego who with his associates had been compelled to forsake the common world substance prior to the sun separation. In this species of human being not only the

215

life body had remained partly untouched by the Luciferic influence, but also the physical body.

In the case of the inferior kinds of human beings, however, the life body was not sufficiently protected to enable it to withstand the Luciferic influence. These human beings could extend the unruly power of their ego's fire spark to such a degree that they were able to call forth in their environment powerful, destructive fire effects. The consequence was a tremendous terrestrial catastrophe. The fire storms caused a large part of the inhabited earth of that time to perish and with it the human beings who had lapsed into error. Only the smallest part who had remained partly untouched by error was able to escape to a district of the earth that had remained until then protected from corrupting human influence. Such a dwelling place, which was especially appropriate for the new mankind, appeared in the land that existed on the spot of the earth now covered by the Atlantic Ocean. It was to this place those human beings withdrew who were most untouched by error. Only scattered human groups inhabited other regions of the earth. The earth region existing at that time, situated between modern Europe, Africa, and America, is called "Atlantis" by spiritual science. (In the corresponding literature reference is made, in a certain way, to the phase of human evolution characterized above that precedes the Atlantean period. The name "Lemurian age" is given to the period of the earth that preceded the Atlantean age. On the other hand, the age in which the moon forces had not yet unfolded their chief activity is designated the "Hyperborean." Preceding this age there was still another that coincides with the very first period of the physical *Earth* evolution. In the biblical tradition, the period before the influence of the Luciferic beings was active is described as the age of Paradise, and the descent of the human being out of this region to the earth, and his subsequent entanglement in the world of the senses, as the expulsion from Paradise.)

Evolution on Atlantis is the time of the actual separation of mankind into the Saturn, Sun, Jupiter, and Mars men. Before that, there had been only the predisposition toward this separation. The division into waking and sleeping states had special consequences for the human being that appeared especially in Atlantean humanity. During the night, man's astral body and ego were in the realm of the beings standing above him—right up to the realm of the Spirits of Personality. By means of that portion of the life body not united with the physical body, the human being was able to have a perception of the Sons of Life (the Angels), and the Spirits of Fire (the Archangels). For he was able to remain united during sleep with the part of the life body not permeated by the physical body. The perception of the Spirits of Personality remained indistinct because of the Luciferic influence. Beside the Angels and Archangels, other beings also became visible to man when in the state described above, beings who, having remained behind on the sun and moon, could not enter earth existence. They had to remain in the world of soul and spirit. Man, however, drew them—by means of the Luciferic nature—into the realm of his soul that was separated from the physical body. Thus he came in contact with beings who worked upon him in a corrupting way. They increased the urge toward error in his soul, especially the urge toward the misuse of the forces of growth and reproduction that were under his control through the separation of the physical and life body.

It was possible, however, for individual men of the Atlantean period to entangle themselves to a small degree in the realm of the senses. Through them the Luciferic influence was transformed from an obstacle to human evolution into an instrument of higher advancement. Through this Luciferic influence they were in the position of unfolding the knowledge of earthly things earlier than would otherwise have been possible. In doing so, these human beings sought to remove erroneous ideas from their thought life, and through the phenomena of the world to fathom the original purposes of spirit beings. They kept themselves free from the impulses and desires of the astral body, which were only inclined toward the world of the senses. In this way they became ever freer from the errors of the astral body. This produced conditions in them by means of which they perceived only with that part of the ether body that was separated from the physical body in the manner described. In these conditions the physical body's power of perception was practically extinguished and the body itself was as though dead. These human beings were then completely united through the ether body with the realm of the Spirits of Form and were able through them to learn how they were being led and guided by the exalted Being Who held the leadership at the time of separation of sun and Earth. Later, through this exalted Being an understanding of the Christ unfolded itself in human beings. Such men were initiates. But since the individuality of man had, as already described above, entered the region of the moon

218

spirits, these initiates also remained, as a rule, untouched directly by the Spirit of the Sun. He could be shown to them only by the moon spirits as though in a reflection. Thus they did not see the Being of the Sun directly, but saw only His splendor. They became the leaders of the other portion of mankind to whom they could communicate the mysteries they beheld. They trained disciples to whom they indicated the paths leading to the state resulting in initiation. The knowledge, previously revealed through Christ, could be attained by human beings only who belonged—in the way described—to the order of "sun men." They cultivated their mysterious wisdom and the functions leading to it in a special place on the earth, which will be called here the Christ or Sun oracle—*oraculum* meaning the place where the purposes of spiritual beings are heard. What is said here about the Christ will only be understood if we keep in mind the fact that supersensible knowledge perceives in His appearance on earth an event that was foreseen for ages by wise men as taking place at some future time, wise men who were familiar, long before this event, with the meaning of *Earth* evolution. We would be in error were we to presuppose in the case of these initiates a connection with the Christ that was made possible only through this event. But they could comprehend prophetically and make their disciples understand that whoever is touched by the power of the Sun Being sees the Christ approaching the earth.

Other oracles came into being through the members of the Saturn, Mars, and Jupiter humanities; their initiates directed their vision only up to the beings who could reveal themselves in their ether bodies as the corresponding higher egos. There thus arose adherents of Saturn, Jupiter, and Mars wisdom. Besides these methods of initiation, there were others for human beings who had acquired too much of the Luciferic nature to allow as large a portion of their ether body to be separated from the physical body as was the case with the sun men. Their astral body retained a greater part of the life body in the physical body, nor could they be brought, by means of the described state of initiation, to a prophetic revelation of the Christ. On account of their astral body, which was considerably influenced by the Luciferic principle, they were compelled to go through more complicated preparations, and then, in a less body-free state than the others, they were unable to behold the manifestation of the Christ Himself, but only that of other higher beings. There were certain spiritual beings who at the time of the sun separation had forsaken the Earth, but who had not yet attained a sufficiently high development to enable them to participate permanently in the sun evolution. After the separation of sun and Earth they withdrew a portion of the sun as a dwelling place. This we know as Venus. The leader of these spiritual beings became the higher ego of the above described initiates and their adherents. Something similar occurred in regard to the leading spirit of Mercury for another kind of human being. In this way the Venus and Mercury oracles had their origin. Certain human individuals who were affected most by the Luciferic influence were able to reach up only to a certain being who, with his associates, had been the earliest to be expelled from the sun development. This being has not a special planet in the cosmos, but lives in the environment of the earth itself, with which he has been again united since his return from the sun. The human beings to whom this being manifested himself as higher ego may be called members of the "Vulcan oracle." Their eyes were turned more toward earth phenomena than was the case with the other initiates. They laid the first foundation for what appeared later on among human beings as "science" and "art." The Mercury initiates, on the other hand, laid the basis for the knowledge of the more supersensory things, and to a still higher degree, this was done by the Venus initiates. The Vulcan, Mercury, and Venus initiates distinguished themselves from the Saturn, Jupiter, and Mars initiates through the fact that the latter received their mysteries more as a revelation from above, in a more finished state, whereas the former received their knowledge revealed more in the form of their own thoughts, of their own ideas. In the middle stood the Christ initiates. They received, together with the direct revelation, the ability to clothe their mysteries in the form of human concepts. The Saturn, Jupiter, and Mars initiates had to express themselves by way of symbols; The Christ, Venus, Mercury, and Vulcan initiates were able to make their communications in the form of definite concepts.

What was attained in this manner by the Atlantean humanity came about in an indirect way through the initiates. But the rest of humanity also gained special abilities through the Luciferic principle, because through the lofty cosmic beings certain faculties, which might otherwise have led to disaster, were transformed into a blessing. One such faculty is speech. It was bestowed upon man through his solidification within physical matter and through the separation of a part of his ether body from the physical

221

body. During the time after the moon separation the human being felt himself at first united to his physical forebears through the group ego. This common consciousness, however, which united descendants with forefathers, was gradually lost in the course of generations. The later descendants had then an inner memory reaching back only to a not very distant ancestor, not any longer to the earlier forebears. Only in a state similar to sleep, in which the human beings came in touch with the spiritual world, did the picture of this or that ancestor emerge again in memory. Human beings, in certain instances, then felt themselves at one with this ancestor whom they believed had reappeared in them. This was an erroneous concept of reincarnation, which emerged chiefly in the last part of the Atlantean period. The true teaching about reincarnation could only be learned in the schools of the initiates. These latter perceived how, in the disembodied state, the human soul passes from one incarnation to another, and they alone could impart the truth about it to their disciples.

The physical form of man was, in the primeval past that is under discussion here, still widely different from the present human shape. It was to a high degree still the expression of soul faculties. The human being consisted of a finer, softer substance than the one he acquired later. What today is solidified was in the limbs soft, supple, and easily molded. A human being who expressed more intensely his soul and spiritual nature had a delicate, active and expressive body structure. Another with less spiritual development had crude, immobile, less easily molded bodily forms. Advancement in soul qualities contracted the limbs; the figure remained small. Retardation in soul development and entanglement in the world of the senses expressed itself in gigantic size. While man was in the period of growth, the body, in accordance with what occurred in the soul, assumed forms of a certain kind that to the present-day human mind must appear fabulous, indeed, fantastic. Moral corruption through passions, impulses, and instincts resulted in an enormous increase in the material substance in man. The present-day human physical form has come into existence through contraction, condensation, and solidification of the Atlantean; whereas before the Atlantean age the human being was a faithful copy of his soul nature, the processes of the Atlantean evolution bore the causes in themselves that led to the post-Atlantean human being who in his physical shape is solid and little dependent on soul qualities. (The animal kingdom became denser in its forms at much earlier periods of the earth than the human being.) The laws that lie at present at the foundation of form-fashioning in the kingdoms of nature are not valid under any circumstances for the more distant past.

Toward the middle of the Atlantean period of evolution a great evil gradually began to manifest itself within mankind. The mysteries of the initiates ought to have been carefully guarded from individuals who had not purified their astral bodies of error through preparation. When such human beings acquire a certain insight into mystery knowledge, into the laws by which the higher beings guide the forces of nature, they then place these laws at the service of their perverted needs and passions. The danger was all the greater, since human beings, as already described, came into the realm of lower spiritual beings who, unable

223

to carry out the regular *Earth* evolution, acted contrary to it. These spiritual beings influenced human beings constantly by arousing in them interests that were, in truth, directed against the welfare of mankind. But human beings had still the ability to use the forces of growth and reproduction of animal and human nature for their own purposes.—Not only ordinary human beings, but also a number of the initiates succumbed to the temptations of lower spiritual beings. They went so far as to use the described supersensible forces in a way that ran counter to the development of mankind, and for this activity they sought associates who were not initiated and who—for lower ends—seized upon the mysteries of the supersensible working of nature. The consequence was a great corruption of mankind. The evil spread further and further, and since the forces of growth and reproduction, when diverted from their natural functions and used independently, stand in a mysterious connection with certain forces that work in air and water, mighty, destructive nature forces were unfettered by human deeds. This led to the gradual destruction of the Atlantean region through terrestrial catastrophes of air and water. The Atlantean humanity—insofar as it did not perish in the storms—was compelled to emigrate. At that time the earth received through these storms a new face. On the one side, Europe, Asia, and Africa received gradually the shapes they bear today. On the other side, America. To these lands went great migrations. For our present day the most important of these migrations were those that went eastward from Atlantis. What is now Europe, Asia, Africa, became gradually colonized by the descendants of the Atlanteans. Various folk established their

224

abode in these continents. They stood at varying degrees of development, but also at varying degrees of depravity. In the midst of these migrating peoples marched the initiates, the guardians of the oracle mysteries. These guardians founded in various regions of the earth institutions in which the services of Jupier, Venus, and other oracles were cultivated in a good, but also in an evil manner. The betrayal of the Vulcan mysteries exercised an especially adverse influence, because the attention of their adherents was chiefly directed toward earthly matters. Mankind, through this betrayal, was made dependent upon spiritual beings who, in consequence of their previous development, held a negative attitude toward everything that came from the spiritual world, which had evolved through the separation of the Earth from the sun. According to the capacity thus developed, they acted in the element that was formed in the human being through his having perceptions of the sense world, behind which the spirit is concealed. These beings acquired henceforth a great influence over many human inhabitants of the earth, and this influence made itself evident through the fact that the human being was more and more deprived of the feeling for the spirit.— Since in these times the size, form and flexibility of the human physical body was still affected to a large degree by the qualities of the soul, the consequence of this betrayal of the mysteries came to light in changes in the human race in this respect also. Where the corruption of the human beings became especially evident through the placing of supersensible forces at the service of lower impulses, desires, and passions, grotesque human shapes were created, monstrous in size and structure. These were not able to

225

continue in existence beyond the Atlantean period. They died out. The post-Atlantean humanity has fashioned itself physically after the model of the Atlantean ancestors in whom already such a solidifying of the bodily shape had taken place that this did not surrender to the influence of soul forces that had become contrary to nature.—There was a certain period of time in the Atlantean evolution in which, through the laws holding sway in and around the earth, conditions prevailed for the human form under which it had to solidify itself. To be sure, the human racial forms that had solidified prior to this period were able to reproduce themselves for a long time; nevertheless, the souls incarnating in them gradually became so narrowly confined that such races had to die out. Many of these racial forms, however, continued in existence on into the post-Atlantean period; certain forms that had remained sufficiently supple continued to exist in a modified form for a long time. Human forms that had remained flexible beyond the characterized period now became chiefly the bodies for souls that experienced intensively the detrimental influence of the betrayal of the Vulcan mysteries as already indicated. They were destined to die out quickly.

Thus, since the middle of the Atlantean period of evolution, beings had asserted themselves within the realm of human development whose activity affected mankind in such a way that it became acquainted with the physical sense world in a non-spiritual manner. In certain instances this went so far that instead of the true shape of this world manifesting itself, it appeared to the human being in phantoms, chimeras and illusions of all sorts. Not only was man exposed to the Luciferic influence, but also to the influence of the other beings about whom we have spoken above, and whose leader may be called Ahriman in accordance with the designation he received later on in the Persian cultural period. (Mephistopheles is the same being.) After death man came through this influence under powers that allowed him to appear also in that realm only as a being who is inclined toward earthly-sensory conditions. The free view into the processes of the spiritual world was by degrees taken away from him. He was obliged to feel himself in the power of Ahriman and to a certain degree had to be excluded from union with the spiritual world.

Of special significance was one oracle sanctuary that in the universal decline had preserved the ancient cultus in its purest form. It belonged to the Christ oracles, and on account of this it was able to preserve not only the Christ mystery itself, but also the mysteries of the other oracles. For through the manifestation of the most exalted Sun Spirit, the regents of Saturn, Jupiter, and other oracles, were also revealed. The sun oracle knew the secret of producing, for this or that individual, the kind of human ether bodies that were possessed by the highest initiates of Jupiter, Mercury, and other oracles. With the means at their disposal, which are not to be discussed any further here, counterparts of the most perfect ether bodies of the ancient initiates were preserved and later implanted into the individuals best fitted for the purpose. Through the Venus, Mercury, and Vulcan initiates, such processes could take place also for the astral bodies.

There came a time when the leader of the Christ initiates found himself isolated with some of his associates to whom he was able to communicate the mysteries of the world

227

only to a very limited degree. For the associates were the kind of human beings upon whom nature had bestowed physical and etheric bodies with the least degree of separation between them. Such men were the best suited, in this epoch, for the further advancement of mankind. Gradually they had fewer and fewer experiences in the realm of sleep. The spiritual world had become more and more closed for them. But they were also lacking the understanding for all that had unveiled itself in ancient times when man was not in his physical but only in his ether body. The human beings in the immediate neighborhood of this leader of the Christ oracle were the most advanced in regard to the union of the physical body with that part of the ether body that previously had been separated from it. This union appeared by degrees in mankind in consequence of the transformation of Atlantis and the earth generally. The physical and ether bodies of human beings coincided more and more with one another. As a result, the previous unlimited faculty of memory was lost and human thought life began. The part of the ether body bound to the physical body transformed the physical brain into the actual organ of thought, and only from that time onward did the human being feel his ego in the physical body. Only then did self-consciousness awake. At the outset, this was the case with a small portion of mankind only, chiefly with the immediate companions of the leader of the Christ oracle. The other groups of human beings who were scattered over Europe, Asia, and Africa, preserved in the most varied degrees the remnants of the ancient states of consciousness. They, therefore, experienced the supersensible world directly.—The companions of the Christ initiate were human beings with highly developed intelligence, but of all human beings of that time their experiences in the realm of the supersensible were the least. With them, this Christ initiate migrated from west to east, toward a certain region in inner Asia. He wished to protect them from coming in contact with the people of less advanced states of consciousness. He educated these companions in accordance with the mysteries revealed to him, and chiefly worked in this way upon their descendants. Thus he trained a host of human beings who had received into their hearts the impulses that corresponded to the mysteries of the Christ initiation. From this host he chose the seven best in order that they might have ether and astral bodies corresponding to the counterparts of the ether bodies of the seven greatest Atlantean initiates. He thus trained initiates to be the successors of the Christ initiate, of the Saturn, of the Jupiter, and of the other oracle initiates. These seven initiates became the teachers and leaders of the people who in the post-Atlantean epoch had settled in the south of Asia, chiefly in ancient India. Since these great teachers were endowed with the counterparts of the ether bodies of their spiritual ancestors, what was contained in their astral bodies, that is to say, their own self-wrought knowledge and understanding, did not extend to what was revealed to them through their ether body. They had to silence their own knowledge and understanding when these revelations strove to manifest in them. Then out of them and by means of them the high beings spoke who had spoken also for their spiritual ancestors. Except during the periods

229

when these high beings spoke through them, they were simple men gifted with the degree of understanding and sympathy that they themselves had acquired.

In India there lived at that time a kind of human being which had preserved chiefly a living memory of the ancient soul state of the Atlanteans, a state which permitted experiences in the spiritual world. In a large number of these human beings there was also present a tremendous urge of the heart and mind to experience this supersensible world. Through the wise guidance of destiny the main body of this kind of men, representing the best sections of the Atlanteans, had reached South Asia. Besides this main body, other sections had settled there at various times. The Christ initiate already mentioned appointed his seven great disciples as teachers for this assemblage of human beings. They gave their wisdom and their laws to this people. For many of these ancient Indians little preparation was needed to arouse in them the scarcely extinct faculties that led to a perception of the supersensible world. For the longing for this world was a fundamental mood of the Indian soul. The Indian felt that in this supersensible world was the primeval home of mankind. From it he was removed into a world that is revealed only through the perceptions of the outer senses and grasped by the intellect bound to these perceptions. He felt the supersensible world as the true one and the sensory world as a deception of human perception, an illusion (Maya). By all possible means the human being strove to gain insight into the true world. He was unable to develop any interest in the illusory sense world, or at least only insofar as it proved to be a veil over the supersensible world. It was a mighty power

230

that the seven great teachers exercised upon such people. What could be revealed through this power penetrated deeply into the Indian souls. Since the possession of the transmitted life and astral bodies endowed these teachers with sublime powers, they were able to act magically upon their disciples. They did not actually teach. They produced their effects from person to person as though through magic powers. Thus a culture arose that was completely permeated by supersensible wisdom. What is contained in the books of wisdom of India—in the Vedas—is not the original form of the exalted wisdom, which in the most primeval ages was fostered by the great teachers; it is but a feeble echo of this wisdom. Only supersensible retrospection can discover an unwritten primeval wisdom behind the written records. A particular characteristic of this primeval wisdom is the harmonious concordance of the wisdom of the various oracles of the Atlantean age. For each of these great teachers was able to unveil the wisdom of one of these oracles, and the different aspects of wisdom produced a perfect concordance because behind them stood the fundamental wisdom of the prophetic Christ initiation. The teacher, however, who was the spiritual successor of the Christ initiate did not present what this Christ initiate himself was able to reveal. The latter had remained in the background of evolution. At the outset, he could not transmit his high office to any member of the post-Atlantean civilization. The difference between the Christ initiate of the seven great Indian teachers and the Christ initiate of the Atlantean sun oracle was that the latter had been able to transform completely his perception of the Christ mystery into human concepts, whereas the Indian Christ initiate could only represent a reflection of this mystery in signs and symbols. This was so because his humanly acquired conceptual life did not extend to this mystery. But the result of the union of the seven teachers was a knowledge of the supersensible world, presented in a great panorama of wisdom, of which in the ancient Atlantean oracles only the various parts could be proclaimed. Now the great regencies of the cosmic world were revealed, and the one great Sun Spirit, the "Concealed One," was gently alluded to—He Who was enthroned above those other regents who were revealed by the seven teachers.

What is meant here by the "ancient Indians," is not what is usually understood by the use of that term. There are no external documents of that period of which we are speaking here. The people usually designated as Indian corresponds to an evolutionary stage of history that came into existence a long time after the period under discussion here. We are able to recognize a primal post-Atlantean epoch in which the characterized Indian culture was dominant. Then a second post-Atlantean epoch began in which the dominant culture, as spoken of in this book, was the ancient Persian; still later, the Egypto-Chaldean culture evolved; both of these have still to be described. During the unfolding of these second and third post-Atlantean cultural epochs, ancient India also experienced a second and a third cultural period. What is usually spoken of as ancient India originated in this third epoch. Therefore, what is presented here should not be confused with the ancient India of history.

Another aspect of this ancient Indian culture is what later led to a division of men into castes. The inhabitants

232

of India were the descendants of Atlanteans who belonged to various human races: Saturn men, Jupiter men, and other planetary men. By means of supersensible teaching it was understood by these ancient Indians that it was not by accident that a soul was placed in this or that caste, but rather by self-determination. Such a comprehension of the supersensible teaching was facilitated especially through the fact that many human beings could arouse the above-characterized inner remembrance of their ancestors, which, however, led easily to an erroneous idea of reincarnation. Just as in the Atlantean period the true idea of reincarnation could be acquired only by coming in contact with the initiates, in the most ancient India it could be obtained only by becoming in direct contact with the great teachers. The above-mentioned erroneous idea of reincarnation was spread most widely among the peoples who, as a result of the submergence of Atlantis, were scattered over Europe, Asia, and Africa, and because certain initiates, who during the Atlantean evolution had followed false paths, had also communicated this mystery to immature disciples, human beings mistook more and more the false doctrine for the true. In many instances these human beings retained a sort of dreamlike clairvoyance as an inheritance of the Atlantean period. Just as the Atlanteans entered the region of the spiritual world during sleep, so their descendants experienced this spiritual world in an abnormal intermediate state between waking and sleeping. Then there arose in them images of an ancient time to which their ancestors had belonged. They considered themselves reincarnations of human beings who had lived in such an age. Teachings about reincarnation that were in

233

contradiction to the true ideas of the initiates spread over the whole earth.

In the regions of the Middle East a community of people had settled as a result of the long continued migrations that had spread from the west eastward since the beginning of the destruction of Atlantis. History knows the descendants of these people as the Persians and their related tribal branches. Supersensible knowledge, however, must go back much further than the historical periods of these people. At the outset we have to consider the earliest ancestors of the later Persians, from whom—after the Indian —the second great cultural period of the post-Atlantean evolution arose. The peoples of this second period had a different task from the Indian. In their longings and inclinations they did not turn merely toward the supersensible; they were eminently fitted for the physical-sensory world. They grew fond of the earth. They valued what the human being could conquer on the earth and what he could win through its forces. What they accomplished as warriors and also what they invented as a means of gaining the earth's treasures is related to this peculiarity of their nature. Their danger did not lie in the fact that because of their love of the supersensible they might turn completely away from the "illusion" of the physical-sensory world, but because of their strong inclination toward the latter they were more likely to lose their soul connection with the supersensible world. Also the oracle establishments that had been transplanted into this region from their homeland, ancient Atlantis, carried in their methods the general character of the Persians. By means of forces, which man had been able to acquire through his experiences in the super-

234

sensible regions and which he was still able to control in certain lower forms, the phenomena of nature were employed to serve personal human interests. This ancient people still possessed, at that time, a great power with which it controlled certain nature forces that later were withdrawn from all connection with the human will. The guardians of the oracles controlled inner powers that were connected with fire and other elements. They may be called Magi. What they had preserved for themselves from ancient times as heritage of supersensible knowledge and power was, to be sure, insignificant in comparison with what the human being had once been able to do in the far distant past. It took on, nevertheless, all sorts of forms, from the noble arts whose purpose was only the welfare of mankind, to the most abominable practices. In these people the Luciferic nature ruled in a special manner. It had brought them into connection with everything that led the human being away from the intentions of higher beings who, without the Luciferic influence, would have simply advanced human evolution. Those sections of this people who were still endowed with the remnants of ancient clairvoyance—that is to say, with the remnants of the above described intermediate state between waking and sleeping —felt themselves also much attracted to the lower beings of the spiritual world. To this people a special spiritual impetus had to be given that counteracted these characteristics. A leadership was given to this people from the same source from which the ancient Indian spiritual life had also sprung, that is, from the guardian of the mysteries of the sun oracle.

The leader of the ancient Persian spiritual culture who

235

was chosen by the guardian of the sun oracle for the people now under consideration may be called by the same name that history knows as Zarathustra or Zoroaster. But it must be emphasized that the personality designated here belongs to a much earlier age than the historical bearer of this name. It is not a question here of outer historical research but of spiritual science, and whoever must think of a later age in connection with the bearer of the name Zarathustra, may reconcile this fact with spiritual science by realizing that the historical character represents a successor to the first great Zarathustra whose name he assumed and in the spirit of whose teaching he worked.—Zarathustra gave his people an impulse by pointing out that the physical world of the senses is not merely something devoid of spirit that confronts man when he comes under the exclusive influence of the Luciferic being. Man owes to this being his personal independence and his sense of freedom, but this Luciferic being should work within him in harmony with the opposing spiritual being. It was important for the prehistoric Persian to be aware of the presence of this spiritual being. Because of the Persian's inclination toward the physical sense world he was threatened by a complete amalgamation with the Luciferic beings. Zarathustra, however, had been initiated by the guardian of the sun oracle and through this initiation the revelations of the exalted sun beings could be imparted to him. In exceptional states of consciousness, into which his training had brought him, he was able to perceive the leader of the sun beings who had taken under his protection the human ether body in the previously described manner. He knew that this Being directs human evolution, but also that He could descend to the earth from cosmic space only at a certain point in time. In order that this might come about it was necessary that He should affect the astral body of a human being to the same degree that He affected the human ether body since the beginning of the interference of the Luciferic being. For that purpose a human being had to appear on earth who had retransformed the astral body to a condition to which this body, without Lucifer, would have attained in the middle of the Atlantean evolution. Had Lucifer not appeared, the human being would have attained this same condition much earlier, but without personal independence and without the possibility of freedom. Now, however, despite these characteristics the human being was to regain this same high condition. Zarathustra was able to foresee by means of his clairvoyance that in the future of mankind's evolution it would be possible for a definite human personality to possess such a required astral body. He knew also that it would be impossible to find the spiritual sun powers on earth prior to this future age, but that it was possible for supersensible perception to behold them in the region of the spiritual sun. He was able to behold these powers when he directed his clairvoyant glance toward the sun, and he divulged to his people the nature of these powers that, for the time being, were to be found only in the spiritual world and that later were to descend to the earth. This was the proclamation of the sublime Sun or Light Spirit—the Sun Aura, Ahura Mazdao, Ormuzd. This Spirit of Light reveals Himself to Zarathustra and his followers as the Spirit who turns His countenance from the spiritual world toward mankind and who prepares the future within mankind. It is the Spirit who points to the Christ before His advent on earth, whom Zarathustra proclaims as the Spirit of Light. On the other hand, Zarathustra represents in Ahriman—Angra Mainju —a power whose influence upon the life of the human soul causes the latter's deterioration when it surrenders itself onesidedly to it. This power is none other than the one previously characterized who, since the betrayal of the Vulcan mysteries, had gained especial domination over the earth. Besides the evangel concerning the Spirit of Light, Zarathustra also proclaimed the doctrine of the spiritual beings who become manifest to the purified sense of the seer as the companions of the Spirit of Light and to whom a contrast was formed by the tempters who appeared to the unpurified remnants of clairvoyance that was retained from the Atlantean period. Zarathustra strove to make clear to the prehistoric Persian how the human soul, as far as it was engaged in the activities and strivings of the physical-sensory world, was the field of battle between the power of the Light God and His adversary and how the human being must conduct himself so as not to be led into the abyss by this adversary but whose influence might be turned to good by the power of the Light God.

A third post-Atlantean cultural period began with the peoples who, by participation in the migrations from Atlantis, had finally assembled in the Middle East and North Africa. Among the Chaldeans, Babylonians, Assyrians on the one hand and the Egyptians on the other, this culture was developed. Among these peoples the understanding for the physical world of the senses was evolved in a way different from that of the prehistoric Persians. They had developed, much more than others, the spiritual capacity that is the foundation for the ability to think, for intellectual endowment, which had come into existence since the last Atlantean epochs. It was the task of the post-Atlantean humanity to unfold in itself the soul faculties that could be gained through the awakened powers of thought and feeling that are not directly stimulated by the spiritual world, but come into existence by man's observation of the sense world, by becoming familiar with it, transforming it. The conquest of this physical-sensory world by means of these human faculties must be considered the mission of post-Atlantean humanity. From stage to stage this conquest advances. Although in ancient India the human being was directed toward this world by means of his soul state, he still considered this world an illusion and his spirit was turned toward the supersensible world. In contrast to this, there arose in the prehistorical Persian people the desire to conquer the physical world of the senses, but this was attempted, to a large measure, with the powers of soul that had remained as heritage of a time when man could still reach up directly into the supersensible world. In the peoples of the third cultural epoch the soul had lost to a large degree its supersensible faculties. It had to investigate the revelations of the spirit in the sensory surroundings and by means of discovery and invention of the cultural means, springing from this world, develop itself. Human sciences arose by means of research within the physical sense world into the spiritual laws standing behind it; human technique and artistic activities and the tools and instruments used to advance them were developed by recognizing the forces of this world and the need of employing them. For the human being of ancient Chaldea and

239

Babylonia the sense world was no longer an illusion, but with its nature kingdoms, its mountains and seas, its air and water, it was a revelation of the spiritual deeds of powers standing behind these phenomena, whose laws he endeavored to discover. To the Egyptian the earth was a field of activity given to him in a condition which he had to transform through his own intellectual capacity, so that it bore the imprint of human power. Oracle establishments of Atlantis, originating chiefly from the Mercury oracle, had been transplanted into Egypt. There were, however, others also, for example, the Venus oracle. A new cultural germ was planted into what could thus be fostered in the Egyptian people through these oracle establishments. It originated with a great leader who had undergone his training within the Persian Zarathustra mysteries. He was the reincarnation of a personality who had been a disciple of the great Zarathustra himself. If we wish to adhere to a historical name, he may be called "Hermes." By absorbing the Zarathustra mysteries he could find the right path on which to guide the Egyptian people. This folk, in earth life between birth and death, directed its mind to the physical sense world in such a way that although it could behold the spiritual world behind the physical only to a limited degree, it recognized in the physical world the laws of the spiritual world. Thus the Egyptian could not be taught that the spiritual world was a world with which he could become familiar on earth. But he could be shown how the human being would live in a body-free condition after death with the world of the spirits who during the earth period appear through their imprint in the realm of the physical-sensory. Hermes taught that to the degree the human being employs his forces on earth in order to act within it according to the aims of spiritual powers, it is possible for him to be united after death with these powers. Especially those who have been most zealously active in this direction during life between birth and death will become united with the exalted Sun Being—with Osiris. On the Chaldean-Babylonian side of this cultural stream the directing of the human mind to the physical-sensory was more marked than on the Egyptian side. The laws of this world were investigated and from the sensory counterparts perception was directed to the spiritual archetypes. The people, nevertheless, remained stuck fast in the world of the senses in many respects. Instead of the spirit of the star, the star itself, and instead of other spiritual beings, their earthly counterparts were pushed into the foreground. Only the leaders acquired really deep knowledge of the laws of the supersensible world and their interaction with the sense world. Here a contrast between the knowledge of the initiates and the erroneous beliefs of the people came into evidence more strongly than anywhere else.

Quite different conditions prevailed in Southern Europe and Western Asia where the fourth post-Atlantean cultural epoch flourished. We may call this the Greco-Latin cultural epoch. In these countries the descendants of human beings of the most varied regions of the ancient world had gathered. There were oracle establishments that followed the example of the various Atlantean oracles. There were men who possessed, as a natural faculty, the heritage of ancient clairvoyance, and there were some who were able to attain to it with comparatively little training. In special places the traditions of the ancient initiates were not only

241

preserved, but there arose worthy successors who trained pupils capable of raising themselves to exalted stages of spiritual perception. Simultaneously, these people bore the impulse in themselves to create a realm within the sense world that expressed in perfect form the spiritual within the physical. Beside much else, Greek art is a consequence of this impulse. One need only penetrate into the Greek temple with spiritual vision to recognize that in such a marvel of art the physical material is transformed by the human being in such a way that every detail is an expression of the spiritual. The Greek temple is the "dwelling place of the spirit." In its forms is to be seen what otherwise only the spiritual vision of supersensible perception can recognize. A Zeus or Jupiter temple is shaped in such a way that for the physical eye it represents a worthy abode for what the guardian of the Zeus or Jupiter initiation perceived with the spiritual eye. Thus it is with all Greek art. In mysterious ways the wisdom of the initiates poured into poets, artists, and thinkers. In the cosmogonies of the ancient Greek philosophers we find again the mysteries of the initiates in the form of concepts and ideas. The influence of spiritual life and the mysteries of the Asiatic and African centers of initiation flowed into these peoples and their leaders. The great Indian teachers, the companions of Zarathustra, and the adherents of Hermes had trained their pupils. These or their successors now founded initiation centers in which the ancient knowledge was revived in a new form. These are the mysteries of antiquity. Here the pupils were prepared to reach states of consciousness through which they were able to attain a perception of the spirit world.[1] From these initiation centers wisdom flowed to those who fostered spiritual impulses in Asia Minor, in Greece, and Italy. (In the Greek world the important initiation centers of the Orphic and Eleusinian mysteries arose. In the Pythagorean school of wisdom the after-effects of the great doctrines and methods of the wisdom of primeval ages appeared. In his wide journeying Pythagoras had been initiated into the secrets of the most varied mysteries.)

*   *   *

The life of man between birth and death—in the post-Atlantean age—had, however, its influence also upon the body-free state after death. The more the human being turned his interest toward the physical-sensory world, the greater was the possibility of Ahriman penetrating into the soul during earth life and of his retaining power beyond death. Among the peoples of ancient India this danger was still insignificant, because they had, during earth life, felt the physical world of the senses to be an illusion. As a result, they were able to elude the power of Ahriman. The danger of the prehistoric Persian people was much greater, because in the life between birth and death they had turned their interest toward the physical world of the senses. They would have fallen prey to Ahriman to a high degree, had Zarathustra not through his teaching about the God of Light drawn attention in an impressive manner to the fact that behind the physical-sensory world there exists

---

[1] More detailed descriptions of these mysteries of antiquity are to be found in my book, *Christianity as Mystical Fact*. More on this subject is given in the last chapter of this book.

243

the world of the Spirits of Light. In proportion to the absorption into the soul of this visualized world by the people of the Persian culture did they escape from the clutches of Ahriman during earth life and likewise during the life after death, when they prepared for a new earth life. During earth life the power of Ahriman leads to the consideration of physical-sensory existence as the only one, thus barring all outlook into the spiritual world. In the spiritual world this power leads the human being to complete isolation, to concentration of all interests only upon himself. Human beings who at death are in the power of Ahriman are reborn as egotists.

At present we are able in spiritual science to describe life between death and a new birth as it is when the Ahrimanic influence has been overcome to a certain degree. In this way it has been described by the writer of this book in other writings and in the first chapters of this book, and thus it must be described in order to make plausible what the human being can experience in this state of existence when he has gained the true spiritual perception of what really exists. Whether the individual experiences it to a greater or lesser degree depends on his victory over the Ahrimanic influence. Man approaches more and more what is possible for him to be in the spiritual world. How this degree of attainment can be impaired by other influences must here be held clearly in mind in considering the path of human evolution.

It was the task of Hermes to see that the Egyptians prepared themselves during earth life for companionship with the Spirit of Light. Since, however, during that time human interests between birth and death were already shaped in such a way that it was possible only to a slight degree to penetrate the veil of the physical-sensory, the spiritual perception of the soul remained also clouded after death. The perception of the world of light remained dim.—The veiling over of the spiritual world after death reached a climax for the souls who entered the body-free state from an incarnation in the Greco-Latin culture. During earth life they had brought the culture of the sensory-physical existence to full flower, and they had thus doomed themselves to a shadow existence after death. The Greek, therefore, felt that his life after death was only a shadow-like existence; and it was not mere empty talk but the feeling for truth when the hero of that age, turning toward the sense world, says, "Rather a beggar on earth than a king in the realm of the shades." This was still more evident among those Asiatic peoples who also in their reverence and adoration had only directed their gaze toward the sensory counterparts instead of toward the spiritual archetypes. During the time of the Greco-Latin cultural period a large part of mankind was in the condition here described. We can see how the mission of man in the post-Atlantean epoch, which consisted of his mastery of the physical sense world, had to lead of necessity to an estrangement from the spiritual world. Thus what is great on the one hand is of necessity connected with what is decadent on the other. —In the mysteries, the connection of the human being with the spiritual world was fostered. The initiates of these mysteries were able, in special states of the soul, to receive the revelations of this world. They were more or less the successors of the Atlantean guardians of the oracles. What was concealed through the impulses of Lucifer and Ahriman was unveiled to them. Lucifer concealed from the human being that part of the spiritual world that, without his cooperation, had poured into his astral body right up to the middle of the Atlantean epoch. If the ether body had not been partially separated from the physical, man would have been able to experience this region of the spirit world as an inner soul revelation. Because of the Luciferic impulse he could only experience it in special states of the soul. Then a spiritual world appeared to him in the vesture of the astral. The corresponding beings revealed themselves in shapes that bore only the higher members of human nature, and in these members they carried the astrally visible symbols of their special spiritual powers. Superhuman forms manifested themselves in this way.— After the encroachment of Ahriman another kind of initiation was added to this one. Ahriman has concealed all that part of the spiritual world that would have appeared behind physical sense-perception, if his encroachment had not occurred after the middle of the Atlantean epoch. The initiates owed the revelation of this part of the spiritual world to the fact that they practiced in their souls all those faculties that the human being had acquired since that time to a degree far greater than the one required in order to gain the impressions of sensory-physical existence. Through it the spiritual powers lying behind the forces of nature were revealed to them. They were able to speak of the spiritual beings behind nature. The creative powers of the forces active in nature below the human being revealed themselves to them. What had continued to be active from the *Saturn, Sun* and the ancient *Moon* evolutions and had formed the human physical, ether, and astral bodies, as

246

well as the mineral, plant, and animal kingdoms, formed the content of one type of mysteries. These mysteries were under Ahriman's influence. What had led to the development of sentient, intellectual, and consciousness soul was revealed in a second type of mystery. What, however, was only possible to be prophesied by the mysteries was that in the course of time a human being would appear with an astral body in which, despite Lucifer, the light world of the Sun Spirit would become conscious through the ether body without special soul states. And the physical body of this human being must be of such a nature that that part of the spiritual world would be manifest to him that Ahriman is able to conceal up to the time of physical death. Physical death cannot change anything for this human being during life; that is to say, physical death cannot have any power over him. In such a human being the ego manifests in such a way that the physical life contains at the same time the whole spiritual life. Such a being is the bearer of the Spirit of Light, to Whom the initiate lifts himself in a twofold way, either by being led to the spirit of the super-human or to the being of the powers of nature in special states of the soul. Since the initiates of the mysteries predicted that such a human being would appear in the course of time, they were the prophets of Christ.

As special prophet in this sense, a personality arose in a people that through natural heritage bore within itself the characteristics of the peoples of the Middle East and, through education, the teachings of the Egyptians; these people were the Israelites. The prophet was Moses. So many influences of initiation had entered the soul of Moses that in special states of consciousness the spiritual

247

being who had assumed, in the normal course of *Earth* evolution, the role of molding human consciousness from the moon, manifested himself to him. In thunder and lightning Moses recognized not only the physical phenomena, but the manifestations of the spirit just described. At the same time, however, the other kind of mysteries had affected his soul to such a degree that he perceived in astral visions how the super-human spirit becomes human through the ego. Thus the Being Who had to come revealed Himself to Moses from two directions as the highest form of the Ego.

With Christ there appeared in human form what the high Sun Being had prepared as the exalted paragon of earthly man. With this appearance all mystery wisdom had in a certain regard to assume a new form. Previously this wisdom existed exclusively in order to enable the human being to bring himself to a soul state that allowed him to behold the kingdom of the Sun Spirit outside of earthly evolution. Now mystery wisdom was allotted the task of making the human being capable of recognizing the Christ Who had become man, and from this center of all wisdom to understand the natural and spiritual world.

At the moment in the life of Christ Jesus, when His astral body contained everything that the Luciferic impulse can conceal, He assumed His mission as teacher of mankind. From this moment onward the aptitude was implanted in human earth evolution for receiving the wisdom through which the physical earthly goal can by degrees be attained. At the moment when the event of Golgotha was accomplished, the other aptitude was injected into mankind by which it is possible to turn the influence of Ahriman to good. Henceforth the human being is able to carry

248

with him out of life through the portals of death what releases him from isolation in the spiritual world. The event of Palestine is not only the center of the physical evolution of mankind, but it is also the center of the other worlds to which the human being belongs. When the "Mystery of Golgotha" was accomplished, when "Death on the Cross" was suffered, the Christ appeared in the world in which souls tarry after death, and in that region He set bounds to the power of Ahriman. From this moment the realm that was named by the Greeks the "kingdom of the shades" was illuminated by that spiritual lightning flash that showed its inhabitants that henceforth light would again appear in it. What was attained through the Mystery of Golgotha for the physical world threw its light into the spiritual world.—Thus the post-Atlantean human evolution was, up to this event, an ascent for the physical world of the senses, but it was at the same time a descent for the spiritual. Everything that flowed into the world of the senses poured forth from what had already existed in the spiritual world from primeval ages. Since the Christ event, human beings who elevate themselves to the Christ mystery are able to carry with them into the spiritual world what they have acquired in the sense world. It flows back again from the spiritual world into the earthly-sensory world by human beings bringing back with them into reincarnation what the Christ impulse has become for them in the world of spirit between death and rebirth.

What the Christ event bestowed upon mankind's evolution acted within it like a seed. The seed can ripen only gradually. Only the very smallest part of the new wisdom's profundity has penetrated physical existence up to the present. This existence stands just at the beginning of Christian evolution. During the succeeding centuries that have elapsed since that event, Christian evolution has been able to unveil only as much of its inner nature as human beings, peoples, were capable of receiving, were capable of absorbing with their mental capacities. The first form into which this knowledge could be poured may be described as an all-encompassing ideal of life. As such it opposed what in the post-Atlantean humanity had fashioned itself as modes of life. We have already described the conditions that prevailed in the evolution of mankind since the re-population of the earth in the Lemurian age. The human beings, as to their soul nature, may thus be traced back to various beings who, returning from other worlds, incarnated in the bodily descendants of the ancient Lemurians. The various human races are a result of this fact, and, in consequence of their karma, the most varied life-interests appeared in the reincarnated souls. As long as the after-effects of all this prevailed, the ideal of a "common humanity" could not exist. Mankind proceeded from a unity, but *Earth* evolution up to the present has led to differentiation. In the Christ-concept an ideal is given that counteracts all differentiation, for in the human being Who bears the name of Christ live also the forces of the exalted Sun Being in Whom every human ego finds its origin. The Israelites felt themselves still as a folk, the human being as a member of this folk. At the outset the fact that in the Christ Jesus lives the ideal man Who is not touched by the conditions of separation was only comprehended in thought, and Christianity became the ideal of an all-encompassing brotherhood. Disregarding all separate inter-

250

ests and separate relationships, the feeling arose that the inmost ego of every human being has the same origin. (Alongside all earthly forefathers the common father of all human beings appears. "I and the Father are One.")

In Europe in the fourth, fifth, and sixth centuries A.D. a cultural age was prepared that began in the fifteenth century and still continues today. It was gradually to replace the fourth, Greco-Latin, period. It is the fifth post-Atlantean culture period. The peoples, which after various migrations and most manifold destinies had made themselves pillars of this age, were descendants of those Atlanteans who had had the least contact with what had occurred in the meantime in the four preceding cultural epochs. They had not penetrated into the regions in which the cultures in question took root, but they had in their way continued the Atlantean cultures. There were among them many people who had preserved to a high degree the heritage of the ancient dreamlike clairvoyance, the intermediate state between waking and sleeping already described. Such individuals were acquainted with the spiritual world through their own experience and were able to communicate what takes place in that world to their fellow-men. A treasure house of narrative about spiritual beings and spiritual events was built up. The treasures of folk fairy tales and myths arose originally from such spiritual experiences. For the dreamlike clairvoyance of many people lasted right on into times not far removed from our present day. There were other human individuals who had lost their clairvoyance but who acquired the faculties of perception in the sensory-physical world through feelings and sensations that corresponded to these clairvoyant experiences. Here, also, the Atlantean oracles had their successors. There were mysteries everywhere. In these mysteries, however, the kinds of secrets of initiation were predominantly developed that led to the revelation of the region of the spirit world that Ahriman keeps concealed. It is the spiritual powers behind the forces of nature that were revealed in these mysteries. In the mythologies of the European nations are contained the remnants of what the initiates of these mysteries were able to communicate to human beings. These mythologies, however, contained also the other concealed wisdom, although in less complete form than it was contained in the Southern and Eastern mysteries. Superhuman beings were also known in Europe. Yet they appeared in a state of constant strife with the companions of Lucifer. The God of Light was proclaimed, but in such a form that it was impossible to say whether He would overcome Lucifer. But as a compensation for this, the future Christ form shone also into these mysteries. It was proclaimed that His kingdom would replace the kingdom of the other God of Light. (All myths about the Twilight of the Gods—the *Götterdämmerung*—and similar events have their origin in this knowledge of the European mysteries. Such influences caused a cleavage in the soul of the human beings of the fifth cultural epoch that still continues on into the present and shows itself in the most manifold phenomena of life. The soul did not preserve from ancient times the urge toward the spirit so strongly that it would have been able to retain the connection between the spirit and sense worlds. It retained it merely in the development of its feelings and sensations, but not, however, as a direct perception of the supersensible world.

252

On the other hand, the attention of the human being was directed more and more toward the world of the senses and its control. The powers of the intellect that awoke in the last part of the Atlantean epoch, all the forces in the human being of which the physical brain is the instrument were developed for the sense world and for its knowledge and control. Two worlds, so to speak, developed in the human breast. One is turned toward sensory-physical existence, the other is receptive to the revelation of the spiritual in order to penetrate it through feeling and sensation, but without perceiving it. The tendencies toward this cleavage of the soul were already present when the teaching of Christ streamed into the regions of Europe. This evangel of the spirit was received into human hearts, penetrated sensation and feeling, but could not find the connection with what the intellect, directed toward the senses, explored in the physical-sensory existence. What we know today as the contrast of outer science and spiritual knowledge is but a consequence of this fact. The Christian mysticism of Eckhardt, Tauler, and others, is a result of the permeation of feeling and sensation with Christianity. The science of the sense world and its results in life are the consequences of the other side of the soul's capacities. We owe the progress in the field of outer material culture entirely to this separation of capacities. Because the human faculties that have the brain as their instrument turned onesidedly to physical life, they were able to attain to the increase in power that made possible modern science and technology. This material culture could originate only among the nations of Europe, for they are the descendants of Atlantean ancestors who developed the tendency for the physical sense world into faculties only when this tendency had attained a certain maturity. Previously these descendants let it slumber, and they were nourished by the heritage of Atlantean clairvoyance and the communications of their initiates. While outwardly spiritual culture had yielded only to these influences, the sense for the material domination of the world gradually matured.

At present, however, the dawn of the sixth post-Atlantean cultural period already proclaims itself. For what is to arise in human evolution at a certain time begins to ripen in the preceding age. What is already able to show its beginnings at present is the discovery of the link that unites the two impulses in the human breast: material culture and life in the world of the spirit. For this purpose it is necessary that the results of spiritual perception are comprehended, and also that the manifestations of the spirit are recognized in the observations and experiences of the sense world. The sixth cultural epoch will bring the harmony between these two impulses to complete development. With this, the considerations of this book have advanced to a point where they can pass over from a view of the past to one of the future. It is, however, better if this view is preceded by a consideration of the knowledge of the higher worlds and of initiation. Then we shall have an opportunity to present briefly this view of the future, as far as this is possible within the framework of this book.

V

COGNITION OF THE
HIGHER WORLDS. INITIATION.

B ETWEEN birth and death man, at his present evolutionary stage, lives in ordinary life through three soul
states: waking, sleeping, and the state between them,
dreaming. Dreaming will be briefly considered later on in
this book. Here let us first consider life in its two chief alternating states—waking and sleeping. Man acquires a
knowledge of higher worlds if he develops a third soul state
besides sleep and waking. During its waking state the soul
surrenders itself to sense-impressions and thoughts that are
aroused by these impressions. During sleep the sense-
impressions cease, but the soul also loses its consciousness.
The experiences of the day sink into the sea of unconsciousness. Let us now imagine that the soul might be able
during sleep to become conscious despite the exclusion of
all sense-impressions as is the case in deep sleep, and even
though the memories of the day's experiences were lacking.

255

Would the soul, in that case, find itself in a state of nothingness? Would it be unable to have any experiences? An answer to these questions is only possible if a similar state of consciousness can actually be induced, if the soul is able to experience something even though no sense-activities and no memory of them are present in it. The soul, in regard to the ordinary outer world, would then find itself in a state similar to sleep, and yet it would not be asleep, but, as in the waking state, it would confront a real world.— Such a state of consciousness can be induced if the human being can bring about the soul experiences made possible by spiritual science; and everything that this science describes concerning the worlds that lie beyond the senses is the result of research in just such a state of consciousness. —In the preceding descriptions some information has been given about higher worlds. In this chapter—as far as it is possible in this book—we shall deal with the means through which the state of consciousness necessary for this method of research is developed.

This state of consciousness resembles sleep only in a certain respect, namely, through the fact that all outer sense-activities cease with its appearance; also all thoughts are stilled that have been aroused through these sense-activities. Whereas in sleep the soul has no power to experience anything consciously, it is to receive this power from the indicated state of consciousness. Through it a perceptive faculty is awakened in the soul that in ordinary life is only aroused by the activities of the senses. The soul's awakening to such a higher state of consciousness may be called *initiation*.

The means of initiation lead from the ordinary state of

waking consciousness into a soul activity through which spiritual organs of observation are employed. These organs are present in the soul in a germinal state; they must be developed.—It may happen that a human being at a certain moment in the course of his life, without special preparation, makes the discovery in his soul that such higher organs have developed in him. This has come about as a sort of involuntary self-awakening. Such a human being will find that through it his entire nature is transformed. A boundless enrichment of his soul experiences occurs. He will find that there is no knowledge of the sense world that gives him such bliss, such soul satisfaction, and such inner warmth as he now experiences through the revelation of knowledge inaccessible to the physical eye. Strength and certainty of life will pour into his will from a spiritual world.—There are such cases of self-initiation. They should, however, not tempt us to believe that this is the one and only way and that we should wait for such self-initiation, doing nothing to bring about initiation through proper training. Nothing need be said here about self-initiation, for it can appear without observing any kind of rules. How the human being may develop through training the organs of perception that lie embryonically in the soul will be described here. People who do not feel the least trace of an especial impulse to do something for the development of themselves may easily say, "Human life is directed by spiritual powers with whose guidance no one should attempt to interfere; we should wait patiently for the moment when such powers consider it proper to open another world to the soul." It may indeed be felt by such human beings as a sort of insolence or as an unjustified de-

257

sire to interfere with the wisdom of spiritual guidance. Individuals who think thus will only arrive at a different
point of view when a certain thought makes a sufficiently
strong impression upon them. When they say to themselves, "Wise spiritual guidance has given me certain faculties; it did not bestow them upon me to be left unused, but
to be employed. The wisdom of this guidance consists in
the fact that it has placed in me the germinal elements of a
higher state of consciousness. I shall understand this guidance only when I feel it obligatory that everything be revealed to the human being that can be revealed through
his spiritual powers." If such a thought has made a sufficiently strong impression on the soul, the above doubts
about training for a higher state of consciousness will disappear.

Other doubts, however, can still arise about such training. We may say, "The development of inner soul capacities penetrates into the most concealed holy of holies of
the human being. It involves a certain transformation of
his entire nature. The means for such a transformation
cannot, by its very nature, be thought out by ourselves.
For the way of reaching higher worlds can only be known
to him who knows the way into these worlds through his
own experience. If we turn to such a personality, we permit
him to have an influence over the soul's most concealed
holy of holies."—Whoever thinks thus would not be especially reassured even though the means of bringing about a
higher state of consciousness were presented to him in a
book. For the point of the matter is not whether we receive
this information verbally or whether someone having the
knowledge of this means presents it in a book that we then

read. There are persons, however, who possess the knowledge of the rules for the development of the spiritual organs of perception and who are of the opinion that these rules ought not to be entrusted to a book. Such people usually do not consider it permissible to publish certain truths relating to the spiritual world. This view, however—considering the present stage of human evolution—must, in a certain sense, be declared outmoded. It is correct, in regard to the publication of the rules in question, that we may do so only to a certain point. Yet the information given leads far enough for those who employ it for soul training to reach a point in the development of their knowledge from which they can then continue on the path. One can only visualize the further direction of this path correctly by what one has experienced previously on it. From all these facts, doubts may arise about the spiritual path of knowledge. These doubts disappear if one holds in mind the nature of the course of development that is indicated by the training appropriate to our age. We shall speak here about this path. Other methods of training will only be briefly touched upon.

The training to be described here places in the hands of the person who has the will for his higher development the means for undertaking the transformation of his soul. Any dangerous interference with the inner nature of the disciple would only occur were the teacher to undertake this transformation by means that elude the consciousness of the pupil. No *proper* instruction for spiritual development in our age employs such means. A proper instruction does not make the pupil a blind instrument. It gives him the rules of conduct, and he then carries them out. There is no

259

need to withhold the reason why this or that rule of conduct is given. The acceptance of the rules and their employment by a person who seeks spiritual development need not be a matter of blind faith. Blind faith should be completely excluded from this domain. Whoever considers the nature of the human soul, as far as it is possible through ordinary self-examination without spiritual training, may ask himself after encountering the rules recommended for spiritual training, "How can these rules be effective in the life of the soul?" It is possible to answer this question satisfactorily prior to any training by the unprejudiced employment of common sense. We are able to *understand* correctly the way of working of these rules prior to their practice. But it can be *experienced* only during training. The experience, however, will always be accompanied by understanding if we accompany each step with sound judgment, and at the present time a true spiritual science will only indicate rules for training upon which sound judgment may be brought to bear. Anyone who is willing to surrender himself to such training only, and who does not permit himself to be driven to blind faith by prejudice of any kind, will find that all doubts disappear. Objections to a proper training for a higher state of consciousness will not disturb him.

Even for a person whose inner maturity can lead him sooner or later to self-awakening of the spiritual organs of perception such training is not superfluous, but on the contrary it is quite especially suited to him. For there are but few cases in which such a person, prior to self-initiation, is not compelled to pass through the most varied, crooked and useless byways. Training spares him these deviations.

It leads straight forward. If self-initiation takes place for such a soul, it is caused by its having acquired the necessary maturity in the course of previous lives. It may easily happen, however, that just such a soul has a certain dim presentiment of its maturity and through this presentiment is inclined to reject the proper training. This presentiment may produce a certain pride that hinders faith in a true spiritual training. It is possible that a certain stage of soul development may remain concealed up to a certain age in human life and only then appear, but training may be just the right means of bringing forth this stage. If the individual pays no heed to such training, it may happen that his ability remains concealed during his present life and will only reappear in some subsequent life.

In regard to the training for supersensible knowledge described here, it is important to avoid certain obvious misunderstandings. One of these may arise through thinking that training would transform man into a different being in regard to his entire life-conduct. It cannot, however, be a question of giving man general instructions for his conduct of life, but of telling him about soul-exercises which, properly performed, will give him the possibility of observing the supersensible. These exercises have no direct influence upon the part of his life-functions that lies outside the observation of the supersensible. *In addition* to these life-functions the human being acquires the gift of supersensible observation. The function of this observation is as much separated from the ordinary functions of life as the state of waking is from that of sleeping. The one cannot disturb the other in the least. Whoever, for example, wishes to permeate the ordinary course of life with impressions of supersensible perception resembles an invalid whose sleep would be continually interrupted by injurious awakenings. It must be possible for the free will of the trained person to induce the state in which supersensible reality is observed. Training, to be sure, is *indirectly* connected with certain instructions concerning conduct in as far as, without an ethically determined conduct of life, an insight into the supersensible is impossible or injurious. Consequently, much of what leads to the perception of the supersensible is at the same time a means of ennobling the conduct of life. On the other hand, as a result of insight into the supersensible world, higher moral impulses are recognized that are also valid for the sensory-physical world. Certain moral necessities are only recognized from out this world.—A second misunderstanding would arise were it believed that any soul function leading to supersensible knowledge might produce changes in the physical organism. Such functions have nothing whatsoever to do with anything in the realm of physiology or other branches of natural science. They are pure soul-spirit processes, entirely devoid of anything physical, like sound thinking and perception. Nothing happens in the soul through such a function—considering its character—that is different from what takes place when it thinks or judges in a healthy fashion. Just as much or as little as sound thinking has to do with the body, so do the processes of true training for supersensible cognition have to do with the body. Anything that has a different relationship to man is not true spiritual training, but its distortion. What follows is to be taken in the sense of what has been said here. Only because supersensible knowledge is something that proceeds from the entire soul of man will it ap-

262

pear as if things were required for this training that would transform man into something else. In truth it is a question of instruction about functions enabling the soul to bring into its life moments in which the supersensible may be observed.

*   *   *

The attainment of a supersensible state of consciousness can only proceed from everyday waking consciousness. In this consciousness the soul lives before its elevation. Through the training the soul acquires a means of lifting itself out of everyday consciousness. The training that is under consideration here offers among the first means those that still may be designated as functions of everyday consciousness. The most important means are just those that consist of quiet activities of the soul. They involve the opening of the soul to quite definite thoughts. These thoughts exercise, by their very nature, an awakening power upon certain hidden faculties of the human soul. They are to be distinguished from the visualizations of everyday waking life, which have the task of depicting outer things. The more truly they do this, the truer they are, and it is part of their nature to be true in this sense. The visualizations, however, to which the soul must open itself for the purpose of spiritual training have no such task. They are so constructed that they do not depict anything external but have in themselves the peculiarity of effecting an awakening in the soul. The best visualizations for this purpose are emblematic or symbolical. Nevertheless, other visualizations may also be employed, for it is not a question of what they contain, but solely a question of the soul's directing its

263

powers in such a way that it has nothing else in mind but the visualized image under consideration. While the powers of everyday soul-life are distributed in many directions —the visualized mental representations changing very rapidly—in spiritual training everything depends upon the concentration of the entire soul-life upon one visualization. This visualization must, by means of free will, be placed at the center of consciousness. Symbolic visualized images are, therefore, better than those that represent outer objects or processes, for the latter have a point of attachment to the outer world, making the soul less dependent upon itself than when it employs symbolic visualizations that are formed through the soul's own energy. The essential is not *what* is visualized; what is essential is the fact that the visualization, through the way it is visualized, liberates the soul from dependence on the physical.

We understand what it means to immerse ourselves in a visualized image if we consider, first of all, the *concept of memory*. If, for instance, we look at a tree and then away from it so that we can no longer see it, we are then able to re-awaken the visualization of the tree in the soul by recollecting it. This visualization of the tree, which we have when the eye no longer beholds the latter, is a *memory* of the tree. Now let us imagine that we preserve this memory in the soul; we permit the soul, as it were, to rest upon the visualized memory picture; and at the same time we endeavor to exclude all other visualizations. Then the soul is *immersed* in the visualized memory picture of the tree. We then have to do with the soul's immersion in a visualized picture or image; yet this visualization is the image of an object perceived by the senses. But if we undertake this

264

with a visualized image formed in the consciousness by an act of independent will, we shall then be able by degrees to attain the effect upon which everything depends.

We shall now endeavor to describe an example of inner immersion in a symbolic visualization. Such a visualization must first be fashioned in the soul. This may happen in the following way. We visualize a plant as it roots in the earth, as leaf by leaf sprouts forth, as its blossom unfolds, and now we think of a human being beside this plant. We make the thought alive in the soul of how he has characteristics and faculties which, when compared with those of the plant, may be considered more perfect than the latter. We contemplate how, according to his feelings and his will, he is able to move about hither and thither, while the plant is chained to the earth. Furthermore we say that the human being is indeed more perfect than the plant, but he also shows peculiarities that are not to be found in the plant. Just because of their nonexistence in the plant the latter may appear to me in a certain sense more perfect than the human being who is filled with desire and passion and follows them in his conduct. I may speak of his being led astray by his desires and passions. I see that the plant follows the pure laws of growth from leaf to leaf, that it opens its blossom passionlessly to the chaste rays of the sun. Furthermore, I may say to myself that the human being has a greater perfection than the plant, but he has purchased this perfection at the price of permitting instincts, desires, and passions to enter into his nature besides the forces of the plant, which appear pure to us. I now visualize how the green sap flows through the plant and that it is an expression of the pure, passionless laws of growth. I then visualize how the red blood flows through the human veins and how it is the expression of the instincts, desires, and passions. All this I permit to arise in my soul as vivid thought. Then I visualize further how the human being is capable of evolution; how he may purify and cleanse his instincts and passions through his higher soul powers. I visualize how, as a result of this, something base in these instincts and desires is destroyed and how the latter are reborn upon a higher plane. Then the blood may be conceived of as the expression of the purified and cleansed instincts and passions. In my thoughts I look now, for example, upon the rose and say, In the red rose petal I see the color of the green plant sap transformed into red, and the red rose, like the green leaf, follows the pure, passionless laws of growth. The red of the rose may now become the symbol of a blood that is the expression of purified instincts and passions that have stripped off all that is base, and in their purity resemble the forces active in the red rose. I now seek not merely to imbue my intellect with such thoughts but to bring them to life in my feelings. I may have a feeling of bliss when I think of the purity and passionlessness of the growing plant; I can produce within myself the feeling of how certain higher perfections must be purchased through the acquirement of instincts and desires. This can then transform the feeling of bliss, which I have felt previously, into a grave feeling; and then a feeling of liberating joy may stir in me when I surrender myself to the thought of the red blood which, like the red sap of the rose, may become the bearer of inwardly pure experiences. It is of importance that we do not without feeling confront the thoughts that serve to construct such a symbolic visualization. After we have pondered on such thoughts and feelings for a time, we are to transform them into the following symbolic visualization. We visualize a black cross. Let this be the *symbol* of the destroyed base elements of instincts and passions, and at the center, where the arms of the cross intersect, let us visualize seven red, radiant roses arranged in a circle. Let these roses be the *symbol* of a blood that is the expression of purified, cleansed passions and instincts.[1] Such a symbolic visualization should be called forth in the soul in the way illustrated above through a visualized memory image. Such a visualization has a soul-awakening power if we surrender ourselves to it in inward meditation. We must seek to exclude all other thoughts during meditation. Only the characterized symbol is to hover in spirit before the soul as intensely as possible.—It is not without significance that this symbol is not simply given here as an awakening visualized picture, but that it has first been constructed by means of certain thoughts about plant and man. For the effect of such a symbol depends upon the fact of its having been constructed in the way described before it is employed in inner meditation. If we visualize the symbol without first having fashioned it in our own souls, it remains cold and much less effective than

[1] The point is not whether this or that idea of natural science finds the above thoughts justified or not. For it is a question of the development of such thoughts by means of plant and man that may be gained, without any theory, through simple, direct perception. Such thoughts have indeed their importance also, besides the theoretical ideas about the things of the outer world, which in other connections are of no less importance. Here thoughts do not have the purpose of representing a fact scientifically, but of constructing a *symbol* that proves itself effective in the soul, notwithstanding the objections that may occur to this or that individual in fashioning this symbol.

when it has received, through preparation, its soul-illuminating power. During meditation, however, we should not call forth in the soul all the preparatory thoughts, but merely let the visualized picture hover vividly before our inner eye, at the same time letting the *feeling* hold sway that has appeared as a result of the preparatory thoughts. Thus the symbol becomes a token alongside the feeling-experience, and its effectiveness lies in the dwelling of the soul in this inner experience. The longer we are able to dwell in it without the intervention of other, disturbing, thoughts, the more effective is the entire process. It is well, nevertheless, for us, outside the period dedicated to the actual meditation itself, to repeat the construction of the symbol by means of thoughts and feelings of the above described kind, so that the experience may not fade away. The more patience we exercise in this renewal, the more significant is the symbol for the soul. (In my book, *Knowledge of the Higher Worlds and Its Attainment*, other examples of means for inner meditation are given. Especially effective are the meditations characterized there about the growth and decay of the plant, about the slumbering creative forces in the plant seed, about the forms of crystals, and so forth. In the present book, the nature of meditation was to be described by a single example.)

Such a symbol, as is described here, portrays no outer thing or being that is brought forth by nature. But just because of this it has an awakening power for certain purely soul faculties. To be sure, someone might raise an objection. He might say, It is true, the symbol as a whole is certainly not produced by nature, but all its details are, nevertheless, borrowed from nature—the black color, the red roses, and the other details. All this is perceived by the senses. Anyone who may be disturbed by such an objection should consider that it is not the pictures of sense-perceptions that lead to the awakening of the higher soul faculties, but that this effect is produced only by the *manner of combining* these details, and this combination does not picture anything that is present in the sense world.

The process of effective meditation was illustrated here by a symbol, as an example. In spiritual training the most manifold pictures of this kind can be employed and they can be constructed in the most varied manner. Also certain sentences, formulae, even single words, upon which to meditate may be given. In every case these means to inner meditation have the objective of liberating the soul from sense-perception and of arousing it to an activity in which the impression upon the physical senses is meaningless and the development of the inner slumbering soul faculties becomes the essential. It may also be a matter of meditation upon mere feelings and sensations. This shows itself to be especially effective. Let us take, for example, the feeling of joy. In the normal course of life the soul may experience joy if an outer stimulus for it is present. If a soul with normal feelings perceives how a human being performs an action that is inspired by kindness of heart, this soul will feel pleased and happy about it. But this soul may then meditate on an action of this sort. It may say to itself, an action performed through goodness of heart is one in which the performer does not follow his own interest, but the interest of his fellow-man, and such an action may be designated morally good. The contemplating soul, however, may now free itself from the mental picture of the special case in the outer world that has given it joy or pleasure, and it may form the comprehensive idea of kindness of heart. It may perhaps think how kindness of heart arises by the one soul absorbing, so to speak, the interests of the other soul and making them its own, and it may now feel joy about this moral idea of kindness of heart. This is not the joy in this or that process in the sense world, but the joy in an *idea* as such. If we attempt to keep alive such joy in the soul for a certain length of time, then this is meditation on inner feeling, on inner sensation. The idea is not then the awakening factor of the inner soul faculties, but the holding sway, for a certain length of time, of the feeling within the soul that is not aroused through a mere single external impression. —Since supersensible knowledge is able to penetrate more deeply into the nature of things than ordinary thinking, it is able through its experiences to indicate feelings that act in a still higher degree upon the unfolding of the soul faculties, when they are employed in inner meditation. Although this is necessary for higher degrees of training, we should remember the fact that energetic meditation on such feelings and sensations, as for example have been characterized in the observation of kindness of heart, is able to lead very far.—Since human beings are varied in character, so are the effective means of training varied for the individual man.—In regard to the duration of meditation we have to consider that the effect is all the stronger, the more tranquilly and deliberately this meditation is carried out. But any excess in this direction should be avoided. A certain inner discretion that results through the exercises themselves may teach the pupil to keep within due bounds.

Such exercises in inner meditation will in general have to be carried on for a long time before the student himself is able to perceive any results. What belongs unconditionally to spiritual training is patience and perseverance. Whoever does not call up both of these within his soul and does not, in all tranquility, continuously carry out his exercises, so that patience and perseverance form the fundamental mood of the soul, cannot achieve much.

It will have become evident from the preceding exposition that meditation is a means of acquiring knowledge about higher worlds, but it will also have become evident that not just any content of thought will lead to it, but only a content that has been evolved in the manner described.

The path that has been indicated here leads, in the first place, to what may be called *imaginative* cognition. It is the first stage of higher cognition. Knowledge that rests upon sense-perception and upon the working over of the sense-perceptions through the intellect bound to the senses may be called, in the sense of spiritual science, "objective cognition." Beyond this lie the higher stages of knowledge, the first of which is imaginative cognition. The expression "imaginative" may call forth doubts in those who think "imagination" stands only for unreal imaginings, that is, a visualization of something that has no corresponding reality. In spiritual science, however, "imaginative" cognition is to be conceived as something coming into existence through a supersensible state of consciousness of the soul. What is perceived in this state are spiritual facts and

271

beings to which the senses have no access. Because this state is awakened in the soul by meditating on symbols or "imaginations," the world of this higher state of consciousness may be named the "imaginative" world, and the knowledge corresponding to it "imaginative" cognition. "Imaginative," therefore, means something which is "real" in a different sense from the facts and beings of physical sense-perception. The *content* of the visualizations that fill imaginative experience is of no importance, but of utmost importance is the soul faculty which is developed through this experience.

An obvious objection to the employment of the characterized symbolic visualizations is that their fashioning corresponds to a dreamlike thinking and to arbitrary imagining and therefore can bring forth only doubtful results. In regard to the symbols that lie at the foundation of true spiritual training, doubts of this character are unjustified. For the symbols are chosen in such a way that their connection with outer sense reality may be entirely disregarded and their value sought merely in the force with which they affect the soul when the latter withdraws all attention from the outer world, when it suppresses all impressions of the senses, and shuts out all thoughts that it may cherish as a result of outer stimuli. The process of meditation is best illustrated by a comparison with the state of sleep. On the one hand it resembles the latter, on the other it is the complete opposite. It is a sleep that represents, in regard to everyday consciousness, a higher waking state. The important point is that through concentration upon the visualization or picture in question the soul is compelled to draw forth much stronger powers from its own depths than it employs in everyday life or in everyday cognition. Its inner activity is thereby enhanced. It liberates itself from the bodily nature just as it does during sleep, but it does not, as in the latter case, pass over into unconsciousness, but becomes conscious of a world that it has not previously experienced. Although this soul state may be compared with sleep in regard to the liberation from the body, yet it may be described as an *enhanced waking state* when compared with everyday waking consciousness. Through this the soul experiences itself in its true inner, independent nature, while in the everyday waking state it becomes conscious of itself only through the help of the body because of the weaker unfolding of its forces in that state, and does not, therefore, experience itself, but is only aware of the picture that, like a reflection, the body (or properly speaking its processes) sketches for it.

The symbols that are constructed in the above described manner do, by their very nature, not yet relate to anything real in the spiritual world. They serve the purpose of detaching the human soul from sense-perception and from the brain instrument to which the intellect is bound at the outset. This detachment cannot occur in man prior to his feeling the following: I now visualize something by means of forces in connection with which my senses and my brain do not serve me as instruments. The first thing that the human being experiences on this path is such a liberation from the physical organs. He may then say to himself, "My consciousness is not extinguished when I disregard the sense-perceptions and ordinary intellectual thinking; I can lift myself out of them and then feel myself as a being

273

alongside the one I was previously." This is the first purely spiritual experience: the observation of a soul-spirit ego being. This, as a new self, has lifted itself out of the self that is only bound to the physical senses and the physical intellect. If without meditation the pupil had released himself from the world of the senses and intellect, he would have sunk into the "nothingness" of unconsciousness. The soul-spirit being, naturally, existed *before* meditation had taken place, but it did not yet have any organs of observing the spiritual world. It was somewhat similar to a physical body without eyes to see, or ears to hear. The force that was employed in meditation first has fashioned the soul-spirit organs out of the previously unorganized soul-spirit nature. The individual beholds first, therefore, what he has created. Thus, the first experience is, in a certain sense, self-perception. It belongs to the essence of spiritual training that the soul, through the practice of self-education, is at this point of its development fully conscious of the fact that at first it perceives itself in the world of pictures—imaginations—which appear as a result of the exercises described. Although these pictures appear as living in a new world, the soul must recognize that they are, at the outset, nothing but the reflection of its own being, strengthened through the exercises, and it must not only recognize this with proper discretion, but it must also have developed such a power of will that it can extinguish, can eliminate these pictures from consciousness at any time. The soul must be able to act within these pictures completely free and fully aware. This belongs to true spiritual training at this stage. If the soul were not able to do this it would be in the same circumstances, in the sphere of spiritual experience, in which a soul would find itself in the physical world, were its eyes fettered to the object upon which they gaze, powerless to withdraw them. Only one group of inner imaginative experiences constitutes an exception to this possibility of extinction. These experiences are *not* to be extinguished at this stage of spiritual training. They correspond to the kernel of the soul's own being, and the student of the spiritual recognizes in these pictures what, in himself, passes through repeated earth lives as his fundamental being. At this point the sensing of repeated earth lives becomes a real experience. In regard to everything else the independence of the experiences mentioned must rule, and only after having acquired the ability to bring about this extinction does the student approach the true external spiritual world. In place of what has been extinguished, something else appears that is recognized as spiritual reality. The student feels how he grows in his soul from the undefined into the defined. From the self-perception he then must proceed to an observation of an outer world of soul and spirit. This takes place when the student arranges his inner experiences in the sense that will be further indicated here.

In the beginning the soul of the student of the spiritual is weak in regard to everything that is to be perceived in the spiritual world. He will have to employ great inner energy in order to hold fast in meditation to the symbols or other visualizations that he has fashioned from the stimuli of the world of the senses. If, however, he wishes besides this to attain real observation in a higher world, he must be able *not only* to hold fast to these visualizations, but he must also, after he has done this, be able to sojourn in a

275

state in which no stimuli of the sensory world act upon the soul, but in which also the visualized imaginations themselves, characterized above, are extirpated from consciousness. What has been formed through meditation can only then appear in consciousness. It is important now that sufficient inner soul power be present in order really to perceive spiritually what has been formed through meditation, so that it may not elude the attention. This is, however, always the case with but weakly developed inner energy. What is thus constructed in the beginning as a soul-spirit organism and what is to be taken hold of by the student in self-perception is delicate and fleeting, and the disturbances of the outer world of the senses and its after-effects of memory are great, however much we may endeavor to hold them back. Not only the disturbances that we observe come into question here, but *much more,* indeed, those of which we are not conscious at all in everyday life.—The very nature of the human being, however, makes possible a state of transition in this regard. What the soul at the beginning cannot achieve in the waking state on account of the disturbances of the physical world, is possible in the state of sleep. Whoever surrenders to meditation will, by proper attention, become aware of something in sleep. He will feel that during sleep he does not "fall into a complete slumber," but that at times his soul is active in a certain way while sleeping. In such states the natural processes hold back the influences of the outer world that the waking soul is not yet able to prevent by means of its own power. If, however, the exercises of meditation have already been effective, the soul frees itself during sleep from unconsciousness and feels the world of soul

276

and spirit. This may happen in a twofold way. It may be clear to the human being during sleep that now he is in another world; or he may have the memory on awaking that he has been in another world. To the first belongs, indeed, greater inner energy than to the second. Therefore the latter will be more frequent for the beginner in spiritual training. By degrees this may go so far that the pupil feels on waking that he has been in another world during the whole sleep period, from which he has emerged on waking, and his memory of the beings and facts of this other world will become ever more definite. Something has taken place for the student of the spiritual in one form or another that may be called the continuity of consciousness. (The continuity of consciousness during sleep.) It is not at all meant by this, however, that man is *always* conscious during sleep. Much, however, has already been gained in the continuity of consciousness if the human being, who otherwise sleeps like ordinary man, has at certain times during sleep intervals in which he can consciously behold a world of soul and spirit, or if, after waking, he can look back again in memory upon such brief states of consciousness. It should not be forgotten, however, that what is described here may be only understood as a transitional state. It is good to pass through this state in the course of training, but one should certainly not believe that a conclusive perception in regard to the world of soul and spirit should be derived from it. The soul is uncertain in this state and cannot yet depend upon what it perceives. But through such experiences it gathers more and more power in order to succeed, also while awake, in warding off the disturbing influences of the physical outer and inner worlds, and thus to acquire the faculty of soul-spirit observation when impressions no longer come through the senses, when the intellect bound to the physical brain is silent, and when consciousness is freed even from the visualizations of meditation by means of which we have only prepared ourselves for spiritual perception.—Whatever is revealed by spiritual science in this or that form should never originate from any other soul-spirit observation than from one that has been made during the state of complete wakefulness.

Two soul experiences are important in the process of spiritual training. Through the one, man may say to himself, "Although I now disregard all the impressions the outer physical world may offer, nevertheless, I do not look into myself as though at a being in whom all activity is extinguished, but I look at one who is conscious of himself in a world of which I know nothing as long as I only permit myself to be stimulated by sense impressions and the ordinary impressions of the intellect." At this moment the soul has the feeling that it has given birth, in the manner described above, to a new being in itself as the kernel of its soul nature, and this being possesses characteristics quite different from those that previously existed in the soul.—The other experience consists in now having the old being like a second alongside the new. What, up to the present, the student knew as enclosing him becomes something that now confronts him, in a certain sense. He feels himself at times outside of what he had otherwise called his own being, *his* ego. It is as though he now lived in full consciousness in two egos. One of these is the being he has known up to the present. The other stands, like a being newly born, above it. The student feels how the first ego attains a certain independence of the second, just as the body of the human being has a certain independence of the first ego.—This experience is of great significance. For through it the human being knows what it means to live in the world that he strives to reach through training.

The second, the new-born ego, may now be trained to perceive within the spiritual world. There may be developed in this ego what, for the spiritual world, has the same significance the sense organs possess for the sensory-physical world. If this development has advanced to the necessary stage, then the human being will not only feel himself as a new-born ego, but he will now perceive spiritual facts and spiritual beings in his environment, just as he perceives the physical world through the physical senses. This is a *third* significant experience. In order completely to find his way about at this stage of spiritual training the human being must realize that, with the strengthening of soul powers, self-love and egotism will appear to a degree quite unknown to everyday soul-life. It would be a misunderstanding if someone were to believe that at this point only ordinary self-love is meant. This self-love increases at this stage of development to such a degree that it assumes the appearance of a nature force within the human soul, and in order to vanquish this strong egotism a rigorous strengthening of the will is necessary. This egotism is not produced by spiritual training; it is always present; it only comes to consciousness through spiritual experience. The training of the will must go hand in hand with the other spiritual training. A strong inclination exists to feel enraptured in the world that we have created for ourselves, and we must, in the manner described above, be able to extinguish, as it were, what we have striven to create with such great effort. In the imaginative world that has thus been reached the student must extinguish *himself.* Against this, however, the strongest impulses of egotism wage war.— The belief may easily arise that the exercises of spiritual training are something external, disregarding the *moral evolution* of the soul. It must be said concerning this that the moral force that is necessary for the indicated victory over egotism cannot be attained unless the moral condition of the soul is brought to a corresponding level. Progress in spiritual training is not thinkable without a corresponding moral progress. Without moral force the described victory over egotism is not possible. All talk about true spiritual training not being at the same time moral training does not conform to facts. Only the person who does not know such an experience can make the following objection by asking, "How are we to know that we are dealing with realities and not with mere visions, hallucinations, and so forth, when we *believe* we have spiritual perceptions?"—The facts are such, however, that the student who has reached the characterized stage by proper training is just as able to distinguish his own visualization from spiritual reality as a man with a healthy mind is able to distinguish the thought of a hot piece of iron from an actual one that he touches with his hand. Healthy experience, and nothing else, shows the difference. In the spiritual world also, life itself is the touchstone. Just as we know that in the sense world the mental picture of a piece of iron, be it thought ever so hot, will not burn the fingers, the trained spiritual student knows whether or not he experiences a spiritual fact only in his imaginings or whether *real* facts or beings make an impression upon his awakened spiritual organs of perception. The general rules that we must observe during spiritual training in order not to fall victim to illusions in this regard will be described later.

It is of greatest importance that the student of the spiritual has acquired a quite definite soul state when he becomes conscious of a new-born ego. For through his ego the human being attains to control of his sensations, feelings, thoughts, instincts, passions, and desires. Perception and thought cannot be left to themselves in the soul. They must be regulated through attentive thinking. It is the ego that employs these laws of thinking and through them brings order into the life of visualization and thought. It is similar with desires, instincts, inclinations, and passions. The ethical principles become guides of these soul powers. Through moral judgment the ego becomes the guide of the soul in this realm. If the human being now draws a higher ego out of his ordinary ego, the latter becomes independent in a certain sense. From this ego just as much of living force is withdrawn as is bestowed upon the higher ego. Let us suppose, however, the case in which the human being has not yet developed a sufficient ability and firmness in the laws of thought and in his power of judgment, and he wishes to give birth to his higher ego at this stage of development. He will be able to leave behind for his everyday ego only so much thought power as he has previously developed. If the measure of regulated thinking is too small, then there will appear a disordered, confused, fantastic thinking and judgment in the ordinary ego that has become independent. Because the new-born ego can only be weak in such a personality, the disturbed lower ego will gain domination over supersensible perception, and man will not show equilibrium in his power of judgment in observing the supersensible world. If he had developed sufficient ability in logical thinking, he would be able, without fear, to permit the ordinary ego to have its independence.—This is also true in the domain of the ethical. If the human being has not attained firmness in moral judgment, if he has not gained sufficient control over his inclinations, instincts, and passions, then he will make his ordinary ego independent in a state in which these soul powers act. It may happen that the human being in describing the knowledge he has experienced in the supersensible is not governed by the same high sense of truth that guides him in what he brings to his consciousness in the physical outer world. With such a demoralized sense of truth, he might believe anything to be spiritual reality that in truth is only his own fantastic imagining. Into this sense of truth there must act firmness of ethical judgment, certainty of character, keenness of conscience, which are developed in the lower, first ego, before the higher, second ego becomes active for the purpose of supersensible cognition.—What is said here must not discourage training, but it must be taken very seriously.

Anyone who has the strong will to do what brings the first ego to inner certainty in the exercise of its functions need not recoil from the liberation of his second ego, brought about through spiritual training for the sake of supersensible cognition. But he must keep in mind that self-deception has great power over the human being when it is a question of his feeling himself "mature" enough for some step. In the spiritual training described here, man attains such a development of his thought life that it is impossible for him to encounter the dangers of going astray, often presumed to be inevitable. This development of thought acts in such a way that all necessary inner experiences appear, but that they occur in the soul without being accompanied by damaging aberrations of fantasy. Without corresponding thought development the experiences may call forth a profound uncertainty in the soul. The method stressed here causes the experiences to appear in such a way that the student becomes completely familiar with them, just as he becomes familiar with the perceptions of the physical world in a healthy soul state. Through the development of thought life he becomes, as it were, an *observer* of what he experiences in himself, while, without this thought life, he stands heedless within the experience.

In a factual training certain qualities are mentioned that the student who wishes to find his way into the higher worlds should acquire through practice. These are, above all, control of the soul over its train of thought, over its will, and its feelings. The way in which this control is to be acquired through practice has a twofold purpose. On the one hand, the soul is to be imbued with firmness, certainty, and equilibrium to such a degree that it preserves these qualities, although from its being a second ego is born. On the other hand, this second ego is to be furnished with strength and inner consistency of character.

What is necessary for the thinking of man in spiritual training is, above all, objectivity. In the physical-sensory world, life is the human ego's great teacher of objectivity. Were the soul to let thoughts wander about aimlessly, it would be immediately compelled to let itself be corrected by life if it did not wish to come into conflict with it. The soul must think according to the course of the facts of life. If now the human being turns his attention away from the physical-sensory world, he lacks the compulsory correction of the latter. If his thinking is then unable to be its own corrective, it must become irrational. Therefore the thinking of the student of the spiritual must be trained in such a manner that it is able to give to itself direction and goal. Thinking must be its own instructor in inner firmness and the capacity to hold the attention strictly to one object. For this reason, suitable "thought exercises" are not to be undertaken with unfamiliar and complicated objects, but with those that are simple and familiar. Anyone who is able for months at a time to concentrate his thoughts daily at least for five minutes upon an ordinary object (for example a needle, a pencil, or any other simple object), and during this time to exclude all thoughts that have no bearing on the subject, has achieved a great deal in this regard. (We may contemplate a new object daily, or the same one for several days.) Also, the one who considers himself a thinker as a result of scientific training should not disdain to prepare himself for spiritual training in this manner. For if for a certain length of time we fasten our thoughts upon an object that is well known to us, we can be sure that we think in conformity with facts. If we ask ourselves what a pencil is composed of, how its materials are prepared, how they are brought together afterward, when pencils were invented, and so forth, we then conform our thoughts more to reality than if we reflect upon the origin of man, or upon the nature of life. Through *simple thought exercises* we acquire greater ability for factual thinking concerning the

Saturn, Sun, and *Moon* evolutions than through complicated and learned ideas. For in the first place it is not at all a question of thinking about this or that, but of thinking *factually by means of inner force.* If we have schooled ourselves in regard to factuality by a physical-sensory process, easily surveyed, then thought becomes accustomed to function in accordance with facts even though it does not feel itself controlled by the physical world of the senses and its laws, and we rid ourselves of the habit of letting our thoughts wander without relation to facts.

The soul must become a ruler in the sphere of the will as it must be in the world of thought. In the physical-sensory world, it is life itself that appears as the ruler. It emphasizes this or that need of the human being, and the will feels itself impelled to satisfy these needs. In higher training man must become accustomed to obey his own commands strictly. He who becomes accustomed to this will be less and less inclined to desire the non-essential. Dissatisfaction and instability in the life of will rest upon the desire for things the realization of which we cannot conceive clearly. Such dissatisfaction may bring the entire mental life into disorder when a higher ego is about to emerge from the soul. It is a good practice if one gives oneself for months, at a certain time of the day, the following command: Today, at this definite time, I shall perform this or that action. One then gradually becomes able to determine the time for this action and the nature of the thing to be done so as to permit its being carried out with great exactness. Thus one lifts oneself above the damaging attitude of mind found in, "I should like this, I want that," in which we do not at all consider the possibility of its accomplishment. A great personality—Goethe—lets a seeress say, "Him I love who desires the impossible." [1] And Goethe himself says, "To live in the idea means to treat the impossible as though it were possible." [2] Such expressions must not be used as objections to what is presented here. For the demand of Goethe and his seeress, Manto, can only be fulfilled by someone who has trained himself to desire what is possible, in order then to be able, through his strong will, to treat the "impossible" so that it is transformed through his will into the possible.

In regard to the world of feeling the soul should attain for spiritual training a certain degree of calmness. It is necessary for that purpose that the soul become ruler over expressions of joy and sorrow, of pleasure and pain. It is just in regard to the acquiring of this ability that much prejudice may result. One might imagine that one would become dull and without sympathy in regard to one's fellowmen if one should not feel joy with the joyful and with the painful, pain. Yet this is not the point in question. With the joyful the soul *should* rejoice, with sadness it *should* feel pain. But it should acquire the ability to control the *expression* of joy and sorrow, of pleasure and pain. If one endeavors to do *this*, one will soon notice that one does not become less sensitive, but on the contrary more receptive to all that is joyous and sorrowful in one's environment than one was previously. To be sure, if one wishes to acquire the ability with which we are concerned here, one must strictly observe oneself for a long period of time. One

---

[1] Goethe: *Faust* II.
[2] Goethe: *Verses in Prose.*

must see to it that one is able fully to sympathize with joy and sorrow without losing one's self-control so that one gives way to an involuntary expression of one's feelings. It is not the justified pain that one should suppress, but involuntary weeping; not the horror of an evil action, but the blind rage of anger; not attention to danger, but fruitless fear, and so forth.—Only through such practice does the student of the spiritual attain the tranquility of mind that is necessary to prevent the soul at the birth of the higher ego, and, above all, during its activity, from leading a second, abnormal life like a sort of *Doppelgänger*—soul double— alongside this higher ego. It is just in regard to these things that one should not surrender oneself to any sort of self-deception. It may appear to many a one that he already possesses a certain equanimity in ordinary life and therefore does not need this exercise. It is just such a person who doubly needs it. It may be quite possible to be calm when confronting the things of ordinary life, but when one ascends into a higher world, the lack of equilibrium that heretofore was only suppressed may assert itself all the more. It must be grasped that for spiritual training what one already *appeared* to possess previously is of less importance than the need to *practice,* according to exact rules, what one lacks. Although this sentence appears contradictory, it is, nevertheless, correct. Even though life has taught us this or that, the abilities *we have acquired by ourselves* serve the cause of spiritual training. If life has brought us excitability, we should break ourselves of the habit; if life has brought us complacency, then we should through self-education arouse ourselves to such a degree that the expression of the soul corresponds to the impression re-

287

ceived. Anyone who never laughs about anything has just as little control of his life as someone who, without any control whatever, is continually given to laughter.

For the control of thought and feeling there is a further means of education in the acquirement of the faculty that we may call *positiveness*. There is a beautiful legend that tells of how the Christ Jesus, accompanied by some other persons, passed by a dead dog lying on the roadside. While the others turned aside from the hideous spectacle, the Christ Jesus spoke admiringly of the animal's beautiful teeth. One can school oneself in order to attain the attitude of soul toward the world shown by this legend. The erroneous, the bad, the ugly should not prevent the soul from finding the true, the good, and the beautiful wherever it is present. This positiveness should not be confused with non-criticism, with the arbitrary closing of the eyes to the bad, the false, and the inferior. If you admire the "beautiful teeth" of a dead animal, you *also* see the decaying corpse. But this corpse does not prevent your seeing the beautiful teeth. One cannot consider the bad *good* and the false *true,* but it is possible to attain the ability not to be deterred by evil from seeing good, and by error from seeing truth.

Thought linked with will undergoes a certain maturing if we permit ourselves never to be robbed by previous experiences of the unbiased receptivity for new experiences. For the student of the spiritual the following thought should entirely lose its meaning, "I have never heard that, I do not believe that." It should be his aim, during specific periods of time, to learn something new on every occasion from everything and everybody. From every breath of air, from

288

every leaf, from the babbling of children one can learn something if one is prepared to bring to one's aid a certain point of view that one has not made use of up to the present. It will, however, be easily possible in regard to such an ability to go wide of the mark. One should not in any way disregard, at any particular stage of life, one's previous experiences. One should judge what one experiences in the present by one's experiences of the past. This is placed upon one scale of the balance; upon the other, however, must be placed the inclination of the student continually to experience the new. Above all, there must be faith in the possibility that new experiences may contradict the old.

Thus we have named five capacities of the soul that the student must make his own by correct training: Control of the direction of thought; control of the impulses of will; calmness in joy and sorrow; positiveness in judging the world; impartiality in our attitude toward life. Anyone who has employed certain consecutive periods of time for the purpose of acquiring these capacities will still be subject to the necessity of bringing them into harmonious concord in his soul. He will be under the necessity of practicing them simultaneously in pairs, or three and one, and so forth, in order to bring about harmony.

The exercises just characterized are indicated by the methods of spiritual training because by being *conscientiously* carried out they not only effect in the student what has been designated above as a direct result, but indirectly much else follows, which is needed on the path to the spiritual worlds. Whoever carries out these exercises to a sufficient degree will encounter in the process many shortcomings and defects in his soul-life, and he will find precisely the means required by him for strengthening and safeguarding his intellectual life, his life of feeling, and his character. He will certainly have need of many other exercises, according to his abilities, his temperament, and character; such exercises will follow, however, when those named are sufficiently carried out. The student will indeed notice that the exercises described yield, indirectly and by degrees, what did not in the first place appear to be in them. If, for example, someone has too little self-confidence, he will be able to notice after a certain time that through the exercises the necessary self-confidence has developed. It is the same in regard to other soul characteristics. (Special and more detailed exercises may be found in my book, *Knowledge of the Higher Worlds and Its Attainment*.)—It is significant that the student of the spiritual be able to increase the indicated abilities to ever higher degrees. He must bring the control of thought and feeling to such a stage that the soul acquires the power of establishing periods of complete inner tranquility, during which the student holds back from his spirit and heart all that everyday outer life brings of joy and sorrow, of satisfaction and affliction, indeed, of duties and demands. During such periods only those things should enter the soul that the soul itself permits to enter during the state of meditation. In regard to this, a prejudice may easily arise. The opinion might develop that the student might become estranged from life and its duties if he withdraws from it in heart and spirit during certain periods of the day. In reality, however, this is not at all the case. Anyone who surrenders himself, in the manner described, to periods of inner tranquility and peace will, during these periods, engender so many and such strong forces for the duties of outer life that as a result he will not, indeed, perform his duties more poorly, but, certainly, in a better fashion.—It is of great benefit if in such periods the student detaches himself completely from the thoughts of his personal affairs, if he is able to elevate himself to what concerns not only *himself*, but mankind in general. If he is able to fill his soul with the communications from the higher spiritual world and if they are able to arouse his interest to just as high a degree as is the case with personal troubles or affairs, then his soul will gather from it fruit of special value.—Whoever, in this way, endeavors to regulate his soul-life will also attain the possibility of self-observation through which he observes his own affairs with the same tranquility as if they were those of others. The ability to behold one's own experiences, one's own joys and sorrows as though they were the joys and sorrows of others is a good preparation for spiritual training. One gradually attains the necessary degree of this quality if, after one has finished one's daily tasks, one permits the panorama of one's daily experiences to pass before the eyes of the spirit. One must see oneself in a picture within one's experiences; that is, one must observe oneself in one's daily life as though from outside. One attains a certain ability in such self-observation if one begins with the visualization of detached portions of this daily life. One then becomes increasingly clever and skillful in such retrospect, so that, after a longer period of practice, one will be able to form a complete picture within a brief span of time. This looking at one's experiences backward has a special value for spiritual training for the rea-

son that it brings the soul to a point where it is able to re-
lease itself in thinking from the previous habit of *merely*
following in thought the course of everyday events. In
thought-retrospect one visualizes correctly, but one is not
held to the sensory course of events. One needs this exercise to familiarize oneself with the spiritual world. Thought
strengthens itself in this way in a healthy manner. It is
therefore also good not only to review in retrospect one's
daily life, but to retrace in reverse order, for instance, the
course of a drama, a narrative, or a melody.—More and
more it will become the ideal for the student to relate himself to the life events he encounters in such a way that, with
inner certainty and soul tranquility, he allows them to approach him and does not judge them according to *his* soul
condition, but according to their inner significance and
their inner value. It is just by looking upon this ideal that
he will create for himself the soul basis for the surrender of
himself to the above described meditations on symbolic
and other thoughts and feelings.

The conditions described here must be fulfilled, because
supersensible experience is built upon the foundation on
which one stands in everyday soul life before one enters
the supersensible world. In a twofold manner all supersensible experience is dependent upon the starting point at
which the soul stands before it enters into this world. Anyone who, from the beginning, does not consider making a
healthy judgment the foundation of his spiritual training
will develop in himself supersensible faculties with which
he perceives the spiritual world inexactly and incorrectly.
His spiritual organs of perception will, so to speak, unfold
incorrectly. Just as one cannot see correctly in the sense

world with eyes that are faulty and diseased, one cannot perceive correctly with spiritual organs that have not been constructed upon the foundation of a healthy capacity for judgment.—Whoever makes the start with an immoral soul condition elevates himself to the spiritual world in a way by which his spiritual perception becomes stupefied and clouded. He stands confronting the supersensible worlds like someone observing the sensory world in a stupor. Such a person will, to be sure, make no important statements. The spiritual observer in his state of stupor is, however, more awake than a human being in everyday consciousness. His assertions, therefore, will become errors in regard to the spiritual world.

* * *

The inner excellence of the stage of imaginative cognition is attained through the fact that the soul meditations described are supported by what we may call familiarizing oneself with *sense-free thinking*. If one forms a thought based upon observation in the physical sense world, this thought is not sense-free. It is, however, not a fact that man is able to form *only* such thoughts. Human thought does not need to become empty and without content when it refuses to be filled with the results of sense-observations. The safest and most evident way for the student of the spiritual to acquire such sense-free thinking is to make his own, in thinking, the facts of the higher world that are communicated to him by spiritual science. It is not possible to observe these facts by means of the physical senses. Nevertheless, the student will notice that they can be *grasped* mentally if he has sufficient patience and persistence. We are not able to carry on research in the higher worlds without training, nor can we make observations in that world; yet without higher training we are able to understand the descriptions of spiritual researchers, and if someone asks, "How can I accept in good faith what these researchers say since I am unable to perceive the spiritual world myself?" then this is completely unfounded. For it is entirely possible merely by reflecting on what is given, to attain the certain conviction that what is communicated is true, and if anyone is unable to form this conviction through reflection, it is not because it is impossible to believe something one cannot see, but solely because his reflection has not been sufficiently thorough, comprehensive and unprejudiced. In order to gain clarity in regard to this point we must realize that human thinking, when it arouses itself with inner energy, is able to comprehend more than is usually presumed. For in thought itself an inner entity is already present that is connected with the supersensible world. The soul is usually not conscious of this connection because it is accustomed to developing the thought faculty only by employing it in the sense world. It therefore regards communications from the supersensible world as something incomprehensible. These communications, however, are not only comprehensible to a mode of thinking taught through spiritual training, but for every sort of thinking that is fully conscious of its own power and that wishes to employ it.—By making what spiritual research offers increasingly one's own, one accustoms oneself to a mode of thinking that does not derive its content from sense-observations. We learn to recognize how, in the inner reaches of the soul, thought weaves into thought,

294

how thought seeks thought, although the thought associations are not effected by the power of sense-observation. The essential in this is the fact that one becomes aware of how the thought world has an inner life, of how one, by really thinking, finds oneself already in the region of a living supersensible world. One says to oneself, "There is something in me that fashions a thought organism; I am, nevertheless, at one with this something." By surrendering oneself to sense-free thinking one becomes conscious of the existence of something essential flowing into our inner life, just as the characteristics of sense objects flow into us through the medium of our physical organs when we observe by means of our senses. The observer of the sense world says to himself, "Outside in space there is a rose; it is not strange to me, for it makes itself known to me through its color and fragrance." One needs now only to be sufficiently unprejudiced in order to say to oneself when sense-free thinking acts in one, "Something real proclaims its presence in me that binds thought to thought, fashioning a thought organism." But the sensations experienced by observing the objects of the outer sense world are different from the sensations experienced when spiritual reality manifests itself in sense-free thinking. The observer of sense objects experiences the rose as something external to himself. The observer who has surrendered himself to sense-free thought feels the spiritual reality announcing itself as though it existed *within him;* he feels himself one with it. Whoever, more or less consciously, only admits as real what confronts him like an external object, will naturally not be able to have the feeling, "Whatever has the nature of being in itself may also announce itself to me by my being united with it as though I were one with it." In order in this regard to see correctly, one must be able to have the following inner experience. One must learn to distinguish between the thought associations one creates arbitrarily and those one experiences in oneself when one silences this arbitrary volition. In the latter case one may then say, "I remain quite silent within myself; I produce no thought associations; I surrender myself to what 'thinks in me.'" Then one is fully justified in saying, "Something possessing the nature of being acts within me," just as one is justified in saying, "A rose acts upon me when I see its red color, when I smell its fragrance."—In this connection, there lies no contradiction in the fact that the content of one's thoughts is derived from the communications of the spiritual researcher. The thoughts are, indeed, already present when one surrenders to them; but one cannot think them if one does not, in every case, re-create them anew within the soul. What is important is the fact that the spiritual researcher calls up thoughts in his listeners and readers that they must first draw forth out of themselves, while the one who describes sense reality points to something that may be observed by listeners and readers in the sense world.

(The path is absolutely safe upon which the communications of spiritual science lead us to sense-free thinking. There is, however, still another path that is safer and above all more exact, but it is also more difficult for many human beings. This path is presented in my books, *A Theory of Knowledge Based on Goethe's World Conception*, and *Philosophy of Freedom*. These writings offer what human thought can acquire if thinking does not give itself up to the impressions of the physical-sensory world, but *only to itself.* It

296

is then pure thought, which acts in the human being like a living entity, and not thought that merely indulges in memories of the sensory. In the writings mentioned above nothing is inserted from the communications of spiritual science itself. Yet it is shown that pure thinking, merely active within itself, may throw light on the problems of world, life, and man. These writings stand at an important point intermediate between cognition of the sense world and that of the spiritual world. They offer what thinking can gain when it elevates itself above sense-observation, while still avoiding entering upon spiritual research. Whoever permits these writings to act upon his entire soul nature, stands already within the spiritual world; it presents itself to him, however, as a world of thought. He who feels himself in the position to permit such an intermediate stage to act upon him, travels a safe path, and through it he is able to gain a feeling toward the higher world that will bear for him the most beautiful fruit throughout all future time.)

*   *   *

The object of meditation on the previously characterized symbolic mental images and feelings is, correctly speaking, the development of the higher organs of perception within the human astral body. They are created from the substance of this astral body. These new organs of observation open up a new world, and in this new world man becomes acquainted with himself as a new ego. The new organs of observation are to be distinguished from the organs of the physical sense world through the fact of their being *active* organs. Whereas eyes and ears remain passive, permitting light and sound to act upon them, the soul-spirit organs of

297

perception are continually active while perceiving and they *seize upon* their objects and facts, as it were, in full consciousness. This results in the feeling that soul-spirit cognition is the act of uniting with the corresponding facts, is really a "living within them."—The soul-spirit organs that are being individually developed may, by way of comparison, be called "lotus flowers," according to the forms which they present imaginatively to supersensible consciousness. (Granted, it must be clear that such a designation has nothing more to do with the case than the expression "chamber" has to do with the case when we speak of the "chamber of the heart.") Through quite definite methods of inner meditation the astral body is affected in such a way that one or another of the soul-spirit organs, one or another of the "lotus flowers," is formed. After all that has been described in this book it ought to be superfluous to accentuate the fact that these "organs of observation" are not to be imagined as something that, in the mental representation of its sense-image, is a picture of its reality. These "organs" are supersensible and consist of a definitely formed soul activity; they exist only as far and as long as this soul activity is practiced. The existence of these organs in the human being produces nothing of a sensory character any more than human thinking produces some sort of a physical "vapor." Whoever insists on visualizing the supersensory as something sensory becomes involved in misunderstandings. In spite of the superfluity of this remark, it is made here because again and again there are those who accept the supersensory as a fact, but who, in their thoughts, desire only what is sensory, and because again and again there appear opponents of supersensory cognition who believe that the spiritual researcher speaks of "lotus flowers" as though they were delicate, physical structures. Every correct meditation that is made in regard to imaginative cognition has its effect upon one or another organ. (In my book, *Knowledge of the Higher Worlds and Its Attainment*, certain methods of meditation, and exercises that affect one or another of the organs, are outlined.) Proper training sets up the several exercises of the student of the spiritual and arranges them to follow one another so that the organs are able to develop correspondingly, either singly, in groups, or consecutively. In connection with this development the spiritual student must have great patience and endurance. Anyone having only the measure of patience possessed, as a rule, by most human beings through the ordinary relationships of life will find that this does not suffice. For it takes a long time, often a very long time, before the organs are sufficiently developed to permit their employment by the spiritual student in perceiving the spiritual world. This is the moment when something occurs for him that may be called *illumination,* in contrast to the *preparation* or purification consisting of the exercises that develop the organs. (We speak of purification, because the corresponding exercises purify the student in a certain sphere of his inner life of all that springs only from the sensory world of observation.) It may happen that the student, even before his actual illumination occurs, may experience repeatedly "flashes of light" coming from a higher world. He should accept such experiences gratefully. Through them he can already become a witness for the spiritual world. But he should not waver if this does not occur during this period of preparation, which may perhaps seem to

299

him altogether too long. If he exhibits any impatience whatever "because he does not yet see anything," he has not yet gained the right attitude toward a higher world. This attitude can only be grasped by someone for whom the exercises performed in his training can be, as it were, an end in themselves. These exercises are, in truth, work performed on the soul-spirit nature, that is to say, on the student's own astral body, and although he "sees nothing," he may "feel" that he is working on his soul-spirit nature. If, however, one forms a definite opinion right at the beginning of what one actually expects to "see," one will not have this feeling. Then one will consider as nothing what in truth is of immeasurable significance. But one should be subtly observant of everything one experiences during the exercises and that is so fundamentally different from all experiences in the sense world. One will then certainly notice that one's astral body, upon which one is working, is not a neutral substance, but that in it there lives a totally different world of which one knows nothing in one's life of the senses. Higher beings are working upon the astral body, just as the outer physical-sensory world works upon the physical body, and one encounters this higher life in one's own astral body if one does not close oneself to it. If someone repeatedly says to himself, "I perceive nothing!" then, in most cases, he has imagined that spiritual perception must take place in this or that manner, and because he does not perceive what he imagines he should see, he says, "I see nothing!"

If the student has acquired the right attitude toward the exercises of spiritual training, they will constitute something for him that he loves more and more for its own sake.

He then knows that through the practice itself he stands in a world of soul and spirit, and with patience and serenity he awaits what will result. This attitude may arise in the consciousness of the student most favorably in the following words, "I will do everything that is proper in the way of exercises, and I know that just as much will come to me at the proper time as is important for me. I do not demand it impatiently, but I am ever ready to receive it."

It is not valid to object that "the spiritual student must thus grope about in the dark, perhaps for an immeasurably long time; for he can only know clearly that he is on the right path in his exercises when the results appear." It is untrue that only results can bring knowledge of the correctness of the exercises. If the student takes the right attitude toward them, he finds that the satisfaction he draws from the practice gives him the assurance that what he is doing is right; he does not have to wait for the results. Correct practice in the sphere of spiritual training calls forth satisfaction that is not mere satisfaction, but knowledge— that is to say, the knowledge that he is doing something which convinces him that he is making progress in the right direction. Every spiritual student may have this knowledge at every moment, provided he is subtly attentive to his experiences. If he does not employ this attention then the experiences escape him, as is the case with a pedestrian who, lost in thought, does not see the trees on both sides of the road, although he would see them were he to direct his attention to them.—It is not at all desirable that a result be hastened different from the one that must always occur from correct practice. For this result might easily be only the smallest part of what should actually ap-

301

pear. In regard to spiritual development a partial success is often the reason for a strong retardation of the complete success. The movement among such forms of spiritual life that correspond to the partial success dulls the sensitivity in regard to the influences of the forces that lead to higher stages of evolution, and what we may have gained by having "peered" into the spirit world is only an illusion, for this "peering" cannot furnish the truth, but only a mirage.

*   *   *

The psycho-spiritual organs, the lotus flowers, are fashioned so as to appear to supersensible consciousness, in the student undergoing training, as though located in the neighborhod of certain organs of the physical body. From among these soul organs the following will be mentioned here. First, the one that is felt between the eyebrows—the so-called two-petalled lotus flower; the one in the neighborhood of the larynx—the sixteen-petalled lotus flower; a third in the heart region—the twelve-petalled lotus flower; a fourth in the region of the solar plexus. Other similar organs appear in the neighborhood of other parts of the physical body. (The names "two-petalled" or "sixteen-petalled" may be used because the corresponding organs may be likened to flowers of a corresponding number of petals.)

One becomes conscious of the lotus flowers through the astral body. The moment one has developed one or another of these organs, one is aware of its existence. One feels that one can employ it and through its use really enter into a higher world. The impressions that one receives from that world still resemble in many ways those of the

302

physical-sensory world. He who possesses imaginative cognition will be able to speak of the new, higher world in such a way that he designates the impressions as sensations of heat or cold, as perceptions of tones and words, as effects of light and color, for he experiences them as such. But he is aware that these perceptions in the imaginative world express something quite different from sense reality. He recognizes that behind them stand not physical material, but soul-spirit causes. If he experiences something like an impression of heat, he does not, for instance, ascribe it to a piece of hot iron, but he considers it the outflow of a soul process that, up to the present, he has only known in his inner soul-life. He knows that behind imaginative perceptions stand soul and spiritual things and processes just as behind physical perceptions stand material physical beings and facts.—Beside this similarity of the imaginative with the physical world there is, however, a significant difference. Certain phenomena in the physical world appear quite different in the imaginative world. In the former can be observed a continual growth and decay of things, an alternation of birth and death. In the imaginative world a continual *transformation* of one thing into another takes the place of these phenomena. One sees, for example, the *decay* of a plant in the physical world. In the imaginative world, in proportion to the withering of the plant the growth of another formation makes its appearance that is not perceptible physically and into which the decaying plant is gradually transformed. When the plant has disappeared, this formation stands completely developed in its place. Birth and death are ideas that lose their significance in the imaginative world. In their place appears the concept of *transformation of one thing into another.*—Because this is so, the truths about the being of man become accessible to imaginative cognition, truths that have been described in Chapter II of this book, entitled *"The Essential Nature of Mankind."* To physical-sensory perception only the processes of the physical body are perceptible. They occur in the "region of birth and death." The other members of human nature—life body, sentient body, and ego—come under the law of transformation, and perception of them is acquired through imaginative cognition. Whoever has advanced to this point perceives the releasing itself from the physical body of what at death continues to live on in another state of existence.

Development, however, does not stop with the imaginative world. The human being who might wish to stop in this world would perceive the beings undergoing transformation, but he would be unable to explain the processes of transformation; he would be unable to orientate himself in the newly attained world. The imaginative world is an unstable region. In it there exist everywhere constant motion and transformation; nowhere are there points of rest.— Such points of rest are attained by man only when he has developed himself beyond the stage of imaginative cognition to the stage that may be called "cognition through inspiration."—It is not necessary that a person who seeks cognition of the supersensible world develop himself in such a way that he advance first to the possession of a full degree of imaginative cognition, and then only advance to "inspiration." His exercises may be so arranged that what may lead to imagination and to inspiration proceeds hand in hand. He will then, after a certain time, enter a higher world in which he not only perceives, but in which he is able to orientate himself, and which he can interpret. To be sure, this progress will, as a rule, be of such a character that first of all some of the phenomena of the imaginative world manifest themselves to him; then after a time he will experience the feeling, "Now I am beginning to orientate myself."—The world of inspiration is, nevertheless, something quite new in comparison with the world of mere imagination. Through the latter one perceives the transformation of one process into another; through the former one learns to know the inner qualities of *beings* who transform themselves. Through imagination one learns to know the soul-expression of beings; through inspiration one penetrates into their inner spiritual nature. One recognizes above all a host of spiritual beings and discerns a great number of relationships between one being and another. One has to deal with a multitude of individual beings also in the physical-sensory world; in the world of inspiration, however, this multitude is of a different character. There each being has a quite definite relationship to others, not as in the physical world through external influences, but through its inner constitution. If we perceive a being in the world of inspiration, there is no evidence of an outer influence upon another being, which might be compared with the effect of one physical being upon another, but a relationship exists between two beings through their inner constitution. Let us compare this relationship with a relationship in the physical world, by selecting for comparison the relationship between the separate sounds or letters of a word. Take, for instance, the word "man." It is produced through the concordance of the sounds m-a-n. There is no impulse or other external influence passing over from the m to the a; both sounds act together within the whole through their inner constitution. Therefore observation in the world of inspiration may only be compared with *reading;* and the beings in the world of inspiration act upon the observer like the letters of an alphabet, which he must learn to know and the interrelationships of which must unfold themselves to him like a supersensible script. Spiritual science, therefore, may call cognition through inspiration—speaking figuratively—the *reading of secret or occult script.*

How we may read by means of this occult script, and how we may communicate what is read, will now be made clear by means of the preceding chapters of this book itself. How the human being takes shape out of various members was described at the very outset. It was then shown how the cosmic being, within which the human being develops, passes through the various states of *Saturn, Sun, Moon,* and *Earth.* The perceptions through which one can, on the one hand, cognize the members of the human being and, on the other, the consecutive states of the *Earth* and its preceding transformations, disclose themselves to imaginative knowledge. It is, however, also necessary that it be known what relationships exist between the *Saturn* state and the human physical body, the *Sun* state and the ether body, and so forth. It must be shown that the germinal human physical body has come already into existence during the *Saturn* state, and that it has evolved further to its present form during the *Sun, Moon,* and *Earth* states. It was necessary to show also, for example, what transformations have taken place within the human being as a result of the separation of the sun from the *Earth,* and similarly through the separation of the moon. It was necessary also to describe the powers and beings who co-operated in order that such transformations could occur in humanity as are expressed in the transformations during the Atlantean period and also during the successive periods of the ancient Indian, the ancient Persian, the Egyptian cultures, and the subsequent periods of culture. The description of these relationships does not result from imaginative perception, but from cognition through inspiration, by reading the occult script. For this sort of "reading" the perceptions of imagination are like letter symbols or sounds. This "reading," however, is not only necessary for the purpose of explaining what has just been described, but it would be impossible to understand the life course of the whole human being were it only perceived through imaginative cognition. One would perceive, indeed, how the soul-spiritual members are released at death from what remains in the physical world, but one would not understand the relationships between what happens to the human being after death and the preceding and succeeding states, were one unable to orientate oneself within the imaginatively perceived. Without cognition through inspiration the imaginative world would remain like writing at which we stare but which we cannot read.

When the student of the spiritual advances from imagination to inspiration he soon sees how incorrect it would be to relinquish the understanding of the macrocosmic phenomena and to limit himself only to facts that, so to say, touch upon immediate human interests. Someone who is not initiated into these things might well say the following. "It appears to me only necessary to learn about the fate of the human soul after death; if I am told something about that, it will suffice; why does spiritual science wish to demonstrate such distant things as the *Saturn* or *Sun* state, and the sun and moon separation, and so forth?" Anyone properly informed about these things learns that real knowledge of what he wishes to know is never acquired without an understanding of what seems to him so unnecessary. A description of the human states after death remains completely unintelligible and worthless if man is unable to connect them with concepts that are derived from such remote matters. Even the simplest observation of the scientist of the supersensible makes his acquaintance with such things necessary. If, for example, a plant makes the transition from blossom to fruit, the human observer of the supersensible sees a transformation taking place in an astral being that during the period of flowering has overshadowed the plant from above and enclosed it like a cloud. Had the fructification not occurred, then this astral being would have made a transition into quite a different shape from the one it has assumed in consequence of fructification. Now one understands the entire process perceived by supersensible observation, if one has learned to understand its nature through the macrocosmic process through which the *Earth* and all its inhabitants have passed at the time of the sun separation. Before fructification, the plant is in a position similar to the entire *Earth* prior to the sun separation. After fructification, the plant blossom shows itself in a condition similar to the Earth after the sun had severed itself and the moon forces were still present in it. If one has made one's own the concepts

308

that may be gained by studying the sun separation, one then understands adequately the meaning of the process of plant fructification. One will say that the plant is in a sun state before fructification, in a moon state after it. For it is a fact that even the smallest process in the world may be grasped only if we recognize that it constitutes a copy of macrocosmic processes. Otherwise its very nature remains unintelligible, just as Raphael's *Madonna* would remain unintelligible if nothing were to be seen but a small blue speck when the rest of the picture were covered up.— Everything that occurs in the human being is a copy of macrocosmic processes that have to do with his existence. If one wishes to understand the observations of supersensible consciousness concerning the phenomena occurring between birth and death, and again between death and rebirth, one can do this if one has acquired the faculty of deciphering the imaginative observations through the concepts acquired by the study of the macrocosmic processes.—This study gives us the *key* to the comprehension of human life. Therefore, in the sense of spiritual science, observation of *Saturn, Sun,* and *Moon* is at the same time observation of man.

Through inspiration one acquires the knowledge of the relationships between the beings of the higher world. It is possible through a higher stage of cognition to understand the inner nature of these beings themselves. This stage of cognition may be designated *intuitive cognition.* (Intuition is a word misused in everyday life for an obscure, uncertain insight into a fact, that is, for a certain idea which at times agrees with truth but the justification of which is at the time not provable. What is meant here has naturally nothing to do with this sort of intuition. Intuition denotes here a cognition of the highest, most illuminating clarity, and, if one has it, one is conscious in the fullest sence of its justification.)—To have knowledge of a sense-being means to stand *outside* it and to judge it according to the external impression. To have knowledge of a spiritual being through intuition means to have become completely one with it, to have become united with its inner nature. Step by step the student of the spiritual ascends to such knowledge. Imagination leads him to sense the perceptions no longer as outer characteristics of beings, but to recognize in them the outpouring of something psycho-spiritual; inspiration leads him further into the inner nature of beings. He learns through it to understand what these beings are to each other; with intuition he penetrates into the beings themselves.—The significance of intuition also may be shown by the descriptions given in this book. In the preceding chapters, not only the course of *Saturn, Sun,* and *Moon* evolutions was described, but it was told that beings participate in this development in the most varied ways. Thrones or Spirits of Will, Spirits of Wisdom, of Motion, and others were mentioned. In the *Earth* evolution mention was made of the spirits Lucifer and Ahriman. The construction of the cosmos was traced back to the beings who participate in it. What may be learned about these beings is won through intuitive cognition. This faculty is also necessary if one wishes to have a knowledge of the course of human life. What is released after death from the human bodily nature goes through various states in the subsequent period. The states directly after death might be described in some measure through imaginative cognition.

310

What, however, takes place when man advances further into the period between death and rebirth would have to remain quite unintelligible to imaginative cognition, if inspiration did not come to the rescue. Only inspiration is able to discover what may be said about the life of man in the land of spirits after purification. Then something appears for which inspiration no longer suffices, where it reaches, so to say, the limits of understanding. There is a period in human evolution between death and rebirth when the being of man is accessible only to intuition.— This part of the being of man, however, is *always* present in him; and if we wish to understand it according to its true inner nature, we must investigate it by means of intuition also in the period between birth and death. Whoever wished to fathom the nature of man by means of imagination and inspiration alone, would miss the innermost processes of his being that take place from incarnation to incarnation. Only intuitive cognition, therefore, makes possible an adequate research into repeated earth lives and into karma. The truth communicated about these processes must originate from research by means of intuitive cognition.—If man himself wishes to have a knowledge of his own inner being, he can only acquire this through intuition. By means of it he perceives what progresses in him from earth life to earth life.

* * *

Man is able to attain knowledge by means of inspiration and intuition only through soul-spirit exercises. They resemble those that have been described as meditation for the attainment of imagination. While, however, those exer-

311

cises that lead to imagination are linked to the impressions of the sensory-physical world, this link must disappear more and more in the exercises for inspiration. In order to make clear to himself what has to happen there, let a person consider again the symbol of the rose cross. If he ponders upon this symbol he has an image before him, the parts of which have been taken from the impressions of the sense world: the black color of the cross, the roses, and so forth. The combining of these parts into a rose cross has not been taken from the physical sense world. If now the student of the spirit attempts to let the black cross and also the red roses as pictures of sense realities disappear entirely from his consciousness and only to retain in his soul the spiritual activity that has combined these parts, then he has a means for meditation that leads him by degrees to inspiration. One may place the following question before one's soul. What have I done inwardly in order to combine cross and rose into a symbol? What I have done—my own soul process—I wish to hold fast to; I let the picture itself, however, disappear from my consciousness. Then I wish to *feel* within me all that my soul has done in order to bring the image into existence, but I do not wish to hold the image itself; I wish to live quite inwardly within my own activity, which has created the image. Thus, I do not intend to meditate on an image, but to dwell in my own image-creating soul activity. Such meditation must be carried out in regard to many symbols. This then leads to cognition through inspiration. Another example would be the following. One meditates on the thought of a growing and decaying plant. One allows to arise in the soul the image of a slowly growing plant as it shoots up out of the seed, as it

312

unfolds leaf on leaf, until it develops flower and fruit. Then again, one meditates on how it begins to fade until its complete dissolution. One acquires gradually by meditating on such an image a feeling of growth and decay for which the plant remains a mere symbol. From this feeling, if this exercise is continued with perseverance, there may arise the imagination of the transformation that underlies physical growth and decay. If one wishes, however, to attain the corresponding state of inspiration, one has to carry out the exercise differently. The student must recall his own soul activity that has gained the visualization of growth and decay from the image of the plant. He must now let the plant disappear completely from consciousness and only meditate upon what he has himself done inwardly. Only through such exercises is it possible to ascend to inspiration. In the beginning it will not be entirely easy for the student of the spirit to comprehend completely how he should go about such an exercise. The reason for this is that the human being who is accustomed to have his inner life determined by outer impressions immediately finds himself uncertain and wavering when he has to unfold a soul-life that has discarded all connection with outer impressions. In a still higher degree than in the acquiring of imagination the student must be clear, in regard to these exercises that lead to inspiration, that he ought only to carry them out when he accompanies them with all those precautionary measures that can lead to safeguarding and strengthening of his power of discrimination, his life of feeling, and his character. If he takes these precautions, then he will have a twofold result. In the first place, he will not, through these exercises, lose the equilibrium of his personality during supersensible perception; secondly, he will at the same time gain the faculty of being able actually to carry out what is required in these exercises. He will maintain in regard to them that they are difficult only so long as he has not yet acquired a quite definite soul condition, quite definite feelings and sensations. He will soon gain understanding and also ability for the exercises, if in patience and perseverance he fosters in his soul such inner faculties as favor the unfolding of supersensible knowledge. If he grows accustomed to withdrawing into himself frequently in such a way that he is less concerned with brooding on himself than with quietly arranging and working over his life-experiences, he will gain much. He will see that his thoughts and feelings are enriched if he brings one life-experience into relationship with another. He will become aware to what a high degree he experiences something new not only by having new impressions and new experiences, but also by permitting the old to work in him. If he sets to work in such a way that he lets his experiences, indeed, even his acquired opinions, play back and forth as though he were not at all involved in them with his sympathies and antipathies, with his personal interests and feelings, he will prepare an especially good soil for the forces of supersensible cognition. He will develop, in truth, what may be called a rich inner life. The question of chief importance here, however, is equanimity and equilibrium of the soul qualities. Man is only too easily inclined, if he surrenders himself to a certain soul activity, to fall into one-sidedness. For example, if he becomes aware of the advantage of inner meditation and of dwelling in his own thought world, he may develop such an inclination toward

314

it that he begins to shut himself off from the impressions of the outer world. This, however, leads to the withering and devastation of the inner life. Those go the farthest who preserve, alongside the ability to withdraw inwardly, an open receptivity to all impressions of the outer world. One need not think here merely of the so-called important impressions of life, but *every* man in *every* situation—even in the poorest surroundings—may have sufficient experiences if he only keeps his mind sufficiently receptive. One need not seek the experiences; they are present everywhere.—Of special importance also is *the way* experiences are transformed in the human soul. For example, somebody may discover that a person revered by him or others has this or that quality that may be viewed as a fault of character. Such an experience may cause the human being to meditate in a twofold manner. He may simply say to himself, "Now, that I have recognized this fault, I can no longer revere this person in the same way as formerly." Or he may pose the following question to himself, "How does it happen that this revered person is afflicted with this fault? Should I not consider that this fault is not *merely* a fault, but something due to the circumstances of this person's life, perhaps even to his great capacities?" A human being posing this question to himself will perhaps arrive at the result that his reverence is not in the least to be decreased by the discovery of such a fault. He will have learned something every time he goes through such an experience; he will have added something to his understanding of life. It would, however, certainly be disastrous to the human being were he to let himself be misled by the merit of such a view of life to excuse everything he possibly can in people and things for whom he has a preference, or even to form the habit of disregarding all faults because it brings him advantage for his inner development. This will *not* be the case if he has the subjective impulse not merely to censure faults but to understand them; it will occur when this attitude is demanded by the case in question, regardless of the gain or loss to him who judges. It is entirely correct that one *cannot learn* through condemning faults, but only through understanding them. If, however, because of understanding, one should entirely exclude disapproval, one would not get very far either. Here also it is not a question of onesidedness in either direction, but of equanimity and equilibrium of the soul powers.—It is especially so with a soul quality that is of great significance for the development of the human being; this is what is called the feeling of reverence or devotion. Those who have developed this feeling in themselves or possess it from the outset through a fortunate gift of nature have an excellent basis for the forces of supersensible knowledge. The person who in childhood or youth has been able to look up with self-surrendering admiration to personalities as though to high ideals, possesses something at the foundation of his soul in which supersensible cognition thrives especially well. And whoever with mature judgment in later life looks upon the starry heavens and feels with wonder in complete surrender the revelation of exalted powers makes himself thus mature for knowledge of supersensible worlds. Something similar is the case with those who are able to admire the forces ruling in human life, and it is not of little importance if we, even as mature human beings, can have reverence to the highest degree for other men whose worth we divine or believe we know. Only where such reverence is present can the view into the higher world open up. The person who is unable to revere will in no way advance very far in his knowledge. Whoever does not wish to acknowledge anything in the world will find that the essential nature of things is closed to him.—The person, however, who permits himself to be misled, through an unrestrained feeling of reverence and surrender, to deaden in himself a healthy consciousness of self and self-confidence sins against the law of equanimity and equilibrium. The student will continually work on himself in order to make himself more and more mature; he is then *justified* in having confidence in his own personality and in having faith that its powers will continually increase. If he achieves correct feelings in this direction he may say to himself, "In me there lie hidden forces and I can draw them forth from my inner being. Therefore, when I see something that I must revere because it stands above me, I need not only revere it, but I may hope to develop myself to such a degree that I become similar to what I revere."

The greater the capacity of a human being to direct his *attention* to certain processes of life with which his personal judgment is not, at the outset, familiar, the greater the possibility for him to lay the foundation for a development into the spiritual worlds. An example may make this clear. A man is in a certain situation in life where he may perform a certain deed or leave it undone. His judgment suggests to him: Do this! But there may be a certain inexplicable something in his feelings that holds him back from the deed. Now it may be that he does not pay any attention to this inexplicable something that seeks to restrain him, but simply performs the deed, according to his capacity to judge. Or he may surrender to the urge of this inexplicable something and leave the deed undone. If he then follows up the matter further it may become evident that evil would have been the result had he followed his judgment, but that by non-performance of the deed, a blessing has ensued. Such an experience may lead man's thoughts into a quite definite direction. He may say to himself, "Something lives in me that is a better guide than my present capacity of judgment. I must hold my mind open to this 'something in me' that cannot at all be reached by the present degree of my capacity of judgment." The soul is benefited to the highest degree when it directs its attention toward such occurrences in life. It then becomes aware, as though in a state of *healthy* premonition, that something exists in man that *transcends* his present ability to judge. Through such attention the human being directs his efforts toward an *extension* of soul-life, but here also it is possible that onesidedness may result that is dangerous. Whoever were to form the habit of disregarding his judgment because his "premonitions" impel him to this or that, would become the plaything of all sorts of uncertain impulses, and from such a habit it is not a great distance to complete lack of judgment and superstition.—Any sort of superstition is fatal to the student of the spiritual. He acquires the possibility of penetrating in a true way into the regions of spiritual life only by guarding himself carefully against superstition, fantastic ideas, and day-dreaming. No one can enter the spirit world in the right way who is happy in experiencing something that "cannot be grasped by the human mind." A preference for the "inexplicable" certainly makes no one a student of the spirit. He must completely abandon the notion that "a mystic is someone who presumes wherever it suits him something inexplicable and unfathomable in the world." The student shows the proper feeling by acknowledging this existence of hidden forces and beings everywhere, but also by assuming that the uninvestigated may be investigated if the necessary powers are present.

There is a certain attitude of soul that is important for the student of the spirit at every stage of his development. This consists in not directing his desire for knowledge in a onesided way by asking, "How may this or that question be answered?" but by asking, "How do I develop this or that ability in myself?" If then by inner patient work in himself this or that faculty is developed, the answer to certain questions is received. Students of the spirit will always foster this attitude of soul. Through this they are led to work on themselves, to make themselves more and more mature, and to renounce the desire to force answers to certain questions. They will *wait* until such answers come to them.—If, however, they become onesided here also, they will not advance properly. The student may also have the feeling at a certain point of his development that he, with the degree of his ability, can himself answer the most sublime questions. Here also equanimity and equilibrium play an important role in the attitude of soul.

Many more soul faculties could be described, the fostering and development of which are beneficial when the student strives by means of exercises to attain inspiration. In all of them, we should have to emphasize that equanimity and equilibrium are the soul faculties upon which everything depends. They prepare the understanding and the ability to carry out the exercises outlined for the purpose of acquiring inspiration.

The exercises for the attainment of intuition demand that the student cause not only the images, to which he has surrendered himself in acquiring imagination, to disappear from his consciousness, but also the life within his own soul activity into which he has immersed himself for the acquirement of inspiration. He should then literally retain *nothing* in his soul of previously known outer or inner experiences. Were there to be, however, *nothing* left in his consciousness after this discarding of outer and inner experiences, that is to say, were his consciousness then entirely to disappear and he to sink down into unconsciousness, this would then make it clear to him that he had not yet made himself mature enough to undertake exercises for intuition; he would then have to continue the exercises for imagination and inspiration. A time will surely come when the consciousness is *not* empty after the soul has discarded all inner and outer experiences, but when, after this discarding, something remains in consciousness as an effect, to which we then may surrender in meditation just as we had previously surrendered to what owes its existence to outer or inner impressions. This something is of a quite special character. It is, in contrast to all preceding experiences, something entirely new. When one experiences it one knows, "This I have not known before. It is a perception just as the real tone, heard by the ear, is a perception, but this something can only enter my consciousness through intuition, just as the tone can only enter my consciousness through the ear." Through intuition man's impressions are stripped of the last trace of the sensory-physical; the spiritual world now begins to open itself to cognition in a form that no longer has anything in common with the qualities of the physical world of the senses.

*   *   *

Imaginative consciousness is attained through the development of the lotus flowers in the astral body. Through the exercises that are undertaken for acquiring inspiration and intuition, certain definite motions, forms, and currents appear in the human ether or life body that were not present previously. They are in fact the organs through which man adds to the scope of his faculties the "reading of the occult script," and what lies beyond it. The changes in the ether body of a human being who has attained inspiration and intuition present themselves to supersensible cognition in the following manner. Somewhere in the neighborhood of the physical heart a new center becomes conscious in the ether body, which develops into an etheric organ. From this organ, movements and currents flow to the various members of the human body in the most manifold way. The most important of these currents flow to the lotus flowers, permeating them and their various petals, then proceeding outward, pouring themselves like radiations into external space. The more the human being is developed, the greater the sphere around him within which these radiations are perceptible. The center in the region of the heart does not, however, develop immediately at the start of correct training. It is first prepared. There appears, to begin with, a temporary center in the head; this then moves down into the neighborhood of the larynx and finally settles in the region of the physical heart. Were its development irregular, then the organ of which we have been speaking might immediately be formed in the neighborhood of the heart. In that case there would be danger that the student, instead of attaining quiet and factual supersensible perception, would become a visionary and fantast. As he develops further, the student acquires the ability to free the currents and structures of his ether body from his physical body and to use them independently. In doing this, the lotus flowers serve him as organs through which he brings the ether body into motion. Before this occurs, however, special currents and radiations must have formed in the sphere of the ether body, enclosing it like a fine network and making it into a self-contained being. If that has happened, the movements and currents taking place in the ether body are able to come into unhindered contact with the outer world of soul and spirit and to unite with it, so that outer occurrences in the realm of soul and spirit and inner events in the human ether body flow into one another. If that happens, the moment has arrived when man perceives the world of inspiration consciously. This cognition occurs in a different way from cognition in the sensory-physical world. In the latter we gain perceptions through the senses and form from them mental images and concepts. This is not the case with the knowledge derived from inspiration. What one knows is immediately present in the act; there is no reflection *after* perception. What sensory-physical cognition gains only afterwards in concepts is, in inspiration, given simultaneously with perception. Man would therefore merge with the environment

322

of soul and spirit and would not be able to distinguish himself from it had he not developed the above characterized network in the ether body.

If the exercises leading to intuition are carried out, their effect extends not only to the ether body, but right down into the supersensible forces of the physical body. One should not, however, think that in this way effects take place in the physical body that are accessible to everyday sensory observation. These are effects that only supersensory cognition can judge. They have nothing whatever to do with *external* cognition. They are the results of the maturity of consciousness, when the latter is able to have experiences in intuition, in spite of the fact that it has excluded all previously known outer and inner experiences.—The experiences of intuition are delicate, intimate, and subtle, and the human physical body is, at the present stage of its evolution, coarse in comparison. It offers therefore a strong hindrance to the success of intuition exercises. If these are continued with energy and persistence and with the requisite inner tranquility, the powerful hindrances of the physical body are finally overcome. The student notices this by the fact that gradually certain expressions of the physical body that formerly took place unconsciously now come under his control. He notices it also by the fact that for a short time he feels the need, for example, so to control the breath that it comes into a sort of concord or harmony with what the soul performs in the exercises or otherwise in inner meditation. The ideal of the development is that no exercises be made at all by means of the physical body itself, also no breathing exercises, but that everything that occurs in the physical body in this way should only come about as a consequence of pure intuition exercises.

* * *

If the student of the spirit ascends upon the path into the higher worlds of knowledge, he notices at a certain stage that the cohesion of the forces of his personality assumes a different form from the one in the physical-sensory world, where the ego effects a uniform co-operation of the soul forces, of thinking, feeling, and willing. These three soul forces stand always in a certain relationship to each other in the conditions of ordinary human life. One sees, for example, a certain object in the outer world. It pleases or displeases the soul. That is to say, of necessity the visualizing of a thing will be followed by a feeling of pleasure or displeasure. One may, perhaps, desire the object or have the impulse to alter it in one way or another. That is, the power of desire and will associate with visualizing and feeling. That this co-ordination takes place is caused by the ego uniting visualizing (thinking), feeling, and willing and in this way bringing order into the forces of the personality. This *healthy* order would be interrupted if the ego were to prove powerless in this regard; if, for example, desire should elect to go a different way from feeling or thinking. A human being would not be in a healthy soul condition who might *think* that this or that is right, but who might *want* something of which he is convinced that it is *not* right. The case would be similar if someone did not want what pleases him, but rather what displeases him. The human being now notices that on the path to higher knowledge thinking, feeling, and willing do indeed separate and each

324

assumes a certain independence. For example, a certain thought has no longer an inward urge toward a certain feeling and willing. The matter is as follows. In thinking something may be perceived correctly, but in order to have any feeling or to come to a resolution of the will, we need again an independent impulse from ourselves. During supersensible perception thinking, feeling, and willing do not remain three forces that radiate from the common ego-center of the personality, but they become three independent entities, three personalities, as it were; one must now make one's own ego all the stronger, for it is not merely a matter of its bringing three forces into order, but of leading and directing three entities. This separation, however, must only exist *during* supersensible perception. Here again it becomes clear how important it is that the exercises for higher training be accompanied by those that give certainty and firmness to the power of judgment, and to the life of feeling and willing. For the person who does not bring these qualities with him into the higher world will soon see how the ego proves weak and unable to act as an orderly guide for thinking, feeling, and willing. If this weakness were present, the soul would be as though torn by three personalities in as many directions and its inner unity would cease. If, however, the development of the student proceeds in the right way the described transformation of forces signifies true progress; the ego remains master of the independent entities that now form its soul.—In the further course of this evolution the development continues. Thinking that has become independent stimulates the emergence of a special fourth soul-spirit being that may be described as a direct influx of currents into man, similar to thoughts. The entire cosmos then appears as a thought-structure confronting man as does the plant or animal world in the realm of the physical senses. Likewise, feeling and willing that have become independent stimulate two forces in the soul that act in it like independent beings. Still another seventh power and being appears that is similar to one's own ego itself.

This entire experience is connected with yet another. Before his entrance into the supersensible world, man knew thinking, feeling, and willing only as inner soul experiences. As soon as he enters the supersensible world he perceives objects that do not express the physical-sensory, but the psycho-spiritual. Behind the characteristics of the new world now perceived by him stand soul-spirit beings. These now stand before him as an outer world, just as in the physical realm stones, plants, and animals stood before his senses. The student of the spiritual can now perceive an important difference between the world of soul and spirit that reveals itself to him, and the world that he was accustomed to perceiving through his physical senses. A plant in the world of the senses remains just as it is, whatever the human soul may feel or think about it. With the images of the world of soul and spirit this is, at the outset, not the case. They alter according to what the human being feels or thinks. In this way he gives them form that depends upon his own nature. Let us imagine that a certain picture appears before man in the world of imagination. If, at first, he remains indifferent to it in his soul, it then shows itself in a certain form. At the moment, however, when pleasure or displeasure is felt in regard to the picture, it changes its form. The pictures therefore, in the first instance, express not only what they are, independent of man, but they reflect what man is himself. They are permeated through and through by his own nature. The latter spreads like a veil over the supersensible beings. Although real beings confront him, he does not see them, but instead, his own creation. Thus he may have something true before him and, nevertheless, see something false. Indeed, this is not only the case in regard to what man notices in himself as his own essential nature, but everything that is in him affects this world. He may have, for example, hidden inclinations that do not come into evidence in life because of his education and character; they affect the world of the soul and spirit, which takes on a peculiar coloring through the whole being of man, no matter whether he himself knows much about this being or not.—In order to be able to advance further from this stage of development it is necessary that man learn to distinguish between himself and the outer spiritual world. It is necessary that he learn to eliminate all the effects of himself upon his soul-spirit environment. This cannot be done otherwise than by acquiring a knowledge of what he himself carries into the new world. It is therefore important that he first possess true, thoroughly developed self-knowledge, in order to be able to have a clear perception of the surrounding world of soul and spirit. Now, certain facts of human development demand that such self-knowledge *must* take place quite naturally at the time of the entrance into the higher world. Man develops his ego, his self-consciousness in the everyday physical-sensory world. This ego now acts as a center of attraction for everything belonging to man. All his inclinations, sympathies, antipathies, passions, and opinions

327

group themselves, as it were, around his ego, and this ego is also the point of attraction for what may be designated as the *karma* of man. If this ego were to be seen unconcealed it would show that certain forms of destiny must still be encountered by it in this and in subsequent incarnations, according to the way it has lived in the preceding incarnations and has made this or that its own. Invested with all this, the ego *must* appear as the first image before the human soul when the latter ascends into the world of soul and spirit. This *Doppelgänger* (double or twin likeness) of man must, according to a law of the spiritual world, emerge prior to everything else as his first impression in that world. One may easily make the law underlying this fact understandable if one considers the following. In the life of the physical senses man only perceives himself in so far as he experiences himself inwardly in his thinking, feeling, and willing. This, however, is an inner perception; it does not present itself to the human being like stones, plants, and animals. Also, man learns to know himself only partially through inner perception. He has something in himself that prevents his having more profound self-knowledge. This is an impulse to transform immediately a trait of character if he, as a result of self-knowledge, must admit to it and *does not wish to deceive himself about himself.*

If he does not follow this impulse, if he simply turns his attention away from himself, remaining what he is, then he, naturally, also deprives himself of the possibility of self-knowledge in the point in question. If man, however, penetrates into himself and confronts himself without deception with this or that trait, then he will either be in the position to improve the trait, or he will be incapable of doing so under the present circumstances of his life. In the latter case a feeling will creep over his soul that must be described as a feeling of shame. This is indeed the reaction of healthy human nature: it feels through self-knowledge various kinds of shame. This feeling has even in ordinary life a quite definite effect. The normally thinking human being will take care that what fills him, through himself, with this feeling does not become evident outwardly in effects, does not manifest in outer deeds. Shame is thus a force that impels man to conceal something in his inner being and not allow it to become outwardly perceptible. If we give this due consideration, we shall find it comprehensible that spiritual research ascribes much farther reaching effects to an inner soul experience that is closely related to the feeling of shame. This research finds that there is, concealed in the depths of the soul, a sort of *hidden* shame of which the human being is not conscious in physical-sensory life. This concealed feeling, however, acts in a similar manner to the feeling of shame in everyday life; it prevents the innermost nature of the human being from appearing before him in a perceptible picture. If this feeling were not present, the human being would perceive before him what he is in truth; his thoughts, feelings, and will would not only be experienced inwardly, but would be perceived outwardly just as stones, animals, and plants are perceived. This feeling is thus the concealer of man from himself, and at the same time it is the concealer of the entire world of soul and spirit. Owing to the fact that his inner nature is concealed from him, he is also not able to perceive that by means of which he should develop inner organs in order to

329

cognize the world of soul and spirit; he is unable so to transform his nature that it may unfold spiritual organs of perception.—If, however, through correct training man strives to acquire these organs of perception, what he himself is appears to him as first impression. He perceives his *Doppelgänger*, his double. This self-perception is not at all to be separated from the perception of the rest of the world of soul and spirit. In everyday life of the physical-sensory world, the feeling characterized acts so as constantly to close the door of the world of soul and spirit to the human being. Even the mere attempt to penetrate into this world causes the feeling of shame—which arises immediately, but of which we do not become conscious—to conceal the part of the world of soul and spirit that strives to appear. The exercises characterized open the door to this world. It is a fact, however, that this concealed feeling acts like a great benefactor of man. For all that man acquires of power of judgment, feeling-life, and character without spiritual-scientific training does not enable him to bear without further preparation the perception of his own being in its true form. He would lose through this perception all self-esteem, self-confidence, and self-consciousness. That this may not happen, we must take the necessary precautions which we do undertake, alongside the exercises for higher knowledge, in the fostering of a healthy power of judgment, feeling-life, and character. Through this regular training man learns to know so much of spiritual science— as though without intention—and, moreover, so many means for the attainment of self-knowledge and self-observation become clear to him as are necessary in order to encounter his *Doppelgänger* bravely. The student then only sees in another form, as a picture of the imaginative world, what he has already learned in the physical world. If he has first comprehended the law of karma properly in the physical world through his intellect, he will not be especially shaken when he now sees the beginnings of his destiny engraved in the image of his *Doppelgänger*. If man has made himself acquainted through his power of judgment with the evolution of the cosmos and mankind and knows how, at a certain point of time of this evolution, the forces of Lucifer have penetrated into the human soul, he will bear it without difficulty when he becomes aware that the Luciferic beings with all their effects are contained within the image of his own nature.—We see from this how necessary it is that man does not demand entrance into the spiritual world before he has understood, through his ordinary power of judgment developed in the physical-sensory world, certain truths about the spiritual world. The knowledge given in this book prior to the discussion about "Cognition of the Higher Worlds" should have been acquired by the student of spiritual science by means of his ordinary power of thought in the regular course of development, before he has the desire himself to enter into supersensible worlds.

In a training in which no attention is paid to the certainty and firmness of the power of judgment, of the life of feeling and character, it may happen that the student encounters the higher world before he possesses the necessary inner faculties. In that case the encounter with his *Doppelgänger* would depress him and lead to error. If, however, the encounter were entirely avoided—something that might indeed be possible—and man nevertheless were led into the supersensible world, he would then be just as little in the position to recognize that world in its true shape. For it would be quite impossible for him to distinguish between what he carries over as projections of himself into things and what they are in reality. This distinction is only possible if one perceives one's own being as an image in itself, and if, as a result of this distinction, everything that flows from one's own inner nature becomes detached from the environment.—For man's life in the physical-sensory world, the *Doppelgänger's* effect is such that he becomes immediately invisible through the feeling of shame characterized when man approaches the world of soul and spirit. As a result of this, he conceals the entire latter world also. Like a "guardian" he stands there before that world, in order to deny entrance to those who are not truly capable of entering. He may therefore be called the "guardian of the threshold that lies before the world of soul and spirit." —Besides the described encounter with the guardian at the entrance into the supersensible world, man also encounters him when passing through physical death, and in the course of life between death and a new birth the guardian discloses himself by degrees in the evolution of soul and spirit. There, however, the encounter cannot depress the human being, because he then has knowledge of worlds quite different from those he knows in the life between birth and death. If, without encountering the "guardian of the threshold," man were to enter the world of soul and spirit, he might fall prey to deception after deception. For he would never be able to distinguish between what he himself has carried over into that world and what in reality belongs to it. A proper training must lead the student of spiritual science into the realm of truth only, not into the realm of illusion. This training will of itself be of such a nature that the encounter must of necessity take place sometime. For it is one of the precautionary measures, indispensable for the observation of supersensible worlds, against the possibility of falling prey to deception and the fantastic.—It belongs to the most indispensable measures that every student of spiritual science must take, to work carefully on himself in order not to become a fantast, a human being who might succumb to possible deception and self-delusion. Where the advice for spiritual training is correctly followed, the sources that may bring deception are at the same time destroyed. Naturally, we cannot speak at length here of all the numerous details that have to be considered in regard to such precautionary measures. The important points can only be indicated. Deceptions that have to be considered here are derived from two sources. They originate in part from the coloring of reality through one's own soul nature. In ordinary life of the physical-sensory world there is comparatively little danger from this source of deception; for here the outer world continually impresses its own form sharply upon our observation, no matter how the observer wants to color it according to his own wishes and interests. As soon, however, as man enters the imaginative world, its pictures are transformed through such wishes and interests, and he has before him, like a reality, what he himself has formed, or at least has helped in forming. This source of deception is removed by the student's having learned to recognize, through his encounter with the "guardian of the threshold," his own inner nature, which he might thus carry into the world of soul and spirit.

333

The preparation that the student of spiritual science undergoes before his entrance into the world of soul and spirit acts in such a way that he becomes accustomed to disregarding himself even when observing the physical-sensory world and to permitting the objects and processes to speak to him purely out of their own nature. If the student has thus prepared himself sufficiently, he can calmly await the encounter with the "guardian of the threshold." This encounter will be the final test to determine whether he feels himself really in a position to disregard his own nature also when he confronts the world of soul and spirit.

Besides this source of delusion, there is still another. This comes into evidence when one misinterprets an impression made on one. A simple example of this sort of delusion in the physical sense-life is the delusion that arises when a man sits in a railway coach moving in a certain direction and *believes* the trees and other objects of perception are moving in the opposite direction, while actually it is he himself who is moving with the train. Although there are numerous cases where such delusions in the physical sense-world are more difficult to correct than the simple one quoted, still, it is easy to see that within this world one also finds the means of disposing of such delusions when, with sound judgment, one takes into consideration all that may possibly contribute to an adequate factual explanation. The matter is different, however, as soon as one penetrates into the realms of the supersensible. In the world of the senses facts are not altered as a result of human delusion; therefore it is possible, by means of unprejudiced observation, to rectify the delusion by means of the facts. In the supersensible world this is not immediately possible. If one wants to observe a supersensible process and approaches it with false judgment, one carries this judgment over into the process and it becomes so interwoven with the fact that it is impossible to distinguish the judgment from the fact. The error is then not within the human being and the correct fact outside him, but the error itself is made a component of the outer fact. It cannot, therefore, be rectified simply by an unbiased observation of the fact. We are here pointing to what may be a superabundant source of delusion and the fantastic for those who approach the supersensible world without proper preparation.—The student of the spiritual, besides acquiring the ability to exclude the delusions that arise through the coloring of supersensible world-phenomena with his own nature, must also acquire the ability to make the second indicated source of delusion ineffective. He can exclude what comes from himself if he has first recognized the image of his own *Doppelgänger*. He will be able to exclude the second source of delusion if he acquires the ability to recognize, from the inner *quality* of a supersensible fact, whether it is reality or delusion. If the delusion were to appear exactly like the actual facts, then a distinction would not be possible. This, however, is not the case. Delusions of the supersensible world have qualities *in themselves* by which they are to be distinguished from realities, and it is important that the student of the spiritual know by which qualities he can recognize realities. Nothing is more self-evident than the fact that anyone ignorant of spiritual training may ask, "How is it at all possible to protect myself against delusion, when its sources are so numerous?" And he may continue to ask, "Is there any proof for the student of the spiritual against the fact that all his professed higher knowledge is not something based on mere delusion and autosuggestion?" Anyone who asks such questions does not realize that in true spiritual training, through the very manner of its occurrence, the sources of delusion are stopped up. In the first place, in preparing himself the true spiritual science student will acquire sufficient knowledge about what may cause delusion and autosuggestion, and thus be in a position to protect himself from them. He has, in this regard, more opportunity than any other human being to make himself prudent and capable in judgment on the path of life. Everything that he experiences causes him to disregard indefinite premonitions and suggestions. This training makes him as careful as possible. Besides this, all correct training leads first to concepts about great cosmic events, and thus to things that make necessary the exertion of sound judgment, which becomes, at the same time, more refined and acute. Only someone who might refuse to go into such distant realms and preferred to abide with "revelations" of a world near at hand might lose the strengthening of that sound judgment that gives him certainty in distinguishing between delusion and reality. All of this, however, is not yet the most important. That lies in the exercises themselves that are used in a correct spiritual training. These must be so arranged that the student is always consciously aware of what takes place in the soul during inner meditation. In order to bring about imagination, a symbol is first formed. In this symbol are still contained mental images of outer perceptions. The human being is not alone responsible for the content of these mental images; he does not make it himself. Thus he may delude himself in regard to its origin; he may interpret its origin incorrectly. But the student of spiritual science removes this content from his consciousness when he advances to the exercises of inspiration. Here he contemplates his own soul activity only, which has formed the symbol. Here also error is still possible. Through education, learning, and through other means man has acquired the character of his soul activity. He cannot know everything about its origin. The student of spiritual science now removes even his own soul activity from his consciousness. If now anything remains in his consciousness, *nothing* is attached to it that cannot be surveyed. Nothing can intermingle with it that is not to be judged in regard to its whole content. In intuition, the student of spiritual science has thus a criterion enabling him to recognize how a clear reality of the world of soul and spirit is constituted. If he now applies the signs of soul and spirit-reality thus recognized to everything that comes under his observation, he is able to distinguish between illusion and reality. He may be certain that by employing this law he will remain protected from illusion in the supersensible world just as it cannot happen to him in the physical-sensory world to mistake an *imaginary* piece of hot iron for one that really burns. It is taken for granted that one only takes this attitude toward the knowledge one regards as one's own experiences in the supersensible worlds, and not toward what one receives as communications from other persons and that one comprehends with one's physical intellect and sound feeling for truth. The student of the spiritual will take pains to draw an exact line between what he has acquired in the one way and what he has acquired in the other. He will receive willingly, on the

337

one hand, the communications about the higher worlds and seek to understand them by means of his capacity to judge. If on the other hand he states something as his own experience, his own observation, he will have tested whether this has confronted him with precisely the qualities he has learned to perceive by means of unerring intuition.

*　　*　　*

After the student of the spiritual has encountered the "guardian of the threshold," further experiences await him as he ascends into supersensible worlds. First he will notice that an inner relationship exists between this "guardian of the threshold" and the soul-power that, in the above description, has resulted as the *seventh*, and has shaped itself into an independent principle. Indeed, this seventh principle is in a certain regard nothing else but the *Doppelgänger*, the "guardian of the threshold" himself, and this principle sets the student of the spiritual a special task. He has to direct and lead with his new-born self what he is in his ordinary self and which appears to him in an image. A sort of battle against the *Doppelgänger* will result. The latter will constantly strive for supremacy. To establish the right relationship to this *Doppelgänger* and not permit him to do anything that is not under the influence of the new-born ego strengthens and fortifies man's powers.—In the higher world, self-knowledge is different, in a certain respect, from self-knowledge in the physical-sensory world. Whereas in the physical-sensory world self-knowledge appears only as an inner experience, the new-born self presents itself at once as an outer soul phenomenon. Man be-

338

holds his new-born self as another being standing before him, but he cannot perceive it completely. For whatever stage he may have reached upon the way into the super-sensible worlds, there are always still higher stages. At these stages he will perceive ever more and more of his "higher self." This "higher self" can thus only partially reveal itself to the student of the spiritual at any of these stages. The temptation is extremely great which overtakes the human being when he first becomes aware of some aspect of his "higher self," to observe this "higher self," so to speak, from the standpoint he has gained in the physical-sensory world. This temptation is even good and it *must* appear, if development is to proceed in the right way. We must observe what appears in the *Doppelgänger,* the "guardian of the threshold," and place it before the "higher self" in order to note the contrast between what we are and what we are to become. Through this observation the "guardian of the threshold" begins to take on quite a different form. He presents himself as an image of all the *hindrances* that the development of the higher self must encounter. The student will perceive what a load he must drag in the form of his ordinary self, and if he is not strong enough through his preparations to say, "I will not remain stationary here, but unceasingly strive to reach my higher self," he will slacken his efforts and shrink back before what is in store for him. He has plunged into the world of soul and spirit, but now gives up his efforts. He becomes a prisoner of the form that, through the "guardian of the threshold," now stands before the soul. What is important here is the fact that in this experience he does not have the feeling of being a prisoner. On the contrary, he believes he experiences something quite different. The form that the "guardian of the threshold" calls forth can be of such a nature that it causes the impression in the soul of the observer of having before him, in the pictures that appear at this evolutionary stage, the entire compass of all imaginable worlds, of having attained the pinnacle of knowledge, with no need of striving further. Instead of feeling to be a prisoner he may feel himself as the immeasurably rich possessor of all the world mysteries. The fact that one can have such an experience that depicts the very opposite of the actual facts will, however, not astonish a person who keeps in mind the fact that, when he experiences this, he stands already in the world of soul and spirit and that it is a peculiarity of this world that events may present themselves in reverse order. This fact was pointed out earlier in this book when life after death was discussed.

The figure that one perceives at this stage of development shows the student of the spiritual something in addition to what appeared to him in the first instance as the "guardian of the threshold." In this *Doppelgänger* all the peculiarities were perceived that the ordinary self of man has in consequence of the influence of the forces of Lucifer. Now, however, in the course of human evolution another power has entered the human soul through the influence of Lucifer. This is the power that was designated in an earlier section of this book as the power of Ahriman. It is the power that prevents the human being during physical sense-existence from perceiving the soul-spirit beings of the outer world lying behind the veil of the sensory. The form the human soul has assumed under the influence of this power is shown in a picture by the shape that emerges in the experience described.—The person who is adequately prepared for this experience will be able to interpret it correctly; very soon thereafter another form will appear that we may call the "greater guardian of the threshold" in contrast to the already described "lesser guardian." This greater guardian tells the student of the spiritual that he must not remain stationary at this stage but must energetically work on. He calls forth in the observer the consciousness that the world that is conquered becomes truth, and is not transformed into illusion, only if the work is continued in an adequate manner.—If, because of incorrect spiritual training, a person were to enter upon this experience unprepared, then, in the encounter with the "greater guardian of the threshold," something would pour into his soul that only can be compared to the "feeling of immeasurable horror," of "boundless fear."

Just as the student of the spiritual in his encounter with the "lesser guardian of the threshold" is afforded the possibility of testing whether or not he is protected against delusions arising from the intermingling of his own being with the supersensible world, so can he also test himself by the experiences that finally lead to the "greater guardian of the threshold" whether he is capable of mastering the delusions described above as coming from the second source. If he is able to withstand the gigantic illusion that has been conjured up before him—that the picture world he has gained is a rich possession, while in reality he is only a prisoner—if he is able to resist this delusion, he is then, during the progressing course of his development, guarded from mistaking illusion for reality.

The "guardian of the threshold" will assume, to a certain

degree, an individual shape for each human being. The encounter with him corresponds indeed to the experience by which the personal character of the supersensible observations is overcome and through which the possibility is given of entering a region of experience that is free from personal coloring and applies to every human being.

* * *

If the student of the spiritual has had the above described experiences he is capable of distinguishing, within the surrounding world of soul and spirit, between himself and what lies outside him. He will then recognize that it is necessary to comprehend the cosmic process described in this book, in order to understand man and his life. Indeed, we understand the physical body only when we recognize how it has been fashioned during the *Saturn, Sun, Moon,* and *Earth* evolutions. We understand the ether body when we follow its formations through the *Sun, Moon,* and *Earth* evolutions. Moreover, we understand what at present is connected with the *Earth* evolution when we know how everything has unfolded itself step by step. Through spiritual training the student is placed in the position to recognize the relationship of everything that exists in the human being to corresponding facts and beings of the world outside him. For it is a fact that every member of the human organism stands in a relationship to the whole world surrounding it. In this book it has only been possible to indicate the facts in a sketchy outline. We must, however, consider that the human physical body, for example, was present during the *Saturn* evolution only in its rudimentary beginnings. Its organs—the heart, the lungs, the brain—developed later out of these beginnings during the *Sun, Moon,* and *Earth* evolutions. The heart, lungs, and the other organs are thus related to the *Sun, Moon,* and *Earth* evolutions. It is quite the same with the members of the ether and soul body, the sentient soul, and the other principles. Man is fashioned from the entire surrounding world, and every part of him corresponds to a process or being of the outer world. At the corresponding stage of his development the student becomes acquainted with this relationship between his own being and the great world. We may designate this stage of cognition as the becoming aware of the correspondence between the *lesser* world, the *microcosm,* which is the human being himself, and the *greater* world, the *macrocosm.* If the student has struggled through to such a stage of knowledge, a new experience may occur for him. He begins to feel as though he were intergrown with the entire cosmic structure, in spite of the fact that he feels himself in his complete independence. This feeling is a merging with the entire cosmos, a becoming one with it, but without losing one's own essential being. This stage of development may be designated as the "becoming one with the macrocosm." It is significant that this becoming one, this union, is not to be thought of as though through it the individual consciousness were to cease and the human being were to flow out into the universe, merging with it. Such a thought would be merely the expression of an opinion springing from the untrained power of judgment.—The stages of higher knowledge, in the sense of the process of initiation that has been described in this book, may now be enumerated as follows:

343

I. Study of spiritual science, in which one employs one's power of judgment gained in the physical-sensory world.
II. Acquiring imaginative knowledge.
III. Reading the occult script—corresponding to inspiration.
IV. Living into the spiritual environment—corresponding to intuition.
V. Knowledge of the relationships between microcosm and macrocosm.
VI. Union with the macrocosm.
VII. Total experience of all previous experiences as a fundamental mood of the soul.

These stages need not be thought of as successive experiences. On the contrary, the training may proceed in such a way that, in accordance with the individuality of the student of the spiritual, he may have reached only a certain degree of perfection in a preceding stage when he begins exercises that correspond to a subsequent stage. It may well happen, for example, that the student has only gained a few imaginations with certainty, yet he already performs exercises leading to inspiration, intuition, or the cognition of the relationship between microcosm and macrocosm.

* * *

If the student of the spiritual has experienced intuition, he not only knows the images of the psycho-spiritual world, he cannot merely read their connections in the "occult script," but he attains to knowledge of the spiritual beings themselves through whose co-operation the world, to which the human being belongs, comes into existence. In this way he learns to know himself in the form he possesses as a spiritual being in the world of soul and spirit. He has struggled through to a perception of his higher ego, and he has become aware of how he has to continue his efforts in order to control his *Doppelgänger,* the "guardian of the threshold." He has, however, also encountered the "greater guardian of the threshold," who stands before him as an ever present exhorter to further effort. This "greater guardian" becomes the ideal toward which he strives. If this feeling emerges in the student of the spiritual, he has then acquired the possibility of recognizing *who* it is that stands there before him as the "greater guardian of the threshold." To the perception of the student of the spiritual this guardian now transforms himself into the form of the Christ, Whose Being and participation in *Earth* evolution has been made clear in the previous chapters of this book. The student is now initiated into the exalted mystery that is linked with the name of the Christ. The Christ shows Himself to the student as the "great ideal of man on earth."—If thus through intuition the Christ is recognized in the spiritual world, what occurred historically on earth in the fourth post-Atlantean evolutionary epoch—the Greco-Latin epoch—also becomes comprehensible. The way in which, at that time, the exalted Sun Being, the Christ, has intervened in the *Earth* evolution and how he continues to work within this evolution becomes the personally experienced knowledge of the student of the spiritual. It is thus a revelation of the meaning and significance of *Earth* evolution that the student receives through intuition.

The way to knowledge of the supersensible worlds, which is described here, is one that every human being can follow, no matter what the situation in which he may find himself within the present-day conditions of life. When describing such a path we must consider that the goal of knowledge and truth is the same in all ages of *Earth* evolution, but that the starting points of man have been different in different ages. If the human being wishes to tread the path to the spiritual world he cannot at present begin at the same starting point as, for example, the would-be initiate of ancient Egypt. Therefore, the exercises that were imposed upon the student of the spiritual of ancient Egypt cannot be carried out by the modern man without modification. Since that time, human souls have passed through various incarnations, and this advance from incarnation to incarnation is not without meaning and significance. The faculties and qualities of souls alter from incarnation to incarnation. Whoever considers human historical life, be it only superficially, is able to notice that since the twelfth and thirteenth centuries A.D. all life-conditions have changed when compared with previous centuries; that opinions, feelings, and also abilities of human beings have become different from what they were previously. The path to higher knowledge described here is eminently fit for souls who incarnate in the immediate present. It is one that places the point of departure for spiritual development just where the human being now stands in any situation presented by modern life.—Progressive evolution leads mankind in regard to the path to higher knowledge from period to period to ever changing forms, just as outer life changes its forms, and at all times a perfect harmony must prevail between outer life and initiation.

VI

THE PRESENT AND FUTURE OF
COSMIC AND HUMAN EVOLUTION

IT IS IMPOSSIBLE to know anything of the present and future of human and cosmic evolution in the sense of spiritual science without a knowledge of this evolution in the past. For what presents itself to the perception of the spiritual researcher when he observes the hidden facts of the past contains *simultaneously* all he can know of the present and future. This book has dealt with the evolution of *Saturn, Sun, Moon,* and *Earth.* It is impossible to understand the *Earth* evolution, in the sense of spiritual science, if one does not observe the facts of the preceding evolutionary cycles. For the facts of the *Moon, Sun,* and *Saturn* evolutions are contained in a certain sense within the conditions that confront the human being at present within the sphere of the earth. The beings and things that participated in the *Moon* evolution have evolved further. Everything that belongs to the present earth came out of them.

347

For physical-sensory consciousness, however, not everything is perceptible that, having come from the *Moon*, has become the *Earth*. A part of what has evolved over from the *Moon* becomes evident only at a certain stage of supersensible consciousness. When this knowledge is attained, then we perceive that our earth is bound to a supersensible world, containing the part of the *Moon* existence that has not condensed to the condition of physical sense-perception. This supersensible world contains the uncondensed part of the *Moon* as it is *at present, not* as it was at the time of the ancient *Moon* evolution. Supersensible consciousness, however, is able to obtain a picture of the previous condition. If this supersensible consciousness concentrates upon the perception it can have at the present time, it becomes evident that, quite by itself, it gradually resolves itself into *two* pictures. One of these presents the shape the *Earth* had during its *Moon* evolution; the manner in which the other picture shows itself, however, reveals that it contains a form that is still in its germinal stage and that will only become real in the future in the sense that the earth is now real. Further observation shows that, in a certain sense, the effect of what happens upon the earth streams continually into this future form. In this form we have, therefore, before us what is to be our earth in the future. The effects of earth existence will unite with what happens in the characterized world and out of this will arise the new cosmic being into which the *Earth* will be transformed, just as the *Moon* has transformed itself into the *Earth*. We may call this future form the *Jupiter* evolution. If we observe this *Jupiter* stage with supersensible perception, we can see that in the future certain processes *must* take place, be-

348

cause in the supersensible part of the *Earth* that originated on the *Moon* certain beings and things are present that will assume certain forms when, within the earth of the physical senses, this or that will have taken place. In the *Jupiter* evolution something will, therefore, exist that has already been determined by the *Moon* evolution, and it will contain new factors that enter into the entire evolution only through terrestrial processes. Because of this, supersensible consciousness may learn something of what will happen during the *Jupiter* state. The beings and facts perceived within this field of consciousness do not possess the nature of sense images; they do not even appear as delicate, airy structures from which effects might proceed which remind us of sense-impressions. They give us pure spiritual impressions of tone, light, and warmth. The latter do *not* express themselves through any sort of material embodiment. They can be comprehended only through supersensible consciousness. We may, nevertheless, say that these beings possess a "body." Yet this body shows itself within their soul nature, which reveals itself as their present being, like a sum of *condensed memories* which they bear within their soul. We are able to distinguish in their being between what they *now* experience, and what they have experienced and remember. The latter is contained within them like a bodily nature. They experience it just as the earth man experiences his body. At a stage of supersensible perception higher than the one just described as necessary for the cognition of *Moon* and *Jupiter,* supersensible beings and things become visible that are the further developed forms of what was already present during the *Sun* evolution, but which has attained at present such a high stage of evolu-

349

tion that it does not at all exist for a consciousness that has only attained to the perception of *Moon* forms. The picture of this world also resolves itself into two pictures during inner meditation. One of these leads to the cognition of the past *Sun* evolution, the other presents a future form of the *Earth*; that is to say, the form into which the *Earth* will have transformed itself when the effects of the *Earth* and *Jupiter* processes have streamed into the forms of that world. What we thus observe of this future world may be designated, in the sense of spiritual science, as the *Venus* evolution. In a similar manner there is, for a still more highly developed supersensible consciousness, a future stage of evolution that may be designated *Vulcan* evolution. It has a relationship to the *Saturn* evolution similar to the one the *Venus* evolution has to the *Sun* evolution, and the *Jupiter* evolution has to the *Moon* evolution. We may, therefore, if we consider the past, present and future of *Earth* evolution, speak of *Saturn, Sun, Moon, Earth, Jupiter, Venus,* and *Vulcan* evolutions.—Just as these all-encompassing relationships of the *Earth* evolution result for our consciousness, so also there result observations of a nearer future. *Every* picture of the past corresponds also to one of the future. Yet in speaking of such things something must be emphasized which, of necessity, must be given due consideration. If we wish to recognize such matters we must discard completely the opinion that philosophical reflection, trained merely by external reality, is able to discover anything about them. These things cannot and never should be investigated by such a mode of thinking. If a person were to believe, when he has received communications through spiritual science about the *Moon* evolution,

350

that through such reflection he might discover how things will appear on *Jupiter* by combining the relationships of *Earth* and *Moon,* he will fall prey to enormous deceptions. *Research* into these relationships is only to be made when supersensible consciousness has lifted itself to higher observation. Only when what has thus been discovered is communicated can it be understood without supersensible consciousness.

Concerning the communications about the future, the researcher of the spiritual is in a position different from the position concerning those about the past. The human being cannot, at the outset, confront future events as impartially as he can confront the past. What will occur in the future stirs human feelings and will; the past is endured in quite a different manner. Whoever observes life knows how true this already is for ordinary existence. To what an enormous degree this increases, what forms it assumes in regard to the hidden facts of life only he can know who is cognizant of certain things of the supersensible worlds. This is the reason why the knowledge of these things is fixed within quite definite limits.

Just as the great cosmic evolution can be presented in the succession of its states from the *Saturn* to the *Vulcan* evolution, it is also possible to present smaller time-divisions; those of the *Earth* evolution, for example. Since that enormous catastrophe that brought the ancient Atlantean civilization to an end there have been successive stages within human evolution that in this book have been designated as the ancient Indian, the ancient Persian, the Egypto-Chaldean, and the Greco-Latin epochs of culture. The *fifth* period is the one in which mankind now stands—

351

the *present*. This period gradually began during the twelfth, thirteenth, and fourteenth centuries A.D., after it had prepared itself since the fourth and fifth centuries. From the fifteenth century onward it emerged quite clearly. The preceding Greco-Latin culture began about the eighth century B.C. At the end of its first third, the Christ event occurred. The condition of the human soul and all the human faculties changed with the transition from the Egypto-Chaldean to the Greco-Latin cultural period. In the former there was not yet present what we now know as logical cogitation, as intellectual comprehension of the world. What the human being now acquires as knowledge through his intellect he received in the form that was fitting for that time: directly through an inner, in a certain respect, supersensible knowledge. He perceived objects, and while perceiving them their concept, their image, needed by the soul, arose in its inner being. With the power of cognition described, not only images of the physical sense world emerge, but from the depths of the soul there arises a certain knowledge of non-sensory facts and beings. This was the remnant of ancient dim clairvoyant consciousness, once the common possession of all mankind. During the Greco-Latin period there arose more and more human beings who lacked such faculties. Instead of these faculties, intellectual reflection upon objects began to appear. Human beings were by degrees removed from a direct, dreamlike perception of the world of soul and spirit and were ever more dependent upon a picture of that world, formed by their intellect and feeling. This state continued in a certain respect throughout the entire fourth post-Atlantean period. Only those individuals who had preserved the ancient soul condition

352

like a heritage could still receive the spiritual world directly into their consciousness. These individuals, however, are stragglers of a more ancient epoch. The kind of knowledge they possessed no longer fitted the new age. For it is a consequence of the laws of evolution that an ancient soul faculty loses its full significance when new faculties appear. Human life then adapts itself to these new faculties, and it is no longer able to exercise the old faculties. There were, however, also individuals who in a quite conscious manner began to develop, besides the acquired powers of intellect and feeling, other higher faculties that again made it possible for them to penetrate into the world of soul and spirit. They had to begin to do this in a manner quite different from what was customary for the pupils of the ancient initiates. The latter did not yet have to consider the soul faculties first developed in the fourth cultural period. In that period the method of spiritual training began that has been described in this book as the present-day method. But it was at that time only in its infancy; it could be properly developed only in the fifth cultural period, actually since the twelfth and thirteenth—chiefly the fifteenth—centuries of our era. Human beings who in this way sought to ascend into the supersensible world were able to experience through their own imagination, inspiration, and intuition something of higher realms of existence. Those who remained satisfied with the developed faculties of intellect and feeling could learn only from tradition, what ancient clairvoyance knew, and which was transmitted from generation to generation by word of mouth, or in writing.

Something of the real nature of the Christ event could also be known only from tradition by those born after the event, if they had not attained a perception of the supersensible worlds. There were, however, certain initiates who still possessed the natural clairvoyant perception of the supersensible world and who through their development could elevate themselves to a higher world in spite of the fact that they paid no attention to the new powers of intellect and soul. Through such initiates a transition was created from the old method of initiation to the new. Such personalities existed also in subsequent periods. It was the chief characteristic of the fourth cultural epoch that the soul's exclusion from direct intercourse with the world of soul and spirit strengthened the human being in his powers of intellect and feeling. The souls who were incarnated at that time with highly developed powers of intellect and feeling carried over the result of this development into their incarnations in the fifth cultural period. As a compensation for this exclusion from intercourse with the world of soul and spirit the mighty traditions of primeval wisdom were then available to man—and especially those concerning the Christ event—traditions that by the very power of their content gave the souls a confident knowledge of the higher worlds.—But human beings always existed who developed the higher powers of knowledge in addition to the faculties of intellect and feeling. It was their task to experience the facts of the higher world and chiefly the mystery of the Christ event through direct supersensible cognition. From them there flowed into the souls of other men as much as was comprehensible and good for them.—In harmony with the meaning of *Earth* evolution, the first spreading of Christianity had of necessity to occur just at a time when the powers of supersensible cognition had not

354

been developed in a large portion of mankind. It was because of this that the force of tradition was so powerful at that time. The strongest possible force was needed to lead men, who were themselves unable to behold this world, to a trust in the supersensible world. There were almost always—if we disregard a brief period of exception in the thirteenth century—individuals who were able to elevate themselves to higher worlds through imagination, inspiration, and intuition. These men are the post-Christian successors of the ancient initiates, of the leaders and members of the institutions of mystery wisdom. They had the task of recognizing, by means of their own faculties, what had been comprehensible through ancient mystery wisdom, to which they had to add the knowledge of the essential nature of the Christ event.

A knowledge thus arose among these new initiates that included everything that was the subject of ancient initiation, but in the center of this knowledge there radiated the higher wisdom of the mysteries of the Christ event. Only in a small degree could such knowledge flow into general life, while the human souls of the fourth period of culture had to consolidate the faculties of intellect and feeling. Thus it was at that time a very "hidden knowledge." Then the dawn of the new age broke, which is to be designated as the fifth cultural period. Its nature consists in the advance of the evolution of the intellectual faculties, which have unfolded to an exuberant blossoming and will unfold still further in the present and into the future. This prepared itself slowly, beginning with the twelfth and thirteenth centuries, in order to accelerate its advance from the sixteenth century onward into the present time. Under these influences, the chief objective of the evolution of the fifth cultural epoch was the fostering of the powers of the intellect, whereas the confident knowledge of former ages, traditional knowledge, lost more and more of its power over the human soul. But in its place there developed what may be called an increasingly stronger influx into human souls of the knowledge gained through modern supersensible consciousness. The "hidden knowledge" flows, although quite unnoticed at the beginning, into the mode of thinking of the men of this period. It is only self-evident that, up to the present, intellectual forces reject this knowledge. But what must happen will happen, in spite of all temporary rejection. The "hidden knowledge," which from this side takes hold of mankind now and will take hold of it more and more in the future, may be called symbolically "the wisdom of the Grail." If this symbol, as it is given in legend and myth, is understood in its deeper meaning, we shall find that it is a significant image of the nature of what has been spoken of above as the knowledge of the new initiation, with the Christ mystery at its center. The modern initiates may, therefore, also be called "initiates of the Grail." The way into the supersensible worlds, the first stages of which have been described in this book, leads to the "science of the Grail." This knowledge has the peculiarity that *research* into its facts can be made only if one has acquired the necessary means that have been described in this book. If, however, such research has been made, these facts can then be understood through the soul forces developed in the fifth cultural period. Indeed, it will become more and more evident that these forces, in an ever higher degree, will find satisfaction through this knowledge. We move now in an age in which this knowledge ought to be received more abundantly into general consciousness than was previously the case, and it is from this point of view that this book desires to impart its information. To the degree to which the development of mankind will absorb the knowledge of the Grail, the impulse given through the Christ event can become ever more significant. To the external aspect of Christian development the *inner* aspect will be joined more and more. What may be known through imagination, inspiration, and intuition about the higher worlds in connection with the Christ mystery will increasingly permeate the thought, feeling, and will-life of humanity. The "concealed knowledge of the Grail" will be revealed; as an inner force it will permeate more and more the manifestations of human life.

Throughout the fifth cultural period the knowledge of supersensible worlds will flow into human consciousness, and when the sixth period begins, mankind will have been able to re-attain at a higher stage what it has possessed of non-sensory perception at an earlier period in a still dim way. The new possession will, however, have a form quite different from the old. What the soul knew in ancient times of higher worlds was not permeated by its own power of intellect and feeling; that knowledge came as an inspiration. In the future the soul will not merely have inspirations, but it will comprehend them and feel them as being of its own being. If knowledge about this or that being or thing dawns upon the soul, the intellect will then find it justified through its own nature; if a knowledge of a different kind asserts itself—knowledge of a moral law, or a human relationship—the soul will then say to itself: My

357

feeling can only justify itself when I act in accordance with this knowledge. Such a soul state is to be developed by a sufficiently large number of human beings of the sixth cultural period.—What the third, the Egypto-Chaldean cultural period, has bestowed upon human evolution repeats itself, in a certain way, in the fifth period. In the third period the soul still perceived certain facts of the supersensible world, but the perception of this world was disappearing. The intellectual powers were preparing themselves for their evolution, and they were, for the time being, to exclude the human being from the higher world. In the fifth cultural period the supersensible facts, which in the third period were perceived by a hazy clairvoyance, again become manifest. Now they are permeated with the forces of human intellect and personal feeling. They become permeated also with what can be imparted to the soul through the knowledge of the Christ mystery. Hence they assume quite a different form from the one possessed previously. Whereas the impressions received from the supersensible worlds were felt in ancient times as forces giving impulses to the human being from an external spiritual world in which he did not dwell, these impressions will be felt, through the development of the modern age, as proceeding from a world into which the human being grows and in which he participates progressively more and more. No one should believe that the Egypto-Chaldean culture will repeat itself in such a way that the soul will simply receive what existed at that time and has been handed down by tradition. The Christ impulse, rightly understood, works in such a way that the human soul who has received it feels, recognizes, and conducts itself as a member of a spiritual

358

world, outside of which it had previously dwelt.—Whereas in this way the third epoch reappears in the fifth, in order to permeate human souls with what the fourth epoch has brought as something completely new, something similar will be the case with the sixth epoch in regard to the second and the seventh in regard to the first, the ancient Indian epoch. All the marvels of wisdom of ancient India that the great teachers of that time could proclaim will be able to reappear as truth of life of human souls in the seventh cultural epoch.

The transformations in the things of the earth existing outside the human being occur with a certain relationship to humanity's own evolution. After the seventh cultural period has run its course, the earth will be visited by a catastrophe that may be likened to what occurred between the Atlantean and post-Atlantean ages, and the transformed earth conditions after this catastrophe will again evolve in seven time periods. Human souls who will then be incarnated will experience, at a higher stage, the union with the higher world experienced by the Atlanteans at a lower stage. Only those human beings, however, in whom are incarnated souls that have developed in a manner possible through the influences of the Greco-Latin epoch and the subsequent fifth, sixth, and seventh cultural epochs of the post-Atlantean evolution will be able to cope with the newly formed earth conditions. The inner being of such souls will correspond to what the earth has then become. Other souls will then *have* to remain behind, whereas previously they would have had the choice of creating the conditions for advancement. Souls who will have created the possibility for themselves, in the transition from the fifth to the sixth post-Atlantean period, of penetrating supersensible knowledge with the forces of intellect and feeling, will have the maturity for the corresponding conditions following the next great catastrophe. The fifth and sixth periods are, so to speak, decisive. In the seventh, the souls who will have reached the goal of the sixth will develop correspondingly further; the other souls, however, will, under the changed conditions of the environment, find but little opportunity of retrieving what they have neglected. Only at some future time will conditions appear again that will permit this.—Evolution thus advances from age to age. *Supersensible* cognition not only observes such future changes in which the earth alone takes part, but it is also aware of changes that occur in co-operation with the heavenly bodies in its environment. A time will come when the evolution of the earth and mankind will have advanced so far that the spiritual powers and beings that had to sever themselves from the earth during the Lemurian age, in order to make possible the continued progress of the earth's beings, will be able to unite themselves again with the earth. The moon will then reunite with the earth. This will occur because at that time a sufficiently large number of human souls will possess so much inner strength that they will use these moon forces for the benefit of further evolution. This will occur at a time when, alongside the high level of development that will have been reached by a certain number of human souls, another development will occur that has taken the direction toward evil. The laggard souls will have accumulated in their karma so much error, ugliness, and evil that they will form, for the time being, a special union of evil and aberrant human beings who violently oppose the community of good men.

The good humanity will through its development acquire the use of the moon forces and thereby so transform the evil part also that, as a special realm of the earth, it may participate in further evolution. Through this work of the good humanity, the earth, united with the moon, will be able, after a certain period of evolution, to reunite also with the sun and with the other planets. Then, after an intermediate stage, which presents itself as a sojourn in a higher world, the *Earth* will transform itself into *Jupiter*. Within this state, what is now called the mineral kingdom will no longer exist; the forces of this mineral kingdom will be transformed into plant forces. The plant kingdom, which in contrast to the present plant kingdom will have an entirely new form, appears during the *Jupiter* state as the lowest kingdom. To this a higher kingdom is added, the transformed animal kingdom; above it there is a human kingdom, which proves to be the progeny of the evil community that arose on the earth; above all these are to be found the descendants of the good community of earth men, a human kingdom of a higher order. A great part of the activity of this latter human kingdom consists in the work of ennobling the fallen souls of the evil community, so that they may still be able to find their way back into the actual human kingdom. The *Venus* evolution will be one in which the plant kingdom also will have disappeared; the lowest kingdom at that time will be the re-transformed animal kingdom; this will be joined on an ascending scale by three human kingdoms of different degrees of perfection. During the *Venus* state the earth remains united with the sun; during the *Jupiter* state, however, evolution proceeds in such a way that at a certain point of time the sun departs once more from *Jupiter* and the latter receives its effects from the outside. After a time, the union of sun and Jupiter[1] again occurs and the transformation gradually proceeds over into the *Venus* state. During that state a special cosmic body splits off that contains all the beings who have resisted evolution, a so to speak "irredeemable moon," which now moves toward an evolution, for the character of which no expression can be found because it is too dissimilar to anything that man can experience on earth. The evolved mankind, however, advances in a completely spiritualized existence to the *Vulcan* evolution, the description of which does not lie within the scope of this book.

We see that the highest imaginable ideal of human evolution results from the "knowledge of the Grail": the spiritualization that man acquires through his own efforts. For this spiritualization appears finally as a result of the harmony that he produces in the fifth and sixth cultural periods of present evolution between the acquired powers of intellect and feeling and the knowledge of the supersensible worlds. What he there produces in the inmost depths of his soul is finally itself to become the outer world. The human spirit elevates itself to the tremendous impressions of its outer world and first divines and afterwards recognizes spiritual beings behind these impressions; man's heart feels the boundless sublimity of the spiritual. The

---

[1] Jupiter minus the sun in contradistinction to *Jupiter* with the sun. (Tr.)

human being can also recognize that his inner experiences of intellect, feeling, and character are the indications of a nascent world of the spirit.

Whoever believes that human freedom is not compatible with foreknowledge and predestination of the future condition of things, should consider that free human action in the future depends just as little upon the character the predestined things will have as this freedom depends upon his resolve to live in a house a year hence, the plan of which he determines today. He will be as free as it is possible for him to be according to his inner nature, precisely in the house he has built for himself; and he will be as free upon *Jupiter* and *Venus* as his inner life permits just *within* the conditions that will arise there. Freedom will not depend upon what has been predestined by antecedent conditions, but upon what the soul has made of itself.

* * *

Within the *Earth* evolution is contained what has evolved during the preceding *Saturn, Sun,* and *Moon* evolutions. The earth man finds "wisdom" in the processes that take place in his environment. This wisdom is present as the result of what had happened previously. The *Earth* is the descendant of the ancient *Moon* which, with all that belonged to it, formed itself into the "cosmos of wisdom." The *Earth* is the beginning of an evolution through which a new force is added to this wisdom. It brings the human being to the point where he feels himself an independent member of the spirit world. This rests on the fact that his ego is fashioned by the Spirits of Form during the *Earth* evolution, just as upon *Saturn* the Spirits of Will formed his physical body, upon the *Sun* the Spirits of Wisdom his life-body, and upon the *Moon* the Spirits of Motion his astral body. The manifestation of wisdom appears through the co-operation of the Spirits of Will, Wisdom, and Motion. The *Earth* beings and *Earth* processes can harmonize in wisdom with the other beings of their world through the work of these three classes of spirits. From the Spirits of Form the human being receives his independent ego. In the future this ego will harmonize with the beings of *Earth, Jupiter, Venus,* and *Vulcan* through the power that is added to wisdom by the *Earth* evolution. This is the power of *love.* In earth humanity this power of love must take its beginning, and the "cosmos of wisdom" unfolds itself into a *"cosmos of love."* Everything that the ego is able to unfold within itself is to become *love.* The exalted Sun Being Whom we are able to characterize in the description of the Christ evolution manifests Himself as the all-encompassing "archetype of love." Thus the seed of love is planted into the innermost core of human nature. And from there it is to flow into the whole of evolution. Just as the previously formed wisdom reveals itself in the forces of the sensory external world of the earth, in the present-day "nature forces," so in the future love will reveal itself in all phenomena as a new nature force. It is the mystery of all evolution into the future that knowledge and all that the human being does through a true understanding of evolution is a sowing of seed that must ripen as *love,* and the greater the force of love coming into being, the greater will be the accomplishments of creative force in the future. In what will be created from love will lie the strong forces leading to the above described culminating result of spiritualization. The greater the amount of spiritual cognition that flows into human and earth evolution, the greater will be the number of fertile seeds for the future. Spiritual knowledge is transmuted by its very nature into love. The entire process that has been described, beginning with the Greco-Latin cultural epoch and extending through our present epoch, shows how this transformation is to take place, and also shows that the *beginning* of development into the future has been made. What has been prepared during the *Saturn, Sun,* and *Moon* evolutions as wisdom acts in the physical, ether, and astral body of man; there it shows itself as "cosmic wisdom"; in the "ego," however, it becomes "inner wisdom." From the *Earth* stage onward, "wisdom of the external world" becomes inner wisdom of man. Intensified in the inner life, it becomes the seed of *love.* Wisdom is the pre-condition of love; love is the result of wisdom reborn in the ego.

Whoever could be misled by the preceding expositions into believing that the described evolution bears a fatalistic stamp, would have misunderstood them. Whoever were to believe that in such an evolution a certain number of men would be condemned to belong to the kingdom of "evil humanity," fails to perceive how the mutual relationship between outer world and the world of soul and spirit takes shape in this evolution. Both outer world and the world of soul and spirit form, within certain limits, separate evolutionary streams. Through the forces inherent in the sensory stream there arise the forms of the "evil human kingdom." The necessity for a human soul to incarnate in such a form will only occur if this soul itself has created the conditions for it. The case might also arise that the forms originating

365

from the forces of the sensory could not find human souls originating in the previous age, for these souls might be too good for that type of body. These forms would then have to be ensouled from the cosmos by something quite different from former human souls. Human souls will incarnate in the forms characterized only when they have made themselves ready for such an incarnation. Supersensible cognition is bound to state what it perceives concerning this sphere, namely, that in the future indicated there will exist two human kingdoms, one good and one evil, but it does not abstractly *deduce* from the present state of human souls a future state appearing as though with the force of self-evident necessity. Evolution of human forms and evolution of soul-destinies must be sought by supersensible cognition on two quite separate paths; any attempt to mix the two in the conception of the world would be a remnant of a materialistic attitude that, if present, would project itself dangerously into the science of the supersensible.

VII

DETAILS FROM THE REALM OF SPIRITUAL SCIENCE

THE ETHER BODY OF MAN

IF HIGHER members of man are observed by means of supersensible perception, this perception is never completely similar to perception with the outer senses. If the human being touches an object and has a perception of heat, he must distinguish between what comes from the object, what streams out of it, as it were, and what he himself experiences in his soul. The inner soul experience of the sensation of heat is something quite different from the heat streaming from the object. Let us now imagine this soul experience alone, without the outer object. Let us imagine the experience of a sensation of heat in the soul without an outer physical cause. If such an experience were simply present *without* a cause, it would be imaginary. The student of the spiritual experiences such inner percep-

367

tions without physical cause, and above all, without their being caused by his own body. These perceptions appear at a certain stage of development, however, in such a way that he is able to know (as has been shown, through the experience itself) that the inner perception is not imaginary, but that it is caused by a being of the world of soul and spirit in a supersensory outer world just as the usual sensation of heat, for example, is caused by an outer physical-sensory object. This is also the case when one speaks of a color perception. There a distinction must be made between the color of the outer object and the inner sensation of color in the soul. Let us visualize the inner sensation of the soul when it perceives a *red* object of the outer physical-sensory world. Let us imagine that we retain a vivid memory of the impression, but we turn the eye away from the object. Let us now visualize as an inner experience what we then retain as memory picture of the color. We shall then distinguish between the inner experience of the color, and the outer color. These inner experiences are certainly different in content from the outer sense-impressions. They bear much more the character of what is felt as pain and joy than the normal outer sensation. Now think that such an inner experience arises in the soul without an outer physical-sensory object or the memory of such an object as the cause. A person able to have supersensible perceptions may have such an experience. He is also able to know, in the case in question, that it is not imaginary, but the expression of a being of the world of soul and spirit. If this being now calls forth an impression similar to the one made by a red object of the physical-sensory world, it may then be designated red. In the case of a physical-sensory object, the outer impression will always be there first; then comes the inner color experience. In the case of true supersensible perception by the human being of our time, the process must be reversed: first the inner experience, shadowlike, like a mere color memory, and then a picture that becomes ever more vivid. The less attention one pays to the fact that the process must occur in this manner, the less one will be able to distinguish between real spiritual perception and imaginary deception, hallucination, and so forth. Whether the vividness of the picture, in the case of such a perception of the world of soul and spirit, remains entirely shadowlike, like a dim visualization, or whether it produces an intensive effect, like an outer object, will depend entirely upon the development of the student of the spiritual.—It is possible to describe the general impression that the clairvoyant has of the human ether body thus: If the person who has supersensible perception has developed such a power of will that, in spite of the presence of a physical man before him, he is capable of diverting his attention from what the physical eye beholds, then he is able by means of supersensible consciousness to look into the space occupied by the physical human being. Of course, a strong increase of will is necessary in order not only to turn the attention away from something one thinks but from something that stands before one, so that the physical impression becomes entirely extinguished. But this increase of will is possible, and it appears as a result of the exercises for the attainment of supersensible cognition. The one who is thus able to cognize may then have, in the first instance, a general impression of the ether body. In his soul the same inner sensation

369

emerges that he has by looking at the color of the peach blossom; this then increases in intensity and enables him to say that the ether body has the color of the peach blossom. Then he perceives also the individual organs and currents of the ether body. We may, however, describe the ether body further by indicating the experiences of the soul that correspond to the sensations of heat, to the impressions of tone, and so forth. For it is not *merely* a phenomenon of color. In the same sense the astral body and the other members of man's being may be described. Whoever considers this will understand how descriptions are to be taken that are made in the sense of spiritual science. (See Chapter II in this book.)

THE ASTRAL WORLD

As long as we observe only the physical world, the earth as a dwelling place of man appears like a separate cosmic body. If, however, supersensible cognition rises to different worlds, this separation ceases. It was, therefore, possible to say that imagination perceives, together with the earth, the *Moon* condition developed right into the present. Not only does the supersensible realm of the earth belong to the world we enter in this way, but embedded in it are still other cosmic bodies, physically separated from the earth. The knower of supersensible worlds does then not merely observe the supersensible nature of the earth, but, *at the outset,* also the *supersensible* nature of other cosmic bodies. (That it is primarily a question of observing the *supersensible nature* of other cosmic bodies should be considered by those who are impelled to ask the question: Why do the clairvoyants not tell us about the conditions on Mars? Such a questioner has the physical-sensory conditions in mind.) In the presentation of this book it was, therefore, possible also to speak of certain relationships of the earth evolution with the simultaneously occurring Saturn, Jupiter, and Mars evolutions, and so forth.—When the human astral body yields to sleep, it does not then belong to the earth conditions only, but to worlds in which still other cosmic realms, stellar worlds, astral worlds, partake. Indeed, these worlds are also active in the astral body of man during the waking state. Therefore, the name "astral body" seems to be justified.

THE LIFE OF MAN AFTER DEATH

In the exposition of this book we have spoken of the time during which, after the death of the human being, the astral body still remains united with the ether body. During this time a gradually fading memory of the whole life just passed is present. (See Chapter III.) The length of this period varies with different human beings. It depends upon the degree of power with which the astral body of the individual human being holds fast to the ether body, upon the degree of force the former exercises upon the latter. Supersensible cognition may have an impression of this power when it observes a human being who, because of his state of body and soul, ought to be asleep, but who remains awake by means of inner strength. It now becomes evident that different people are able to remain awake for greatly varying lengths of time without being overpowered by sleep. For the most extreme length of time that a human

371

being is able to remain awake does the memory of the life just passed through continue after death, that is to say, does the connection of the astral with the ether body last.

*   *   *

When the ether body is released from man after death, a portion of it still remains for the rest of man's future evolution. This may be described as an extract or an essence of this body. This extract contains the fruits of the past life, and it is the bearer of everything that, during man's spiritual development between death and a new birth, unfolds as a germinal beginning of the subsequent life. (Compare Chapter III.)

*   *   *

The length of time between death and a new birth is determined by the fact that, as a rule, the ego returns to the physical-sensory world only after the latter has been changed sufficiently to make it possible for the ego to experience something new. While the ego remains in the spiritual realms, the earthly dwelling place undergoes a change. This change is connected in a certain respect with the great changes in the cosmos, with the changed position of earth and sun, and so forth. These are changes, however, in which certain repetitions take place in connection with new conditions. They express themselves outwardly, for instance, through the fact that the point of the celestial sphere at which the sun rises in the beginning of spring makes a complete circle in the course of 26,000 years. This vernal equinox thus resolves, in the course of that period, from one celestial region to another. In the course of one twelfth of this period, in about 2,100 years, the conditions on the earth have altered so much that the human soul can experience something new after a preceding incarnation. Since the experiences of a human being are different according to his incarnation as a woman or as a man, there occur *as a rule* two incarnations within the characterized period of 2,100 years, one as a man and one as a woman. These things, however, depend also upon the nature of the forces man takes with him from earth existence through the door of death. It should, therefore, be understood that all indications given here are valid in the essentials; in individual cases, however, they show themselves varied in the most manifold way. How long the human being remains in the spiritual world between death and a new birth depends in one way only upon the described conditions in the cosmos. In another regard this depends on the states of development through which man passes during that time. These states lead the ego, after a certain lapse of time, to a spiritual condition that finds no further satisfaction in its inner spiritual experiences, and which develops the longing toward the change of consciousness that finds satisfaction in the reflection through physical experience. Through the co-operation of this inner thirst for incarnation and the possibility offered by the cosmos of finding the corresponding bodily organism the entrance of the human being into earth-life occurs. Since there must be a twofold co-operation, incarnation occurs, in one instance,—although the "thirst for incarnation" has not yet attained its full intensity—because an approximately fitting embodiment can be realized; it occurs, in another instance,—although the thirst for incarnation has overstepped its normal intensity

—because at the corresponding time there was no possibility yet of embodiment. The general mood of life in which a human being finds himself because of the constitution of his bodily nature is connected with these conditions.

THE COURSE OF HUMAN LIFE

The life of the human being as it expresses itself in the succession of conditions between birth and death can only be grasped completely by taking into account not only the sensory-physical body, but also those changes that occur in the supersensory principles of human nature—We may regard these changes in the following manner. Physical birth represents the breaking loose of the human being from the physical maternal sheath. Forces, which the embryonic human being had in common with the maternal body before birth, are present in him after birth only as independent forces. Later in life, however, supersensible events occur for supersensible perception, resembling the sensory events occurring at physical birth. Up to the time of his change of teeth (at the sixth or seventh year), the human being, in regard to his ether body, is surrounded by an etheric sheath. This falls away at this period of life. A "birth" of the ether body takes place. The human being, however, still continues to be enclosed by an astral sheath; this falls away between the twelfth and sixteenth years, (at the time of puberty). The "birth" of the astral body then takes place. And still later the actual ego is born. (The fruitful points of view for education, which result from these supersensible facts, are to be found in my brochure, *The Education of the Child from the Standpoint of Spiritual*

374

Science. In this booklet also may be found a further exposition of what here can only be indicated.) Man, after the birth of the ego, lives so as to fit himself into the conditions of the world and life and is active within them according to the principles working through the ego: sentient soul, intellectual soul, and consciousness soul. Then a time arrives when the ether body retraces the processes of his development from the seventh year onward. Whereas the astral body has previously developed in such a way that it has first unfolded in itself what was already present in him as a possibility at birth, and then, after the birth of the ego, has enriched itself through the experiences of the outer world, it begins from a certain point of time to nourish itself spiritually by its own ether body. It feeds on the ether body. In the further course of life the ether body also begins to feed on the physical body. With this is connected the decline of the physical body in old age.—As a result the course of human life falls into three periods: one in which the physical and ether bodies unfold; another in which the astral body and the ego are developed; finally the third period in which the ether and physical bodies reverse their development. The astral body, however, participates in all processes between birth and death. Through the fact of its being actually born spiritually only between the twelfth and sixteenth years and of its being compelled, during the last period of life, to feed on the forces of the ether and physical bodies, what it is able to do through its own forces develops more slowly than it would were it not in a physical and ether body. After death, when the physical and ether bodies have fallen away, the development during the period of purification (compare Chapter III), therefore, takes place in such a way that it lasts about one third of the duration of life between birth and death.

THE HIGHER REGIONS
OF THE SPIRITUAL WORLD

By means of imagination, inspiration, and intuition supersensible cognition gradually reaches the regions of the spiritual world in which there are accessible to it the beings that participate in the evolution of the cosmos and man. Through this fact it is also possible for this cognition to follow up human evolution between death and a new birth so that this becomes comprehensible. There are, however, still higher regions of existence that can only be briefly alluded to here. If supersensible cognition has raised itself up to the stage of intuition, it then lives in a world of spiritual beings. These beings also undergo development. The concerns of modern mankind extend, so to speak, into the world of intuition. To be sure, the human being also receives influences from still higher worlds in the course of his development between death and a new birth, but he does not experience these influences directly; the beings of the spiritual world convey them to him, and if these are taken into consideration, we then have everything that happens to man. The affairs of these beings, however, what they need for themselves in order to lead human development, can be observed only through cognition that reaches beyond intuition. In this we have a hint concerning higher spiritual worlds that are to be thought of as being of such a character that spiritual matters, which on earth are the most exalted, belong there to those on a lower level. For

376

example, within the earth region, reasoned conclusions are among the highest achievements, while the effects of the mineral kingdom are among the lowest. In those higher regions, reasoned conclusions approximate what are on earth mineral effects. Beyond the region of intuition lies the realm in which, out of spiritual causes, the cosmic plan is spun.

THE MEMBERS OF MAN'S BEING

When it has been said (compare beginning of Chapter IV) that the ego works on the members of man's being—on the physical, ether, and astral bodies—and fashions these, in reverse order, into spirit self, life spirit, and spirit man, this refers to the work of the ego on the being of man by means of the highest faculties, which began their development only in the course of the earth periods. This transformation, however, is preceded by another on a lower stage, and through this the sentient soul, intellectual soul, and consciousness soul are developed. For, while during the course of human evolution the sentient soul is formed, transformations in the astral body take place; the formation of the intellectual soul expresses itself in transformations in the ether body, the formation of the consciousness soul in transformations in the physical body. In the course of the description of the *Earth* evolution given in this book, the details of these processes were indicated. We may thus say, in a certain sense, that the sentient soul is already based upon a transformed astral body, the intellectual soul upon a transformed ether body, and the consciousness soul upon a transformed physical body. We may, however, also say that these three soul principles are parts of the astral body, for the consciousness soul, for example, is only possible through its being an astral entity in a physical body adapted to it. It lives an astral life in a physical body that has been fashioned into its dwelling place.

THE DREAM STATE

The dream state has been characterized, in a certain respect, in the earlier chapter, *Sleep and Death.* It is to be conceived of, on the one hand, as being a remnant of the ancient picture consciousness that man possessed during the *Moon* evolution and also during a large part of *Earth* evolution. For evolution advances in such a fashion that the earlier states play over into the later. Thus, a remnant now appears in the human being during the dream state of what was previously a normal state. On the other hand, however, this state is different from ancient picture consciousness, for the ego, since its development, plays also into the processes of the astral body taking place in sleep while man is dreaming. Thus, in dreams we have a picture consciousness transformed through the presence of the ego. Since the ego, however, does not consciously carry on its activity upon the astral body during the state of dreaming, nothing that belongs to the realm of dream life must be considered as belonging to what in truth can lead to a spiritual-scientific knowledge of supersensible worlds. The same is true for what is often designated as vision, premonition, or second-sight (*deuteroscopy*). These come into existence through the ego's eliminating itself with the result that remnants of ancient states of consciousness arise.

These have no direct use in spiritual science. What is observed by them cannot be considered in the true sense a result of the latter.

THE ACQUIREMENT
OF SUPERSENSIBLE KNOWLEDGE

The path leading to a knowledge of supersensible worlds that has been described more explicitly in this book may also be called the "direct path of knowledge." Another exists beside it that we may designate as the "path of feeling." It would, however, be quite incorrect to believe that the first path has nothing to do with the development of feeling. On the contrary, it leads to the greatest possible deepening of the life of feeling. The path of feeling, however, turns *directly* to feeling only and seeks to ascend from this to knowledge. It is based upon the fact that when the soul surrenders itself completely to a feeling for a certain length of time, this feeling transforms itself into knowledge, into a picture-like perception. If, for example, the soul fills itself completely during weeks, months, or even a longer period, with the feeling of humility, then the content of feeling transforms itself into a perception. One may, by passing step by step through such feelings, also find a path into supersensible regions. This, however, is not easily carried out by modern man under ordinary life-conditions. Seclusion, retirement from present-day life is an almost unavoidable necessity for this path. For the impressions experienced in daily life disturb, especially at the beginning, what the soul reaches through its immersion in certain feelings. In contrast to this, the path of knowledge described

379

in this book can be carried out in every situation of modern life.

OBSERVATION OF SPECIAL EVENTS
AND BEINGS OF THE WORLD OF SPIRIT

The question may be asked whether inner meditation and the other means described of attaining supersensible cognition permit *only* a *general* observation of man between death and a new birth or of other spirtual processes, or whether they permit the observation of quite definite processes and beings, for example, of some particular deceased person. The answer to this must be: Whoever acquires by the described means the faculty of observing the spiritual world, may also reach the point of observing detailed occurrences within it. He makes himself capable of coming in contact with human beings dwelling in the world of spirit between death and a new birth. One must, however, pay heed to the fact that this must happen, in the sense of spiritual science, only after one has gone through the regular training in supersensible cognition. Only then is one able, in regard to special events and beings, to distinguish between delusion and reality. Whoever wishes to observe details without the proper training may fall a victim to many deceptions. Even the most elementary achievement, namely, the understanding of the way in which such impressions of *special* supersensible facts are to be interpreted is not possible without an advanced spiritual training. The training that leads into the higher worlds for the observation of what is described in this book leads also to the ability to follow the life of an individual human being

380

after death. It also leads to the observation and understanding of all special beings of the world of soul and spirit who influence from hidden worlds the outer manifested world. Nevertheless, correct observation of details is only possible upon the basis of cognition of the general, great cosmic and human facts of the spiritual world that concern every human being. Whoever desires the one without desiring the other goes astray. It belongs to the experiences that must be undergone in regard to the observation of the spiritual world that the admission into the realms of supersensible existence for which one *longs* at the very first is granted only when the student has striven on solemn and difficult paths, leading to problems of general knowledge, for that which gives information about the meaning of life. If he has trodden these paths with a pure and unegotistical urge for knowledge, then only is he mature enough to observe details, the observation of which would have been previously only a satisfying of egotistical longings, even though he had persuaded himself that it was only his love of someone who is dead, for example, that had made him strive for an insight into the spiritual world. The insight into the special is only possible for him who, from sincere interest for general spiritual-scientific knowledge, has gained the possibility of accepting also the special without any egotistical desire like an objective scientific truth.

381

VIII

SPECIAL COMMENTS

(a) page 30 and fol. pp.

Expositions of the kind in this book about the faculty of
memory can easily be misunderstood. For those who only
observe external processes will not readily detect the difference between what happens in the animal or even in the
plant when something appears that resembles memory,
and what is here described as actual memory in man. Certainly, if an animal carries out an action a third or fourth
time, it may then so perform it that the outer process appears as though the action were the result of memory and
what is learned through it. Like some natural scientists and
their adherents, one may, indeed, extend the concept of
memory or recollection to such a point that one says that
when the little chick pops from the shell and immediately
pecks at the grain, knowing even how to make the movements of its head and body in order to reach its object, it
could not have learned this in the shell, but that it was

382

learned through the thousands and thousands of creatures from which it has descended. (Ewald Hering, for example, states this.) We may declare that the phenomenon under discussion has the appearance of memory. We shall, however, never gain a real comprehension of man's being if we do not hold in mind what appears quite especially unique in the human being as the process of real perception of previous experiences at subsequent times, not merely as an influence of past states into later ones. Here in this book this *perception* of the past, not merely the reappearance— even though changed—of the previous in the subsequent, is called memory. If one were to use the word memory for the corresponding processes in the plant and animal kingdoms, then one ought to have a different word for the processes of memory in man. It is not the word, however, that is important in the above presentation, but, for the sake of understanding the human being, the significant thing is the *recognition of the difference* between what occurs in man on the one hand, and in animal and plant on the other. What may appear as highly intelligent actions in animals has also no connection whatever with what is *here* called memory.

(b) page 39 and fol. pp.

No fixed boundary can be drawn between the changes resulting from the activity of the ego in the astral body and those taking place in the ether body. They pass over into each other. If man learns something and through it gains a certain power of discrimination, then a change has occurred in the astral body; if however, this judgment or discrimination so alters his soul condition that he becomes accustomed, after he has learned something about a matter, to *feel* differently about it from previously, a change has then taken place in the ether body. Everything that becomes a possession of the human soul that can be recalled in memory is based upon a change in the ether body. What becomes, by degrees, an immutable treasure of memory, rests on the fact that the work performed on the astral body has been transferred to the ether body.

(c) page 51 and fol. pp.

The connection between sleep and *fatigue* is, in most cases, not viewed in a manner demanded by the facts. Sleep is supposed to be a result of fatigue. That this thought is much too simple is shown by the fact that a man, not at all tired, may fall asleep while listening to an uninteresting lecture, or on some similar occasion. Whoever maintains that such an occasion tires the listener, tries to explain by a method that lacks a serious scientific attitude. Unprejudiced observation must lead to the conclusion that waking and sleeping present different relationships of the soul to the body, which must appear in the regular course of life in rhythmical sequence like the right and left swing of a pendulum. The result of such unprejudiced observation is that the filling of the soul with the impressions of the outer world awakes in it the desire, after experiencing this state, to enter another in which it is absorbed in the enjoyment of its own bodily nature. Two soul states alternate: the state of surrender to outer impressions and the state of surrender to one's own bodily nature. In the first state the desire for the second is unconsciously produced; the second state then takes its course in unconsciousness. The expression of the desire for the enjoyment of one's own bodily nature is fatigue. We must then actually say that we feel tired, because we wish to go to sleep, not that we wish to go to sleep because we feel tired. Since the human soul can, through habit, arbitrarily call forth in itself the states that of necessity appear in normal human life, it is possible that, when the soul makes itself insensitive to a given outer impression, it calls forth in itself the desire for enjoyment of its own bodily nature; that is to say, the soul goes to sleep, even though this state is not induced by the inner condition of the human being.

(d) p. 89

The statement that, if the personal talents of a human being were subject only to the law of heredity, they would have to show themselves not at the end but at the beginning of a blood relationship, might easily be misunderstood. It might be said that talents cannot show themselves at the beginning, for they must first be developed. But this is not a valid objection. For, if we wish to prove that something is inherited from a forebear, we must show how there is to be found again in the descendant what existed already previously. If it were shown that something was present at the beginning of a blood relationship that would be found again in the further course of its evolution, we might then speak of heredity. We cannot do this, however, if at the end something appears that previously did not exist. The reversal of the above sentence was only to show that in this case the idea of heredity is an impossible one.

(e) p. 110

In certain chapters of this book it has been indicated how the world of man and the human being himself pass through the states that have been designated by the names *Saturn, Sun, Moon, Earth, Jupiter, Venus, Vulcan.* Indications have also been given concerning the relationship between human evolution and celestial bodies co-existing with the earth, such as Saturn, Jupiter, Mars, and so forth. These latter celestial bodies naturally go through their evolution also. In the present age they have reached a stage in which their physical parts are shown to perception as what is called in physical astronomy Saturn, Jupiter, Mars, and so forth. If now, in the sense of spiritual science, the present Saturn is studied, it shows itself, so to speak, as a reincarnation of ancient *Saturn*. It has come into existence because, before the separation of the sun from the earth, certain beings were present who were unable to participate in this separation, since they had absorbed into themselves so many of the characteristics belonging to the *Saturn* state that they could not abide in an environment where especially the sun characteristics were unfolded. The present Jupiter has arisen, however, through the presence of beings who possessed characteristics that can only unfold on the future *Jupiter* of general cosmic evolution. An abode came into existence for them in which they are able to anticipate this future evolution. Similarly, Mars is a celestial body on which beings dwell who have passed through the *Moon* evolution in such a way that the earth could offer them no further advancement. Mars is a reincarnation of the ancient *Moon* at a higher stage. The present Mercury is the dwelling place of beings who, by having developed certain earth characteristics in a form higher than it can occur on this earth planet, are in advance of the evolution of the *Earth*. In a similar way the present Venus is a prophetic anticipation of the future *Venus* state. From all this we are justified in choosing the designations for the states that have preceded the *Earth* and that will follow it from their present representatives in the cosmos. It is self-evident that there will be many objections to what has been brought forth here by those who wish to subject the paralleling of the supersensibly perceived *Saturn, Sun* and other cosmic states of evolution with the similarly named physical celestial bodies to the judgment of an intellect trained in outer observation of nature. But just as it is possible, by means of mathematical concepts, to place the solar system before the soul as an image of time-space occurrences, so is it possible for supersensible cognition to permeate the mathematical picture with a soul content. Then it takes on a form that justifies the above indicated parallels. This permeation with a soul content is a natural consequence of the further application of a strictly natural scientific mode of observation. This latter mode of observation limits itself at present to seeking a reciprocal relationship between the solar system and the earth according to purely mathematical-mechanical concepts. By doing so, the natural science of the future will of itself be driven to concepts that will extend the idea of a mechanical cosmos to one endowed with soul. To show—which could very well be done—that such an extension ought already to occur on the basis of modern natural scientific concepts would require the writing of another book. Here the matter in question can only be indicated; as a consequence, this indication is exposed to misunderstandings of one sort or another. The disagreement of spiritual science with natural science is often *only apparent,* because the latter science still refuses at present to form thoughts that are not only demanded by supersensible congnition but also, in truth, by a cognition that adheres strictly to the physical-sensory. An unprejudiced observer is able to see everywhere in the results of modern natural scientific observation allusions to other fields of purely physical-sensory observation, which will have to be investigated in the future in a purely natural scientific manner and which will show that what supersensible perception reveals is completely verified by a physical observation of nature insofar as supersensible cognition is concerned with those supersensible cosmic occurrences to which physical-sensory manifestation corresponds.

DATE DUE